INSPIRE / PLAN / DISCOVER / EXPERIENCE

SCOTLAND

SCOTLAND

CONTENTS

DISCOVER 6

EXPERIENCE 66

NEED TO KNOW 268

Left: Scottish Parliament, designed by Enric Miralles
Previous page: Kilchurn Castle, Loch Awe
Front cover: Glenfinnan Monument, Loch Shiel

DISCOVER

Neolithic Ring of Brogdar, Orkney

WELCOME TO
SCOTLAND

Rugged shores and wild Highland glens. Stern castles and haunting battlefields. World-class museums and internationally renowned festivals. Scotland offers enough bucket-list experiences to draw visitors back year after year. Whatever your dream trip entails, this DK Eyewitness Travel Guide is the perfect companion.

1 Wild red stags grazing on a frosty moor in the Scottish Highlands.

2 Visitors admiring the view from the top of Calton Hill, Edinburgh.

3 Dusky skies over Eilean Donan Castle on Loch Duich.

Small but spectacular, Scotland is famed for its majestic mountain landscapes, tranquil lochs and windswept moors, all fringed by thousands of miles of dramatic coastline. The undulating farmlands of Angus, Ayrshire and Aberdeenshire and the verdant pastures of the Borders are a haven of tranquillity, while pocket wildernesses like the Cairngorms, Rannoch Moor and the Trossachs are but a stone's throw from bustling towns and cities such as Edinburgh, Glasgow and Inverness.

Scotland's richly varied hinterland is a joy for outdoor enthusiasts, offering a vast array of activities from gentle country strolls to long-distance hill walking, rock climbing and white-water kayaking. Meanwhile, the museums and art galleries of Scotland's cities are temples to art and culture, and a plethora of pubs, bars and venues offer an impressive roster of live gigs, impromptu folk sessions and comedy. Old-school inns abound, but cool cocktail bars and gastropubs offer an exciting new take on food and drink while still honouring the country's local produce and culinary traditions.

With so much on offer, it is easy to feel overwhelmed. This guide breaks Scotland down into easily navigable chapters, with detailed itineraries, expert local knowledge and comprehensive maps to help you plan your perfect trip. Whether you're here for a flying visit or a grand tour, this DK Eyewitness guide will ensure that you see the very best the country has to offer. Enjoy the book, enjoy Scotland, and *haste ye back*.

REASONS TO LOVE
SCOTLAND

Dramatic coastlines, soaring mountains and spirited cities, each with their own rich and multifaceted culture. There are so many things that make this vibrant country irresistible. Here's a round up of a few of our favourites.

1 DRAMATIC HISTORY

Explore ancient strongholds such as Edinburgh Castle *(p78)*, or be transported to medieval times as you wander the winding, cobbled closes and hidden courtyards of the Royal Mile *(p80)*.

MAJESTIC LANDSCAPES *2*

Venture through the iconic Highland landscapes of Glencoe and the Isle of Skye, and explore rolling moorlands and ravishing coastlines in Torridon and the northwest.

3 HOGMANAY

Party your way into the New Year with world-class bands and awesome midnight pyrotechnics at Edinburgh's famous Hogmanay, then join locals in a "Loony Dook" to blow the cobwebs away.

A FLOURISHING FOODIE SCENE 4

Scotland is in full culinary bloom thanks to creative chefs across the country working their magic with the best locally sourced ingredients.

CITIES OF CULTURE 5

Admire Renaissance gems at Glasgow's Kelvingrove Art Gallery *(p146)* or cutting-edge design at Edinburgh's National Gallery of Modern Art *(p100)* and the V&A, Dundee *(p168)*.

DISTILLERIES GALORE 6

Scotland is a whisky-lover's paradise. Sip ancient malts in distilleries such as Glenlivet in Speyside *(p187)*, or try a new breed of Scotch at an artisan spirit house or cocktail bar.

HIGHLAND CULTURE 7

Experience Highland heritage, tartan pageantry, pipe music, Scottish dance and caber-tossing muscle-men (and women) at Highland games and clan gatherings *(p204)*.

ISLAND GETAWAYS 8

Admire a Hebridean sunset from the shores of Luskentyre Beach on Harris *(p236)*. Remote, rugged and utterly breathtaking, Scotland's many islands will capture your heart.

9 WILDLIFE SPOTTING

Spot seals, whales and dolphins in the chilly waters of the Moray Firth *(p255)*, meet puffins on Handa Island *(p265)*, or go on a Highland safari where you can see red deer and wildcats.

10 CEILIDH TILL THE WEE HOURS

Tap your feet to the rhythms of traditional Scottish jigs and reels at a lively ceilidh, or even better, join in. Just about anyone can get the hang of an Orcadian Strip the Willow.

OUTDOOR ACTIVITIES 11

Ride whitewater rapids on the River Tay, cycle in Galloway Forest Park (p133), or ascend summits like Ben Nevis (p208) and Lochnagar (p211) while walking the West Highland Way.

WORLD-CLASS GOLF 12

Play a breezy round of golf at the iconic St Andrews Links, birthplace of golf and home of the famous Royal and Ancient Golf Club (p170).

EXPLORE
SCOTLAND

This guide divides Scotland into five colour-coded sightseeing areas: Edinburgh, Southern Scotland, Glasgow, Central and Northeast Scotland and the Highlands and Islands, as shown on this map. Find out more about each area on the following pages.

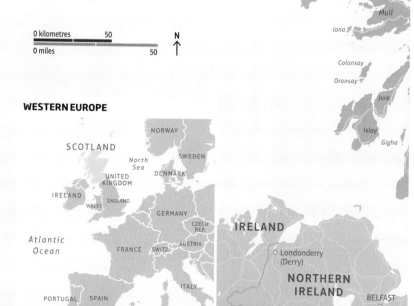

Stornoway

Outer Hebrides

Lewis

Tarbert

Harris

Lochmaddy

Quiraing

North Uist

Skye

Portree

Cuillins

South Uist

Inner Hebrides

Lochboisdale

Canna

Sleat

Barra
Castlebay

Rhum

Eigg

Muck

Coll

Tiree

Mull

Iona

Colonsay

Oronsay

Jura

Islay

Gigha

*Atlantic
Ocean*

| 0 kilometres | 50 |
| 0 miles | 50 |

N ↑

WESTERN EUROPE

NORWAY

SCOTLAND

*North
Sea*

SWEDEN

UNITED
KINGDOM

DENMARK

IRELAND

ENGLAND

WALES

GERMANY

CZECH
REP.

*Atlantic
Ocean*

FRANCE

SWITZ.

AUSTRIA

PORTUGAL

SPAIN

ITALY

IRELAND

○ Londonderry
(Derry)

NORTHERN
IRELAND

BELFAST
○

GETTING TO KNOW
SCOTLAND

Stretching from the rich farmlands of the Borders to a chain of isles just south of the Arctic Circle, the Scottish landscape is distinct and diverse. There is plenty to discover here, from tranquil lochs and rugged hills to clan castles and vibrant cities, each with their own unique charm.

EDINBURGH

PAGE 68

Replete with sights and cultural treasures, Edinburgh is the gateway to Scotland. Dominated by the ramparts of Edinburgh Castle, the Royal Mile runs through the heart of a uniquely intact medieval quarter of the city. To the north, the gracious Georgian New Town is filled with upscale shops, boutique hotels, restaurants and café-bars. Beyond the city lie urban villages, such as Stockbridge and Leith, that have a charming character of their own.

Best for
Sightseeing and culture

Home to
Edinburgh Castle, National Museum of Scotland, Scottish National Gallery

Experience
Panoramic views over the city and beyond from the summit of Arthur's Seat

PAGE 108

SOUTHERN SCOTLAND

Stretching between the North Sea and the Atlantic, Scotland's southern regions are bound in the north by the Firths of Clyde and Forth. Fertile farmlands contrast with upland moors and riverside valleys, while baronial mansions stand alongside evocative ruins of historic abbeys and castles. The delights of this region are within an hour's drive of Edinburgh or Glasgow.

Best for
History and scenery

Home to
Culzean Castle, Abbotsford

Experience
Taking the ferry to Arran and climbing Goatfell, the island's highest peak

→

PAGE 136

GLASGOW

Scotland's biggest city, straddling the River Clyde, buzzes with energy. A legacy of the 18th- and 19th-century mercantile and industrial revolutions, the city centre is studded with several handsome buildings, including the City Chambers and Kelvingrove Art Gallery and Museum. But it is also a city that is constantly reinventing itself, with a lively and youthful nightlife, vibrant shopping districts, and a cosmopolitan array of places to eat and drink.

Best for
Art, shopping and nightlife

Home to
Kelvingrove Art Gallery and Museum, Glasgow Science Centre

Experience
A waverley paddle-steamer cruise on the River Clyde

PAGE 160

CENTRAL AND NORTHEAST SCOTLAND

Encompassing wild uplands and tamer lowland landscapes, Central and Northeast Scotland is a patchwork of farmland and forest, fringed by sandy shores. Each of its cities has a unique history, from the medieval splendour of Stirling Castle and the austere architecture of Aberdeen's St Machar's Cathedral to the industrial heritage of Dundee and Falkirk. Loch Lomond, the Trossachs and Tayside offer a range of outdoor activities and experiences, while Royal Deeside combines natural beauty with regal splendour.

Best for
Royal heritage and whisky

Home to
Aberdeen, Scone Palace, Loch Lomond, Stirling Castle

Experience
Whitewater rafting and canoeing on the River Tay

THE HIGHLANDS AND ISLANDS

For many, the Highlands and Islands epitomize Scotland. This is a vast and sparsely populated region of innumerable lochs, rivers, glens and moors dotted with majestic clan castles and ancient standing stones. Hundreds of islands lie off the coast, many of them within sight of shore or an easy ferry ride from Oban, Mallaig or Ullapool. Inverness, the Highland capital, is an excellent starting point for exploring Loch Ness and the Cairngorms, while Fort William holds the key to Ben Nevis, Britain's highest peak.

Best for
Outdoor adventure and majestic mountains

Home to
Ben Nevis, Cairngorms National Park, Loch Ness

Experience
Walking in the shadow of Ben Nevis or island-hopping on the west coast

2 WEEKS
Around Scotland

Day 1

Start your day at the National Museum of Scotland (*p86*), then stroll to the Royal Mile (*p80*), pausing for a quick snap of Greyfriars Bobby and a lunch stop at one of the many restaurants on George IV Bridge. Deacon Brodies Tavern (*453 Lawnmarket*), where an effigy of the famous 18th-century villain lurks in a corner, is a favourite for a pie and a pint. After lunch, walk up the Royal Mile to Edinburgh Castle (*p76*) and admire the mighty Mons Meg in the castle grounds. Stroll down The Mound to the Scottish National Gallery (*p90*), to admire its world-class collection of Scottish masters and medieval and Renaissance Italian, Dutch and French artworks. Finish the day with a walk up Calton Hill (*p84*) for a sunset vista, then descend to the Gardener's Cottage, which serves an excellent multi-course tasting menu with fine paired wines.

Day 2

A half-hour drive west on the M9 will take you to Falkirk, where The Helix (*p191*) is home to The Kelpies, two colossal equine heads, sculpted in metal by artist Andy Scott, that rear above the Forth and Clyde and Union canals. A further 25-minute drive brings you to Stirling (*p181*) and its legendary castle. Explore within the castle's ancient walls, then head for the nearby towering Wallace Monument, an unmistakable landmark. Climb this Gothic spire for an impressive view of the Castle and learn about Scotland's national hero, William Wallace. Spend the evening in the quaint town of Dunblane, where Chez Roux at Cromlix House (*www.cromlix.com*) offers a light, nouvelle, French-influenced menu.

Day 3

Visit the iconic Doune Castle (*p187*), then drive a further half-hour to Perth (*p188*) where you can pause for lunch and visit the Fergusson Gallery. After lunch, cross the River Tay to Scone Palace (*p174*), a stately home crammed with precious antiques. Stretch your legs in its wooded gardens before embarking on a short drive to your final destination of the day: Dundee (*p168*). Dine in the city's arts quarter, and enjoy live entertainment nearby at Dundee Rep Theatre.

1. Calton Hill at sunset.

2. Modern exterior of the V&A Dundee.

3. Macallan whisky barrels, Speyside.

4. Crathes Castle, Deeside.

5. Skye Bridge, connecting the town of Kyleakin to the mainland.

Day 4

Begin the day with a visit to Dundee's spectacular V&A Museum of Design, where the original interior of Charles Rennie Mackintosh's Oak Room is a highlight, then board RRS *Discovery* and learn about Captain Scott's polar voyages. After a spot of lunch, head north to the haunting ruined clifftop fortress of Dunnottar Castle *(p1)*. Spend the night in Aberdeen *(p164)*, where you can feast on Black Angus steak and North Sea lobster at Chez Mal Brasserie at Malmaison Aberdeen *(www.malmaison.com)*, which also has stylish rooms.

Day 5

On your way to Royal Deeside, stop at Crathes Castle to explore its walled garden and nature trails – a perfect spot for a picnic lunch. Then on to the famous Balmoral Castle and Estate *(p184)*, where you can walk through delightful pine-scented grounds and admire the Baronial architecture. Carry on through the Cairngorms *(p212)* and admire rugged mountain landscapes on your way to Aberlour for the evening.

Day 6

Follow The Malt Whisky Trail® *(p187)* through Speyside to Craigellachie for a fascinating tour around the The Macallan Distillery and Visitor Centre. En route to Inverness, stop off for an afternoon tour of the infamous Culloden Battlefield *(p256)* to imagine the clash of claymores that took place here in 1746. A jumble of friendly pubs and atmospheric restaurants welcomes you to Inverness *(p216)*.

Day 7

First stop Drumnadrochit to join a Loch Ness Monster "research cruise". Admire the ruins of Urquhart Castle *(p218)* from the water, then eat at the Loch Ness Inn's Lewiston Restaurant *(www.staylochness.co.uk)*, which serves local produce with a contemporary twist. Follow the banks of Loch Ness through breathtaking Glen Shiel *(p262)*. Pause for a stroll around the Eilean Donan Castle – Scotland's most photogenic castle – on Loch Duich, then on to Kyle of Lochalsh. Cross the bridge to Skye *(p222)* where a fine dinner and cosy room await at Kinloch Lodge *(www.kinloch-lodge.co.uk)*. →

Day 8

Visit the dinky town of Portree for a colourful snapshot, then head to Dunvegan Castle, stronghold of Clan MacLeod for over eight centuries. Off the main road from Portree to Staffin is the start of a fantastic walk along the Trotternish ridge, leading to The Old Man of Storr, which rewards hikers with fantastic views across the island and beyond. Don't miss a quick stop at the Talisker Distillery for a sip of the whisky nicknamed "the lava of the Cuillins".

Day 9

Take the short ferry crossing from Armadale to the pretty town of Mallaig (p245), famed for its fresh seafood. Stop off at the Sands of Morar and take a stroll where this idyllic sweep of white sand meets aquamarine water. Continue your drive through Glenfinnan (p253) to pay your respects to Jacobite warriors at the Glenfinnan Monument and see the iconic Jacobite Steam Train, which doubles as the Hogwarts Express in the Harry Potter movies, as it chuffs along the Glenfinnan

Viaduct in a billow of smoke. You can even ride the train – a regular service runs between Mallaig and Fort William. Arrive in Fort William (p253) in time to dine at The Crannog (www.crannog.net) while watching a glorious sunset over Loch Linnhe.

Day 10

A short trip from Fort William is Glen Nevis, where you can get a great view of Scotland's highest peak and stretch your legs on many a woodland stroll, or a more energetic munro. If you wish to conquer Ben Nevis (p208), start the day early, and ensure that the weather conditions are right, and that you are well prepared for the demanding ascent.

Day 11

The drive south from Fort William through Glencoe (p252) is real stunner. You'll find great views of Buachaille Etive Mor from the Glencoe Visitor Centre. From here, follow the A82 for an hour and a half, skirting heather-covered Rannoch Moor, to Loch Lomond (p176). Don't miss a

1 The Old Man of Storr, Skye.

2 Jacobite Express crossing the Glenfinnan Viaduct.

3 The pier at Luss, Loch Lomond.

4 Main hall at Kelvingrove Art Gallery and Museum.

5 Hikers exploring the Eildon Hills.

stop in the picturesque town of Luss. Enjoy dinner and drinks overlooking the loch and Ben Lomond at Colquhoun's at the Lodge on Loch Lomond (www.loch-lomond. co.uk), where the menu features grilled steaks, local game and exquisite seafood.

Day 12

Start your day by exploring the beautiful Trossachs National Park aboard a Victorian paddle-steamer boat cruise on Loch Katrine. Spend the rest of the day taking advantage of some of the many activities on offer in the Queen Elizabeth Forest Park, be that biking, walking sections of the West Highland Way or even ziplining above the treetops. Set off on the 45-minute drive to Glasgow in the early evening to arrive in time for dinner out in the bustling city centre.

Day 13

Stroll through Glasgow's Kelvingrove Park to Kelvingrove Art Gallery and Museum (p146) where works by the Scottish Colourists and the Glasgow Boys steal the show. To refuel, visit quirky Ashton Lane where your taste buds will be spoilt for choice. From here, it's a short walk to the Riverside Museum (p153) where you will be wowed by gleaming vintage vehicles. Relax at The Winged Ox at St Luke's (www.stlukesglasgow.com), next to the famous Barrowlands music venue, where you'll find an eclectic menu of food, drink and entertainment.

Day 14

Take a slight detour through the rolling Borders countryside on the way back to Edinburgh, stopping at literary legend Sir Walter Scott's favourite viewpoint of the triple-crowned Eildon Hills (p126). Head north to the last sight on your tour, the enchanting Rosslyn Chapel (p121). Admire its intricately carved stonework, then walk through leafy Roslin Glen before embarking on the short drive back to Edinburgh city centre.

7 DAYS
On the North Coast 500

Day 1

Starting in the Highland capital of Inverness *(p216)*, a short drive along the south shore of the Beauly Firth (keep an eye open for dolphins) then north through Dornoch, will take you to Dunrobin Castle *(p256)*, seat of the Earls of Sutherland and one of the north's great fairytale stately homes. Stop at the Golspie Inn *(www.golspieinn.co.uk)* for a light lunch before continuing north to John O'Groats *(p265)*, then on to windswept Dunnet Head. From there, Scrabster is just 35 minutes away. Catch the 7pm ferry to Stromness *(p228)*, then dine at the Merkister Hotel's Skerries Restaurant *(p229)*, which specializes in Orkney beef and fresh seafood.

Day 2

Explore the wonders of Neolithic Orkney, including the ancient tomb at Maeshowe and the stone megaliths at Stenness and the Ring of Brodgar. In the afternoon, visit Kirkwall to admire St Magnus Cathedral, a 12th-century masterpiece in red and yellow stone.

Day 3

The next morning, return by ferry to the mainland, and begin the winding route along the A836 across the windswept, rugged expanse of Scotland's northern coast, stopping to admire stunning viewpoints and sheer clifftop vistas as you go. Veer off to the appropriately named Côte du Nord *(p265)* for a lunch that fuses the finest local Scottish produce with French cuisine. A mile before you hit Durness, make a stop to venture deep into the eerie caverns of Smoo Cave.

Day 4

As a welcome break from driving, park up and join the ferry and minibus tour from Durness to Cape Wrath *(p266)*, where waves crash beneath savage grey cliffs and hundreds of squaking seabirds perch on towering sea stacks that lie just offshore. Stop for a snap of the white stone lighthouse on the very northwest tip of mainland Britain, where endless views seem to stretch all the way to the edge of the world.

1 Visitors exploring the Ring of Brodgar, Orkney.

2 Stunning interior of St Magnus Cathedral, Kirkwall.

3 Lighthouse, Cape Wrath.

4 Red grouse among the heather at Handa Island.

5 Road to Loch Maree.

Day 5

The route down the West Coast, heading south from Durness, is where the magic really kicks in. First, head to Tarbet, where you can hop on a ferry to the tiny Handa Island *(p265)* where the air is filled with the cries of tens of thousands of seabirds. On your return to the mainland, head south to Eddrachillis Bay, a mirror-calm natural anchorage dotted with heather-tufted islets where seals bask and yachts anchor in summer. Then follow the road that passes through an undulating series of peaks known as the Quinag, and the impressive Ben More Assynt and Conival munros. This wild expanse of mountain and moorland, sliced up by long narrow lochs, is only 18 miles (30 km) from Ullapool *(p263)*, where you can enjoy a night of foot-tapping fiddle music at the Ceilidh Place *(p263)*.

Day 6

Follow the shore of long, narrow Loch Broom, then double back west on a remote road overlooked by the breath-takingly wild summits of Sgurr Mor and An Teallach. Visit the meticulously preened Inverewe Garden *(p262)* on Loch Ewe, where vivid red and purple rhododendrons bloom spectacularly in their very own unique microclimate.

Day 7

Continue on this road alongside the beautifully serene Loch Maree, then fork left at Kinlochewe to drive inland through the desolate but stunningly beautiful moorland of Torridon in Wester Ross to Achnasheen, then return by way of Strathpeffer *(p256)*. Stop en route for a view of the foaming cascades of thundering white water at Rogie Falls, 2 miles (3 km) west of Contin on the A835. Continue along this road to return to Inverness, where a warm welcome in one of the lively Highland capital's many cosy pubs and restaurants awaits.

←

1 Old croft, Harris.

2 Boats line the harbour in Stornoway, Lewis.

3 Freshly caught crabs at the Oban Seafood Hut.

4 The Callanish Standing Stones on the Isle of Lewis.

5 DAYS
Island Hopping in the Hebrides

Day 1

Morning Begin in the bustling port of Oban (p248) where charming shops line the pretty seafront promenade. Stop for an early lunch at the Oban Seafood Hut to sample some of the best lobster and shellfish in town.

Afternoon Board the afternoon ferry for a scenic cruise to Castlebay, the main town on the idyllic wee island of Barra (p238).

Evening Check in at the Dunard Hostel, popular with cyclists embarking on the Hebridean Way (p239). Dine at Café Kisimul (p237) for an unexpected fusion of Indian, Italian and Scottish flavours. A short drive south will take you to Vatersay and it's spectacular white-sand isthmus. With Altantic waves lapping at the shore, it's the perfect spot to enjoy your first Hebridean sunset.

Day 2

Morning Spend the morning touring Barra, stopping off at Traigh Mhòr – a sprawling sandy bay that doubles as a runway when the tide is out. Time your arrival to coincide with scheduled flights (www.hial.co.uk/barra-airport). Lunch at the tiny airport café is an absolute must – this is certainly not your conventional airport dining experience.

Afternoon Take the ferry to Eriskay and drive through the watery landscapes of the Uists and Benbecula to Berneray.

Evening Dine at the Berneray Bistro and stay at John's Bunkhouse (www.johnsbunkhouse.com), a cosy lodge with all the mod cons.

Day 3

Morning Explore Berneray's stunning shell beaches and gentle dunescapes before boarding the ferry accross the Sound of Harris to the small town of Leverburgh.

Afternoon On arrival, fuel up at the no frills Butty Bus (Pier Rd) then hit the road. The drive along the South Harris coast is utterly breathtaking. Stop at the Seilebost lookout for epic views of this stunning turquoise lagoon. A detour off the main road will bring you to Luskentyre, an absolute belter of a bay set against a mountainous backdrop.

Evening Arrive in Tarbert in time for a tour and evening tipple at the famous Harris Distillery. For dinner, choose from an array of specials at the Harris Hotel (p237).

Day 4

Morning Blow away the cobwebs with a bracing ascent up the notorious Clisham, the highest mountain in the Hebrides.

Afternoon On to Lewis (p235) to visit the Callanish Standing Stones and learn of the islands' ancient past before a hearty lunch at the excellent onsite café. Drive on to the Butt of Lewis, the most northerly point on the archipelago, for far-reaching views.

Evening Dine out in style at the Harris and Lewis Smokehouse in Stornoway (p237), the main settlement on Lewis, and end the night with a whisky at McNeil's (11 Cromwell St).

Day 5

Morning Discover the history of island life in the Museum Nan Eilean in Lews Castle.

Afternoon Explore a more modern side to island life at An Lanntair Arts Centre. As Stornoway's creative hub it is home to a stunning collection of contemporary art by local artists, showcasing the creativity of Gaelic culture in the Outer Hebrides.

Evening Dine at the Boatshed (www.royal-stornoway.co.uk) and turn in early for the early morning ferry back to the mainland.

Majestic Mountains

From Arran to Applecross, mountains are in no short supply in Scotland. The highest, Ben Nevis *(p208)*, reigns over an impressive entourage of smaller peaks. Forbidding Lochnagar looms high above the rolling moors of the Cairngorms *(p210)*, while on Skye, the treeless black basalt Cuillin range *(p224)* rises in stark contrast to the island's gentler lowlands.

→

Overlooking the rugged highland landscapes on the Isle of Arran

SCOTLAND FOR
AMAZING
LANDSCAPES

Snow-capped peaks that tower high above mirror-still lochs and windswept moors, fast-flowing rivers that lead to silver firths, and rugged coastlines, pounded by Atlantic waves. It's no wonder that Scotland is best known for its breathtaking scenery and abundance of awe-inspiring landscapes.

Dramatic Coastlines

With its miles of long sandy beaches, narrow sea lochs, calm island-studded bays and castle-topped crags, Scotland is home to Britain's most breathtaking shores.

A scenic drive along the wild and windswept north coast *(p264)* from the sea-pounded cliffs of Cape Wrath to John O'Groat's and the northern tip of the British mainland, is truly unforgettable.

←

Sea stacks at Dunnet Head, the most northerly point in mainland Britain

REFORESTATION

Scotland is famed for its untouched scenery, yet its landscapes were shaped by centuries of human activity. Almost 2,000 years ago, the land was blanketed by thick forest. In the years that followed, most of this vast Caledonian forest was felled for fuel, timber and pasture, while on private estates the ground was razed for grouse shooting and deer stalking. Now, environmentalists are working to bring back mixed woodland and foster biodiversity.

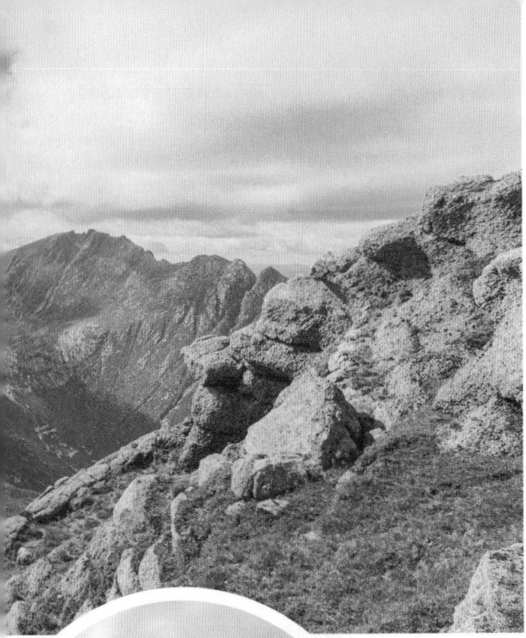

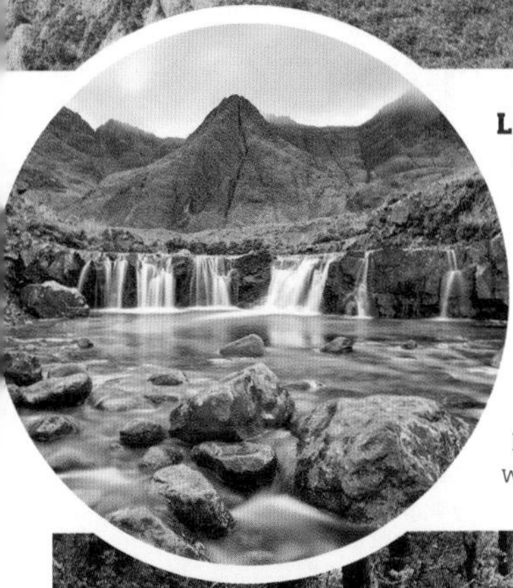

Lochs and Rivers

Scotland is a land shaped by water. Dotted with tree-tufted islands, Loch Lomond *(p176)* is Scotland's loveliest inland sea. Further north, Loch Ness *(p176)* is one in a chain of lochs that form the Great Glen. And of course there are the Fairy Pools on the River Brittle - perfect for a dip in the shadow of Skye's Black Cuillins *(p224)*.

←

Beautifully clear Fairy Pools in Glen Brittle, Skye, with the Cuillin mountains in the background

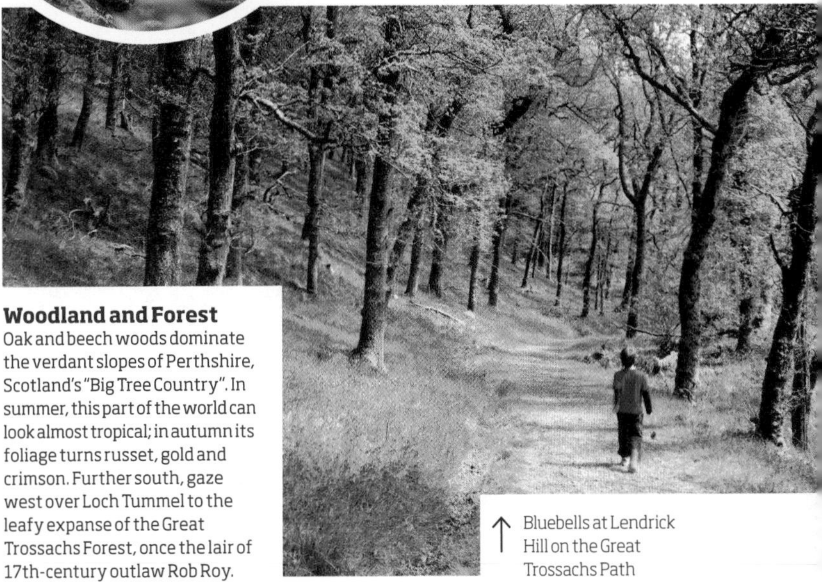

Woodland and Forest

Oak and beech woods dominate the verdant slopes of Perthshire, Scotland's "Big Tree Country". In summer, this part of the world can look almost tropical; in autumn its foliage turns russet, gold and crimson. Further south, gaze west over Loch Tummel to the leafy expanse of the Great Trossachs Forest, once the lair of 17th-century outlaw Rob Roy.

↑ Bluebells at Lendrick Hill on the Great Trossachs Path

Adventures at Sea

Scotland's coastal waters offer endless possibilities for water-based adventures, from sea kayaking to deep-sea diving. Qualified scuba divers can discover vast underwater kelp forests and ghostly shipwrecks such as Scapa Flow in Orkney *(p229)*.

Scuba diver exploring an eerie shipwreck at Scapa Flow, Orkney

SCOTLAND FOR
OUTDOOR
ADVENTURES

Scotland offers a plethora of adrenaline-pumping activities, including hill walking, mountain biking, whitewater kayaking, skiing and scuba diving. Long hours of daylight make summer the perfect season to get out and about, but the great Scottish outdoors is open all year round.

TOP 5 WINTER SPORTS AREAS

Cairngorm Mountain
Home to some 30 km (19 miles) of pistes and cross-country trails.

The Lecht
Pistes for all levels at 2,900 ft (645 m).

Glenshee Ski Centre
Britain's largest ski area with 36 slopes.

Glencoe Mountain
Scotland's steepest ski run with views of Buachaille Etive Mòr and Rannoch Moor.

Nevis Range
A huge network of slopes and back-country routes within sight of Ben Nevis.

Winter Sports

Scotland offers a wealth of options for wintersport fanatics. Zoom down the powdery slopes of Britain's largest resort at Glenshee or try out Nordic skiing on the numerous cross-country trails at Cairngorm Mountain *(p211)*.

→

Cross-country ski touring through the snow-covered forest at Cairngorm Mountain, Aviemore

Inland Waters

Scotland's many rivers and stunning lochs offer plenty opportunities for thrilling whitewater kayaking, rafting and canoeing through breathtaking scenery. More easy-going activities are available on calm stretches of water – ideal for young families and novices. Aberfeldy, on the upper reaches of the River Tay, and Aviemore are hubs for river experiences of all kinds. For a day out on calm waters, sailing dinghies can be hired on inland lochs.

$\rightarrow$

Kayaker descending rapids on the scenic River Tummel

A Hiker's Haven

Scotland has a vast network of long-distance walking routes, and almost nowhere is out of bounds. The West Highland Way (p33) is a particular favourite among keen hikers.

$\leftarrow$

Family hopping across a stream and enjoying a scenic hike in the Highlands

Cycling and Mountain Biking

There are excellent off-road woodland and moorland trails all over Scotland. Great forest rides can be found in Galloway Forest Park (p133) and Glentress near Peebles (p122). Outside ski season, the Nevis Range (p208) and the Lecht offer more challenging trails, while Arran (p250) and the Trossachs (p176) offer gentler journeys.

$\rightarrow$

Mountain biker jumping at speed on a forest mountain-bike trail

WALKING IN SCOTLAND

Whether you wish to stroll for an afternoon or spend weeks on the trail, Scotland is a veritable paradise for ramblers. Established routes, most of which are off-road and traffic-free, are clearly waymarked for the public by the green signs of the Scottish Rights of Way Society. The country's most impressive scenery is reasonably accessible by foot, and the variety of terrain encompasses everything from craggy mountain peaks that beckon the most ambitious of adventurers to gentle river valleys suited to a more leisurely stroll. Scotland also possesses many miles of dramatic coastline, with a large number of offshore islands to explore.

RIGHT OF ACCESS

In Scotland there is a statutory right of access to most land for recreational purposes. The 2003 Land Reform Act granted everyone "freedom to roam". This means that although most of Scotland's land is owned by very few people, the hills, valleys, moors and waters are open to anyone who wants to explore them, as long as they behave responsibly. The Scottish Outdoor Access Code *(www.outdooraccess-scotland.scot)* gives guidance as well as information on restrictions during lambing (Jan–Apr) and deer stalking season (Jul–Oct).

$\longrightarrow$

Hiking in moss-covered woodland near a waterfall in Dumfries and Gallway

CLOTHING AND EQUIPMENT

The weather in Scotland is fickle. It can snow in June or be balmy in February and conditions are liable to change rapidly. When going for a day walk, take waterproof trousers and a fleece or warm sweater. Make your clothing adaptable; several thin layers are better than one thick one. For a walk of more than a couple of hours, take plenty of food and water. Countryside walks demand strong shoes or boots. Sturdy trainers (running shoes) can be worn on roads or firm tracks, but not on rough ground where you may need ankle support.

$\longrightarrow$

Walking in the magnificent wilderness of the Cairngorms National Park

↑ A red deer stag, standing majestically beside a loch in the Scottish Highlands

DAY WALKS

Miles of local path networks provide excellent, safe walking opportunities. Some of the best are in the Borders and around Galloway, in Perthshire (around Dunkeld and Pitlochry), in Aberdeenshire (around Huntly), at Braemar and on the island of Bute, as well as in more remote Wester Ross, the Western Isles, Orkney and Shetland. Most have a cultural or natural history theme. Walk Highlands *(www.walkhighlands.co.uk)* is an excellent resource, detailing the distance, elevation and level of difficulty of each route.

LONG-DISTANCE WALKING ROUTES

From cross-country favourites such as the West Highland Way to lesser known beauties such as the Affric Kintail Way, Scotland's long-distance walking routes offer a great opportunity to experience some of the country's most diverse landscapes and wildlife. You can combine multiple trails as you like, or just walk a small section of a waymarked path. Before setting off, ensure you pick up the latest OS map for the area.

TOP 5 LONG-DISTANCE HIKES

West Highland Way
⌂ 96 miles (154 km)
ⓦ westhighlandway.org
Scotland's best-known long-distance walk.

Southern Upland Way
⌂ 211 miles (340 km)
Coast-to-coast route in southernmost Scotland.

Great Glen Way
⌂ 73 miles (118 km)
From the southwest coast to the northeast.

Speyside Way
⌂ 73 miles (117 km)
ⓦ speysideway.org
Path that follows the course of the River Spey.

Hebridean Way
⌂ 156 miles (252 km)
Covers the length of this spectacular archipelago.

Wild Deer

With over one million wild red deer in Scotland, deer stalking is a controversial yet popular pursuit. Rather than harming the deer, why not join a four-wheel-drive safari in the Cairngorms *(p210)* to shoot these magnificent stags with your camera instead? Boisterous stags can be spotted clashing antlers during the autumn rut, while, in spiring, flocks of hinds and their young are a common sight on open moorland in the Cairngorms and the glens of Argyll.

→

A young stag standing in front of a snow-capped mountain in the Highlands

SCOTLAND FOR
WILDLIFE ENCOUNTERS

From the wide, open spaces of the Highlands and thick wooded riverbanks of Tayside and the Borders, to the rugged cliffs and tidal firths of the Atlantic and North Sea coasts and rocky shorelines of the Scottish isles, Scotland is home to a rich variety of birds and animals large and small.

Protecting Scotland's Native Species

Red squirrel priority woodlands like Glenmore Forest Park *(p210)* are a haven for these cute critters. Safe from the threat of rival greys, their numbers are on the rise. The Scottish wildcat, almost extinct in the wild, can be seen at the Highland Wildlife Park *(p213)*, where bison, lynx and wolves, once native to Scotland, roam in spacious open-air enclosures.

←

Scotland's native red squirrel, a species under threat from invasive grey squirrels.

REWILDING SCOTLAND

Re-establishing native species has had positive results, but it's a controversial issue for some. White-tailed sea eagles and beavers have been successfully reintroduced, despite strong objections from farmers claiming eagles prey on lambs and beavers damage riverbanks. But there has been strident opposition to reintroducing lynx and even wolves. A final decision is yet to be reached on the matter.

Whales, Seals and Dolphins

The waters around Scotland's northern shores and northern and western isles are a refuge for many marine mammals. Take a boat trip from Aberdeen *(p164)* or Inverness *(p216)* to see bottlenose dolphins and harbour porpoises, or explore the waters around Mull to spot minke whales, basking sharks and killer whales (orca). Grey seals and common seals are a frequent sight in the sea lochs and sandbanks of the west coast, in the Firth of Forth and in the Firth of Tay.

→

Grey seals being observed and photographed on a sandy estuary near Aberdeen

Puffins and Seabirds

Seabirds can be spotted from just about anywhere on Scotland's coastline. See the world's largest colony of northern gannets on Bass Rock *(p118)* and, for a close encounter with puffins, head to the remote Handa Island Wildlife Reserve *(p265)* between May and July.

→

An Atlantic puffin, with its distinctive brightly coloured bill, on Handa Island

→ Eilean Donan
Castle on its tiny
island in Loch Duich

SCOTLAND FOR
SPECTACULAR
CASTLES

Imposing fortified strongholds, ghostly shells crowning sea-girt crags,
pocket-sized keeps of Highland and Border lairds and the fanciful 19th-
century inventions of imaginative Victorians: each of Scotland's many
castles has its own secrets, legends and often bloody history.

Rugged Ruins

Dunnottar *(p182)* was, in its
day, a perfect natural fortress.
It was here that Scotland's
crown jewels were hidden
when Cromwell invaded in
1650. Another spectacular
coastal ruin, Tantallon Castle
(p118) is perched high above
the sea near Dunbar. Near the
English border, Caerlaverock
(p130) was the stronghold
of the Maxwell lords.

→ Ruins of Dunnottar Castle
perched on a craggy rocky
outcrop near Stonehaven

Fearsome Fortresses

Edinburgh's iconic castle (*p78*) has changed many times during its tumultuous history. Its position on Castle Rock has been of strategic importance since the 12th century. Many of its buildings date back to the 16th century, but its formidable outer ramparts were later heavily reinforced against the threat of Jacobite rebellion. Outside Inverness, Fort George (*p255*) is another forbidding military relic of that era. More romantic looking is Eilean Donan (*p262*), Scotland's most photogenic castle. Its owners, the MacRae chieftains, were notorious for mounting the severed heads of their foes along the ramparts. Their keep was demolished after the 1715 Jacobite rising and rebuilt by John MacRae-Gilstrap between 1912 and 1932.

Stately Homes and Palaces

The remains of royal palaces at Linlithgow (*p122*) and Falkland (*p194*) tell of grand ambitions of Scottish kings. In the 19th century, Scottish magnates began re-creating their former strongholds into opulent imitations of French chateaux, like Dunrobin Castle (*p257*), home of the Earls of Sutherland, or Gothic piles like Inveraray Castle (*p242*), seat of the dukes of Argyll.

→

Baronial turrets of Dunrobin Castle, and (*inset*) its opulent library

EVOLUTION OF THE SCOTTISH CASTLE

Few sights can match the romance of a Scottish castle set upon a small island in the middle of a quiet loch. These formidable retreats, often in remote settings, were built all over the Highlands, where incursions and strife between the clans were common. From the earliest Pictish brochs (Iron Age stone towers) and Norman-influenced motte and bailey castles, the distinctively Scottish stone tower-house evolved, first appearing in the 14th century. By the mid-17th century fashion had become more important than defence, and there followed a period in which numerous huge Scottish palaces were built.

Did You Know?

Scotland has around 650 castles, ranging from ruins to grand palatial residences.

The motte of earth or rock was sometimes partially man-made.

The keep contained the chief's house, lookout and main defence.

The bailey enclosed dwellings and storehouses.

Crenellated parapet for sentries

Featureless, straight walls contain arrow slits for windows.

Castles through the Years

Motte and Bailey

These castles first appeared in the 12th-century. They stood atop two adjacent mounds enclosed by a wall, or palisade, and defensive ditches. The higher mound, or motte, was the most strongly defended as it held the keep and chief's house. The lower bailey was where the ordinary people lived.

Duffus Castle (c 1150) was atypically made of stone rather than wood. It is one of Scotland's best-preserved motte and bailey castles and is well worth going out of your way to visit. The castle's fine defensive position dominates the surrounding flatlands north of Elgin.

Early Tower-house

Designed to deter local attacks rather than a major assault, the first tower-houses appeared in the 13th-century, and their design lived on for 400 years. They were built initially on a rectangular plan, with a single tower divided into three or four floors. The walls were unadorned, with few windows. Defensive structures were on top, and extra space was made by building adjoining towers. Extensions were vertical, to minimize the area open to attack.

Neidpath Castle, standing upon a steep rocky crag above the River Tweed, is an L-shaped tower-house dating from the late 14th-century.

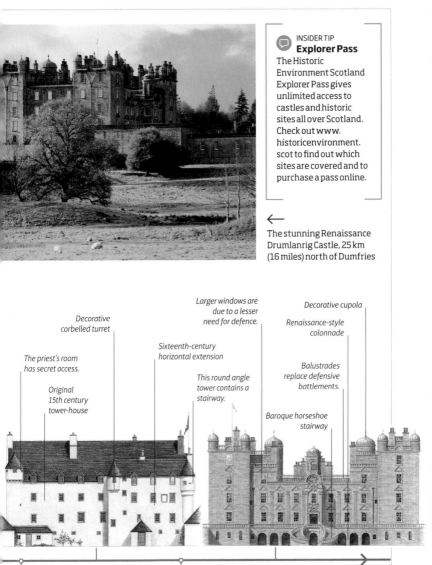

INSIDER TIP
Explorer Pass

The Historic Environment Scotland Explorer Pass gives unlimited access to castles and historic sites all over Scotland. Check out www.historicenvironment.scot to find out which sites are covered and to purchase a pass online.

←

The stunning Renaissance Drumlanrig Castle, 25 km (16 miles) north of Dumfries

Decorative corbelled turret

The priest's room has secret access.

Original 15th century tower-house

Sixteenth-century horizontal extension

Larger windows are due to a lesser need for defence.

This round angle tower contains a stairway.

Decorative cupola

Renaissance-style colonnade

Balustrades replace defensive battlements.

Baroque horseshoe stairway

Later Tower-house

Though the requirements of defence were being replaced by those of comfort, the style of the early tower-house remained popular. By the 17th-century, wings for accommodation were being added around the original tower (often creating a courtyard). The battlements and turrets were kept more for decorative than defensive reasons.

Glamis Castle, one of Scotland's finest castles, was originally a tower house and was embellished in the 17th-century.

Classical Palace

By the 18th-century the defensive imperative had passed and castles were built in the manner of country houses; the vertical tower-house was rejected in favour of a horizontal plan (though the building of imitation fortified buildings continued into the 19th-century with the mock-Baronial trend). Outside influences came from all over Europe, including Renaissance and Gothic revivals, with echoes of French châteaux.

Drumlanrig Castle (p123) was built in the 17th-century and has traditional Scots aspects as well as Renaissance features, such as the decorated stairway.

Edinburgh City of Literature

Few places can match the capital's literary treasury. Discover Scotland's spoken word heritage at the Scottish Storytelling Centre *(p83)*, or walk in the footsteps of the country's greatest authors on the Edinburgh Literary Pub Tour *(www.edinburghliterary pubtour.co.uk)*. Don't miss the Edinburgh International Book Festival which takes place every summer.

→

Robin Mair speaking at Unbound, Edinburgh International Book Festival

SCOTLAND FOR
BOOKWORMS

Scotland has a remarkable literary heritage, and has produced more than its fair share of acclaimed writers and enlightened thinkers. Bookworms will enjoy the wealth of bookish festivals, events and experiences on offer that honour the country's most celebrated literary luminaries.

MEAN STREETS AND TARTAN NOIR

With *Laidlaw* (1977), Scots author William McIlvanney kicked off Scotland's "tartan noir" crime fiction genre, a pantheon including the likes of Ian Rankin's gloomy Inspector Rebus, Christopher Brookmyre's roguish investigator Jack Parlabane, and Denise Mina's DI Alex Morrow, a rare female protagonist in the crime fiction world. Val McDermid's novels were adapted into a cult TV series, *Wire in the Blood*, and Kate Atkinson's Jackson Brodie stars in *Case Histories*.

A National Treasure

One of Scotland's most celebrated and prolific writers, Robert Burns has made his mark all over the country. There are numerous museums and exhibitions in his name. For hard-core fans, the Burns Heritage Trail *(p116)* is a comprehensive tour of where he lived and wrote and the places that inspired him most.

The Bookish Borders

The traditions of the Borders inspired Sir Walter Scott's many tales, and his grandiose home at Abbotsford *(p114)* is a place of pilgrimage for fans of his ballads and historical romances. Meanwhile, book-mad Wigtown *(p128)* in Dumfries and Galloway is home to a plethora of bookshops and bookish cafés; it plays host to a lively ten-day literature festival every autumn.

$\longrightarrow$

Decorative entrance to one of many second-hand bookshops in Wigtown

Glasgow Greats

Edinburgh may steal the literary limelight, but Glasgow has produced an adventurous generation of authors and poets, including Alexander McArthur, James Kelman, multi-talented author and visual artist Alasdair Gray, and Jackie Kay, who was appointed Scotland's makar (poet laureate) in 2016.

$\longleftarrow$

Jackie Kay reciting a poem at the official opening of the Queensferry Crossing, Fife

Land of Inspiration

Scotland's landscapes and architecture have inspired generations of authors. J K Rowling wrote the first of her *Harry Potter* novels in Edinburgh's Elephant House café, overlooking Greyfriars Kirkyard, while *Dracula* author Bram Stoker based his spooky description of the vampire's lair on Slains Castle in Aberdeenshire.

↑ The Auld Brig in Alloway, Ayrshire features in Robert Burns's famous poem *Tam O'Shanter*

↑ Birthplace of Harry Potter, The Elephant House café

Off the Beaten Track

In Glasgow, you don't have to go to a gallery to see great art, as gable ends and derelict walls become canvases for eye-catching works on Glasgow's Mural Trail *(www.citycentremuraltrail.co.uk)*. In Ullapool *(p263)*, An Talla Solais offers visitors the chance to get creative through a variety of hands-on art classes.

↑ *Saint Mungo*, a mural by the Glasgow street artist known as Smug

SCOTLAND FOR
ART LOVERS

Scotland's art galleries span an almost unimagineable breadth of time. Here, elaborately knotted Celtic jewellery sits alongside vivid Modernist masterpieces, while Pictish monoliths rub shoulders with ground-breaking 21st-century artists from around the globe.

Modern Marvels

Dada and Surrealism rule the Scottish National Gallery of Modern Art's permanent collection *(p100)*, but the gallery also hosts exhibitions by contemporary art titans from all over the world. The most recent addition to Scotland's modern art scene is the V&A Dundee *(p168)*, a stunning piece of architecture which opened on Dundee's waterfront in 2018.

←

The striking interior of the V&A Dundee, designed by Kengo Kuma

Scottish Masterpieces

The Scottish National Gallery *(p90)* houses a world-class collection of Scottish and international art. Meanwhile, the stars of the Glasgow Style and Scottish Colourist movements share space with Dalí, Rembrandt and Monet in the halls of the Kelvingrove Art Gallery and Museum *(p146)*.

→

Visitors exploring one of the many rooms at the Scottish National Gallery

Ancient Treasures

Silver torcs, bejewelled gold arm-rings and an intricately carved ivory chess set on display at the Museum of Scotland *(p86)* are evidence of the artistic brilliance of ancient Celtic and Norse cultures. Older still are the enigmatic pinnacles that form the mysterious stone circle at Callanish *(p235)* on the Isle of Lewis. Stop by the visitor centre to uncover the fascinating story of these ancient stones.

←

Lewis Chessmen, carved from walrus ivory by skilled craftsmen.

TOP 5 SCOTTISH ARTISTS

Henry Raeburn (1756-1823)
Royal portraitist knighted by George IV.

Samuel Peploe (1871-1935)
A leading light of the post-Impressionist "Scottish Colourists".

Anne Redpath (1895-1965)
Star of the "Edinburgh School" known for her vivid use of colour.

Eduardo Paolozzi (1924-2005)
Pop art pioneer and creator of massive bronze sculptures.

↑ A curator showing the exhibits at the Hoswick Visitor Centre, Shetland

Arts, Crafts and Textiles

Scotland's local makers create all manner of authentic products, including textiles, pottery, jewellery and glass. In Shetland to Stranraer, you'll discover a dizzying diversity of local artisans on one of Scotland's many art trails, where studios and workshops welcome visitors with open arms.

Headline Acts

Scots love to party, so it's no wonder that this small country is home to some big-name festivals. Glasgow's TRNSMT festival is the summer's highest-profile event, hosting icons like Stormzy and the Arctic Monkeys, home-grown talents such as Lewis Capaldi and Young Fathers, and a supporting cast of up-and-coming stars. The Edinburgh Jazz and Blues Festival (p74) kicks off the festival season with ten days of everything from bebop and samba to swing and soul. On the banks of the River Tay, Solas is a lively gallimaufry of acoustic and electric world music, while the Tiree Music Festival lures folk-rock fusion fans to the shores of Scotland's sunniest isle (p249).

→

Lewis Capaldi performing
in Edinburgh's Princes
Street Gardens

SCOTLAND FOR
MUSIC FANS

Scotland is a nation of music lovers. Plaintive pibrochs recall bygone battles and fiddles set feet tapping at events and venues all over Scotland, while newer rock and pop traditions are represented by guitar-based indie bands and DJs who perform to packed theatres, concert halls and giant stadiums.

Pipers and Pibrochs

Once the exclusive sound of the Highlands, bagpipes have become a national emblem. In summer, Edinburgh's Royal Mile (p70) is teeming with energetic kilted pipers vying for tourists' attention. Some play lesser known pibrochs – slow, melancholy melodies. Find out more at Glasgow's National Piping Centre (p155).

 INSIDER TIP
Glasgow Mela

Enjoy musical performances by Indian dance troupes and African drummers at the Glasgow Mela – Scotland's largest multicultural festival – held in Kelvingrove Park every summer.

→

The Inveraray Pipe
Band parading through
their home town

Toe-Tapping Traditions

Scotland's traditional music festivals attract visitors from all over the world. Scottish folk music embraces not just Celtic sounds but global rhythms and harmonies too. Glasgow's Celtic Connections festival, is the year's biggest folk event. In the Northern Isles, Folk Frenzy, held in July, is Shetland's celebration of the most enduring fiddling tradition in Scotland. But you don't have to go to a festival to experience Scotland's toe-tapping trad. When the Shetland Folk Frenzy is in full swing there are jam sessions in just about every pub in Lerwick..Visiting musos can sit in on - or even join - sessions in folk music pubs like the legendary Sandy Bell's *(www.sandybells. co.uk)* in Edinburgh and the Taybank *(www.thetay bank.co.uk)* in Dunkeld.

← Contemporary folk band Lau performing at Celtic Connections

TOP 4 LIVE MUSIC VENUES

King Tut's Wah-Wah Hut, Glasgow
Ⓦ kingtuts.co.uk
Many legends launched their careers here, among them Oasis.

Barrowland Ballroom, Glasgow
Ⓦ barrowland-ballroom.co.uk
Legendary venue hosting big names as well as up-and-coming bands.

The Jazz Bar, Edinburgh
Ⓦ thejazzbar.co.uk
Scotland's only venue dedicated solely to jazz.

Fat Sam's, Dundee
Ⓦ fatsams.co.uk
This vast club hosts DJs, bands and theme nights.

Glasgow's Musical Heritage

Glasgow is home to a vibrant music scene and its musical history runs deep. Walk in the footsteps of musical greats and discover the stories of legendary performers who have come to define this musical city on a walking tour of Glasgow's Music Mile *(www.glasgowmusiccitytours.com)*. The tour covers iconic gig venues such as the Barrowland Ballroom and King Tut's, dive bars where big names paid their dues, and concert halls of the past and present.

↑ The brightly lit façade of the Barrowland Ballroom

Cookery Courses

Roll up your sleeves, don your apron and brush up your culinary expertise under the tutelage of top Scottish chefs at Nick Nairn's Cook School at Port of Menteith, or add to your skills and innovate with tips from top chefs such as Tony Singh. For cooking with a twist, Praveen and Swarma Kumar share their culinary skills at their Indian cook school in Perth *(p189)*.

→

Learning from culinary expert and top Scottish chef Tony Singh

SCOTLAND FOR
FOODIES

Scotland's humble gastronomic beginnings are very much a thing of the past. Swapping deep-fried Mars Bars for Michelin stars, it is now a top foodie destination, home to a plethora of acclaimed fine-dining restaurants and a wealth of talented chefs working with great local ingredients.

Meet the Makers

Stalls at the monthly Aberdeen Country Fair and the weekly Edinburgh Farmers Market are great places to sample artisan baked goods, charcuterie, cheeses and organic produce, and there are lots of smaller farmers' markets in traditional market towns like Aberfeldy, Banchory, Ayr and Elgin.

↑ Weekend Farmers Market at the foot of Edinburgh Castle

Scotland's Foodie Trails

Themed foodie trails showcase Scotland's flavours, from Arbroath's smoked haddock to the tangy, heather-infused ales of Islay. The Seafood Trail, comprising eight restaurants from Oban to the Kintyre peninsula, is a particular highlight. Surprises include Scotland's Chocolate Trail, where master chocolatier Iain Burnett creates sweet delights like salted raspberry chocolate with Szechuan pepper salt in his shop *(www.high-landchoco-latier.com)*.

←

Velvet chocolate truffles made by the Highland Chocolatier, Pitlochry

TOP 5 SCOTTISH DELICACIES

Haggis
Spiced sheep's offal, oats and seasoning, traditionally eaten with "neeps" (swedes) and "tatties" (potatoes).

Stovies
A mix of potatoes, onions and beef cooked in dripping (fat).

Cullen Skink
Creamy soup made from smoked haddock, milk and potato.

Arbroath Smokies
Haddock split open, salted and smoked.

Venison
The meat of wild red deer is dark and gamey.

💬 INSIDER TIP
Fruit Picking in the Borders

Border Berries near Kelso *(p122)* is one of the few remaining berry farms that ripens fruit in the open air. Visit in July to late August, when the berries are at their best.

Fish and Chips to Fine Dining

Scotland is famous for its fish and chips, but there's much more to delight discerning diners. Edinburgh has four Michelin-starred restaurants, and other temples to gastronomy are scattered far and wide from the Peat Inn near St Andrews to the Isle of Eriska Hotel's fine dining restaurant near Oban to Braidwoods *(p133)* in Ayrshire.

→

Beautiful presentation at the Whitehouse Restaurant, Lochaline

Lowland Whiskies

Lowland whiskies tend to be smooth and their palate gentle. Until recently lowland distilleries were few and far between, but new ones are cropping up, many producing spirits that replicate the light, grassy style of the region.
What to try: Glenkinchie (p121) is made near Edinburgh, while Auchentoshan is triple-distilled in Clydebank. Bladnoch, in tiny Wigtown (p128), is Scotland's most southerly distillery.

→

Casks at the Glenkinchie distillery, a long-standing whisky producer

Did You Know?

Whisky stored in casks evaporates at a rate of around 2% per year. This is called the "angels' share".

SCOTTISH
SPIRIT

No special occasion is complete without a dram of the drink that is the pure essence of Scotland. Although global brands have industrialized whisky-making, their dominance is being challenged by artisan distilleries that produce exciting new malts using age-old skills. Meanwhile, new distillers are creating gins and other spirits such as rum, vodka and absinthe.

Speyside Malts

Many of Scotland's famous malt whiskies come from Speyside, where distillers claim there is a perfect balance of climate, terrain and water from Highland springs.
What to try: Glenlivet and Glenfiddich, matured in Bourbon casks to give them notes of light vanilla and orchard fruits, or sherry-matured, Macallan, the "Rolls Royce of single malts", has notes of dried fruits and sweet spices. Don't miss a visit to the Macallan distillery as part of The Malt Whisky Trail® in Speyside (p187).

←

Glenlivet whisky, one of Speyside's most famous malts, being poured into a glass

Highland Malts

Due to the Highlands' vast and diverse terrain, its single malts can vary considerably. Some are rich and full-bodied, others sweet and fruity.
What to try: Glenmorangie, Scotland's biggest-selling single malt, is light and flowery taste, while Edradour makes a minty, creamy whisky.

$\rightarrow$

A glass of single malt whisky, served "on the rocks" over ice

New Make Spirits and Gins

Gin has become Scotland's trendy tipple of choice alongside "new make" spirits that side-step the ageing process of traditional whisky production.
What to try: Rascally Liquor at Annandale Distillery or go on a "gin jolley" at Pickering's in Edinburgh's Summerhall.

$\leftarrow$

Edinburgh's hand-crafted Pickerings gin served with tonic and a slice of orange

THE BIG BIG GIN FESTIVAL

This award-winning festival in Edinburgh celebrates all things pertaining to this much-loved libation, from old-school favourites to the latest innovations. Sample gins from some of Scotland's leading makers and craft gin distilleries, and enjoy the show as mixologists prepare colourful concoctions with flare and gusto at the cocktail bar. You can even take part in a restorative Yin Yoga class to cure the hangover *(bigbiggin festival.com)*.

↑ Laphroaig distillery produces a distinctively smoky single malt

Island Malts

The malt whiskies of the Hebrides are redolent of heather and peat smoke, while some claim to detect a hint of seaweed and iodine in some island malts. For many they are an acquired taste.
What to try: Islay malts like Laphroaig, Lagavulin and Bowmore, Tobermory from Mull and Talisker from Skye.

WHISKY PRODUCTION IN SCOTLAND

Whisky is to the Scots what champagne is to the French, and a visit to Scotland would not be complete without sampling this fiery, heart-warming spirit. Scotland has many distilleries producing highly rated single malt whiskies, a title that is revered by true whisky connoisseurs. All malt whiskies are produced using much the same process, but the environment, maturity and storage of the whisky have such a strong bearing on its character that every one is a different experience. There is no "best" malt whisky – some are suited to drinking at bedtime, others as an aperitif.

HOW WHISKY IS MADE

Traditionally made from just barley, yeast and stream water, Scottish whisky (from the Gaelic *usquebaugh*, or the "water of life") takes a little over three weeks to produce, though it must be given at least three years to mature, usually in oak casks. The art of blending, pioneered in Edinburgh in the 1860s, became so popular that very little single malt whisky was drunk outside the Highlands until the 1980s when the original vintages were rediscovered and have since regained widespread popularity.

> 💬 INSIDER TIP
> **Anything Goes**
>
> Traditionalists may scoff, but whisky is a drink to be enjoyed. So whether that be straight up, on the rocks, with a drop of water, or mixed in a cocktail – *Sláinte*!

→

Rows of copper pot stills and *(inset)* oak casks in Glenfiddich distillery, producer of the world's best-selling single malt whisky

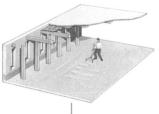

A "mash tun", where ground malt is soaked and dissolved.

Making Whisky

△ Malting is the first stage. Barley grain is soaked in water and spread on the malting floor. With regular turning, the grain germinates, producing a "green malt". Germination stimulates the production of enzymes which turn the starches into fermentable sugars.

△ Drying of the barley halts germination after 12 days of malting. This is done over a peat fire in a pagoda-shaped malt-kiln. The peat-smoke gives flavour to the malt and eventually to the mature whisky. The malt is gleaned of germinated roots and then milled.

△ Mashing of the ground malt, or "grist", occurs in a large vat or "mash tun", which holds a vast quantity of hot water. The malt is soaked and begins to dissolve, producing a sugary solution called "wort", which is then cooled and extracted for fermentation.

Yeast turns to alcohol in a woven vat, or "washback".

Copper pot stills, where the wash is distilled and purified.

Oak casks

△ Fermentation occurs when yeast is added to the cooled wort in wooden vats, or "washbacks". The mixture is stirred for hours as the yeast turns the sugar into alcohol, producing a clear liquid called "wash", ready for distillation to remove impurities.

△ Distillation involves boiling the wash twice so that the alcohol vaporizes and condenses. In copper "pot stills", the wash is distilled - first in the "wash still", then in the "spirit still". Now purified, with an alcohol content of 57 per cent, the result is young whisky.

△ Maturation is the final process. The whisky mellows in oak casks that have held sherry, whisky or other wines, for a legal minimum of three years. Premium brands give the whisky a 10- to 15-year maturation, though some are given up to 50 years.

Furry Friends

Get up close and personal with chimps, pelicans, creepy-crawlies and giant pandas at Edinburgh Zoo *(p101)*. Home to over 1,000 animals, it makes for a great day out for animal lovers of all ages. At the Highland Wildlife Park *(p213)* kids will love spotting bison, polar bears, wolves and wildcats, all of which were once common in the Highlands. Nearby, Britain's only herd of wild reindeer roam free at the Cairngorm Reindeer Centre.

→

Playful penguins cooling off under the sprinklers at Edinburgh Zoo

SCOTLAND FOR
FAMILIES

With an abundance of castles, country parks and exciting museums Scotland is a veritable playground for kids. Even in big cities, you're always close to parks and gardens where tots can romp around safely. Most attractions are family-friendly, leaving the weather as your only worry.

Adventures in Science

Young visitors to Glasgow Science Centre *(p144)* can take an incredible voyage inside the human body, walk among the planets or travel to the far reaches of outer space at fun and exciting exhibits like BodyWorks and the Planetarium.

> **INSIDER TIP**
> **Quids In!**
>
> Children aged 5-15 travelling with adults who purchase an off peak return can travel for £1 each. Tickets can be bought at ScotRail ticket offices and online *(www.scotrail.co.uk)*, and include free entry to some of Scotland's top attractions.

↑ Children playing on a giant hamster wheel at Glasgow Science Centre

Swing From the Treetops

Go Ape offers treetop-level high ropes and zip-wire adventures at outstanding locations throughout Scotland, including the grounds of Crathes Castle near Aberdeen, Queen Elizabeth Forest Park in the Trossachs *(p176)*, and Glentress Forest *(p122)*.

→

Exploring the tree-top canopy on a zipwire at Go Ape

Hit the Slopes

Tobogganing, snowboarding, skiing and ice climbing are among the activities on offer at Snowfactor *(www.snowfactor. com)*, a year-round indoor winter sports centre near Glasgow. Further afield, Aviemore is a family-friendly resort on the slopes of Cairngorm Mountain *(p211)*.

←

Youngsters learning how to snowboard at Snowfactor

Amazing Mazes

Leafy labyrinths are family-friendly features of the gardens and grounds of many of Scotland's stately homes, castles and farms. Every summer, Cairnie Fruit Farm *(www.cairniefruitfarm. co.uk)* in Fife carves a pop-up "mega maze" out of a six acre (2.5 hectare) expanse of 2.5 m (8 ft) maize stalks - offering hours of entertainment and family fun. Elegant Traquair House *(p123)* in the Borders claims its permanent cypress maze is the longest of its kind in Scotland, but it is rivalled by Scone Palace's stunning 800 m (2,620 ft) Murray Star Maze *(p174)*, its mix of copper and green beech designed to match the Earl of Mansfield's family tartan. Here, little ones love to discover the secret fountain in its centre.

↑ Visitors entering the labyrinthine Traquair Maze, the largest hedged-maze in Scotland

Sand in the City

Scotland's biggest cities are never far from the coast, and each has, within a manageable distance from the city centre, their own seaside resort. Once teeming with holidaymakers, these city beaches now offer a quiet escape for both locals and visitors alike. Stroll along the sand, eat fish and chips and ice cream, paddle in the shallows or, if you're feeling brave, swim further out. Portobello Beach *(p103)* offers a breath of fresh sea air only 8 km (5 miles) from central Edinburgh, and it hosts a summer sandcastle competition and sand sculpture festival. Gullane, 35 km (22 miles) from the city, offers long breezy walks on a vast stretch of sand. On the west coast, Largs *(p132)* has been a great escape for Glaswegians since the 19th century.

→

People walking their dogs on the sandy bay at Portobello on a winter afternoon

SCOTLAND FOR
BEACHGOERS

Scottish seaside resorts fell from favour in the 1960s, when affordable air travel lured Scots to the Mediterranean and beyond. But seaside thrills now attract sporty visitors and sunseekers back to city beaches and even further afield to the spectacular white sands and windy bays of the West Coast.

Surf's Up

The Atlantic rollers that sweep Tiree's shores make this tiny island a surfers' mecca *(p249)*. Year-round Atlantic swell and the sheer variety of surf on offer make this an ideal destination for both seasoned surfers and beginners. On the North Coast *(p264)*, Thurso is another favourite spot for bold surfing pilgrims who dare breakers that reach 5 m (15 ft). Less remote is Belhaven Bay on the East Lothian Coast *(p118)* which is home to the new Belhaven Surf Centre *(www. belhavensurfcentre.org)*.

←

Surfer catching a wave on the windswept island of Tiree, a surfing hotspot

Hebridean Beauties

Nowhere are Scotland's beaches more impressive than in the Hebrides. The vast sands of Traigh Mhòr on Barra *(p238)* double as the island's airport, with planes landing on the sandy bay at low tide. Hit up another stunner and head across the causeway that links Barra to the even smaller island of Vatersay. Its crescents of white sand are surely among the most beautiful of all Scotland's beaches.

← Plane landing on Traigh Mhòr on Barra

→ Turquoise waters and white sands of remote Seilebost Beach, South Harris

THE GULF STREAM

The ocean current known as the Gulf Stream curves northeast from the Caribbean across the Atlantic towards Scotland's western shores, where its influence creates coastal and island microclimates that are surprisingly warm for such northerly latitudes. The island of Tiree *(p249)* is only 10° south of the Arctic Circle, but local air temperatures never fall below zero and in midsummer they can reach up to 17°C – which is practically tropical by Scottish standards. That said, sea temperatures never rise above 15°C, so heavy duty wetsuits are still a must for anyone who might fancy a dip.

Scotland's Epic Coastline

The thousands of beaches scattered around Scotland's 10,000-mile (16,500-km) coastline range from tiny, hidden coves to seemingly endless white sandy bays and turquoise lagoons that, on a sunny day, look more like the Caribbean than Scotland. The Sands of Morar *(p267)*, north of Fort William, is famed for its chain of pink and silver beaches, while island gems like Seilebost on Harris *(p236)* astound with stunning aquamarine colour palettes and dazzling white sands.

◁ Trainspotting (1996)

Edinburgh city council was so shocked by Irvine Welsh's gritty, realistic and somewhat gruesome tragi-comedy of Edinburgh low-life that it refused permission to shoot the movie in Leith, where the original novel was set. It was filmed instead in the more film business-friendly (and less shockable) Glasgow.

▷ James Bond's Scottish Roots

It will come as no surprise to true 007 fans that Britain's most suave secret agent has Scottish roots, with his native homeland featuring heavily in the Bond movie franchise. Drive through Glencoe's stunning mountain pass to James Bond's family home as depicted in *Skyfall* (2012), or visit Eilean Donan Castle, which starred as the Scottish headquarters of MI6 in *The World is Not Enough* (2012).

SCOTLAND
ON SCREEN

From gritty urban realism to fantastic sagas of dungeons and dragons, Scotland's spectacular landscapes, picturesque castles and quaint villages have inspired directors and producers the world over. Take a cinematic journey round Scotland to see iconic movie and television backdrops for yourself.

◁ Outlander (2014)

The much-loved time-travel series *Outlander* was filmed against some of the most evocative historic buildings and landscapes in Scotland. Castle Leod, near Strathpeffer, serves as Castle Leoch, a key setting for the series. Other locations include Aberdour and Falkland in Fife (which doubled as 18th-century Inverness), Blackness Castle, Kinloch Rannoch, the Cairngorms and the Highland Folk Museum at Kingussie.

◁ Harry Potter and the Hogwarts Express

The multi-arched Glenfinnan Viaduct railway bridge features in the eight Harry Potter movies, carrying the Hogwarts Express on its way to the now legendary school of witchcraft and wizardry. In summer, you can ride the Jacobite Express steam train, which doubled as the Hogwarts Express in the films, on its way across the viaduct from Fort William to Mallaig. Standard trains also cross it daily all year round.

◁ Braveheart (1995)

With an Australian-American starring as Scots hero William Wallace, Braveheart was shot almost entirely outside Scotland. This is because the scenes of Wallace's great battles against the English are now engulfed in the urban sprawls of Stirling and Falkirk. However, a mock-medieval village was built in Glen Nevis for early scenes, some of which were shot against the spectacular backdrop of Glencoe, the Mamore hills and Loch Leven.

TOP 5 SCOTTISH MOVIE STARS

Sean Connery
The original and best James Bond.

Ewan McGregor
McGregor was young Obi-Wan Kenobi in the Star Wars prequels.

Robbie Coltrane
Best known as Hagrid in the Harry Potter movies.

Kelly MacDonald
MacDonald played Renton's girlfriend in Trainspotting.

James McAvoy
McAvoy starred in the X-Men chronicles.

△ Doune Castle, Perthshire

The majestic Doune Castle (p187), on the fringes of the Trossachs, is a particular favourite among location scouts and has starred in Monty Python and the Holy Grail (1975), Ivanhoe (1952) and The Bruce (1996), plus TV drama Outlander. The castle also posed as Winterfell in the pilot episode of Game of Thrones (2011-19), but was dropped in favour of cheaper locations.

A YEAR IN
SCOTLAND

Pagan fire festivals, torchlight parades, piping championships, fiddle frenzies, Highland games and Viking battle re-enactments; there really is no shortage of exciting goings on in Scotland. In fact, it seems that there's an event to mark just about any occasion.

Spring

As the snows melt and temperatures start to rise, walkers and cyclists begin venturing out on the country's many long-distance trails. Sports fans, meanwhile, enjoy a Six Nations rugby match in Edinburgh or a game of shinty, the most traditional of all Scottish sports, in the Highlands. In May, major whisky festivals take place in Speyside and Islay alongside smaller ones in Stirling and Campbeltown.

1. Scotland play Wales in the Six Nations rugby tournament

Summer

Summer sees the Scottish festival season in full swing, with the Edinburgh International Festival as the headline act. Meanwhile, other towns and villages throughout the country stage their own Highland Games – the most well known take

HOGMANAY

No one enjoys a party more than the Scots, and Hogmanay is the perfect excuse for a knees up. Street parties are held throughout Scotland; the largest takes place in the capital, which sees in the New Year with fire-works and a rousing rendition of "Auld Lang Syne" at midnight.

place in Braemar and Cowal. Also popular are the many piping and folk festivals, among them HebCelt and the Shetland Folk Frenzy, held in July and August respectively.

2. Street entertainer Mullet Man performing at Edinburgh International Festival

Autumn

As the weather cools and the nights draw in, September sees the Scottish countryside ablaze in scarlet, orange, cardinal reds and yellow ochre. It's the perfect season to walk the many trails without the crowds and observe wildlife, such as red deer in the Highlands, geese on Islay and grey seals on Orkney. The end of autumn is signalled by St Andrews Day, which honours the country's patron saint.

3. Autumn colours in the Highlands

Winter

In December skiers and snowboarders hit the slopes of Scotland's mountain resorts. Christmas is keenly celebrated across the country, as is New Year, where Edinburgh's legendary Hogmanay sees it in with a bang. On 25 January, Scotland's most cherished annual tradition, Burns Night, commemorates the country's greatest poet with a Burns Supper of haggis, neeps and tatties, washed down with a wee dram.

4. Skiers on Cairngorm Mountain, and (inset) Burns Night celebrations

3

4

Spirit of Speyside Whisky Festival (Apr)
Scotland's largest whisky-producing region hosts some 700 events over six days.

Islay Festival of Music and Malt (May)
A boisterous, week-long festival of music, dance, poetry, and whisky on Islay, an island known for its peaty malts.

Highland Whisky Festival (May)
Highland whisky is celebrated at eight distilleries along the North Coast 500 route.

Campbeltown Malts Festival (May)
A small but lively event at the Springbank distillery on Kintyre.

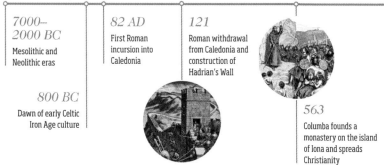

A BRIEF
HISTORY

Scotland has been torn apart by religion and politics, coveted by a powerful neighbour, and wooed and punished for 400 years in the power struggles between England, France and Spain. The country has risen and fallen through the ages, but has always demonstrated an irrepressible spirit.

In the Beginning

Stone Age settlers arrived in Scotland in around 7000 BC. By 2000 BC their Neolithic descendants were erecting impressive megalithic stone structures like those at Callanish (p235), which were to become a focus for ritual activity during the Bronze Age, and stone villages like Skara Brae (p228). By around 800 BC they had learned to forge iron, evolving into what Tacitus called the Picts, the "painted people". Often regarded as savage warriors, recent studies suggest that the Picts were in fact a sophisticated people who could read, write and convey their culture and history through art.

1 Antique map of Scotland.

2 Depiction of Pictish warriors circa 300 BC.

3 Ancient remains of Hadrian's Wall.

4 Painting of William the Conqueror.

Timeline of events

7000–2000 BC
Mesolithic and Neolithic eras

800 BC
Dawn of early Celtic Iron Age culture

82 AD
First Roman incursion into Caledonia

121
Roman withdrawal from Caledonia and construction of Hadrian's Wall

563
Columba founds a monastery on the island of Iona and spreads Christianity

Romans and Caledonians

The Romans invaded Scotland in AD 82–84, but by AD 121, after several defeats at the hands of the Picts, they were forced to retreat to Hadrian's Wall, which marked the northwest frontier of the Roman Empire for nearly 300 years. The traditional view is that Hadrian's Wall was constructed to keep the Caledonians from raiding and pillaging the civilized Roman Empire; however, some historians believe its real purpose was much less noble: that it was designed to intimidate and extract taxes from tribes on both sides of the border. A later attempt to secure Rome's frontier in the form of the Antonine Wall, between the Clyde and Forth, failed and the Romans abandoned Britain in AD 410.

New Invaders

In 1072 William the Conqueror led the first Norman incursion into Scotland, with little success. The border between Scotland and England was already under dispute, and centuries of conflict were still to follow. At this time, Scotland was made up of a number of loosely connected regions lead by Scottish kings and clan chiefs who gave lands to Anglo-Norman barons in return for serving in Scotland's wars.

BIRTH OF A NATION

The Scottish nation emerged from centuries of conflict and warfare between Picts, Scots, Britons, Angles, Norsemen and incomers from Ireland and even the Roman Empire, who could not conquer the land they called "Caledonia". In 843 AD the Scots and Pictish realms merged to form the Kingdom of Alba, and by the 11th century this included most of what we know today as Scotland.

794
The first Vikings cross the treacherous North Sea to raid, trade and eventually settle in Scotland

843
Union of Scots and Picts creates the Kingdom of Alba

1040
Macbeth rules over the Kingdom of Alba until 1057

1154
Loss of "southern countries" to England

1124
King David I imposes a Norman feudal system. A clan system prevails in the Highlands

The Wars of Independence

After the death of Alexander III in 1286, Edward I of England installed a puppet king by the name of John Balliol. When the Scots rebelled, King Edward's army invaded. In pursuit of independence from the English crown, rebels rallied behind a commoner, William Wallace, who lead them in their fight for independence as Guardian of the Kingdom of Scotland. After he was captured and executed, their support shifted to the now famed warrior, Robert the Bruce. Scion of a Norman-Scots dynasty, and with a claim to the throne, Bruce forged nobles, commoners and clansmen into an army that won a decisive victory at the Battle of Bannockburn in 1314, successfully re-establishing Scotland's status as an independent country.

The Unlucky Stuarts

The Stuart dynasty began with Robert the Steward, who became king in 1371. They were an ill-fated line: James I and James III were assassinated, James II was blown up by one of his own cannons, James IV died in battle, as did James V. His baby daughter became Mary Queen of Scots and was executed on the orders of Elizabeth I of England, the last monarch in the

1 Robert the Bruce rallying his troops at the Battle of Bannockburn.

2 Mary, Queen of Scots.

3 Battle of Dunbar.

4 Wedding portrait of William of Orange and Mary II.

Did You Know?

The name Steward was changed to Stuart to make it easier for the French to pronounce.

Timeline of events

1287
Edward I of England and his troops are defeated by Scots at the Battle of Stirling Bridge

1314
Scots defeat Edward II of England at the Battle of Bannockburn

1320
The Declaration of Arbroath affirms Scotland's status as an independent country

1326
Meeting of the first Scottish Parliament

1513
10,000 Scots including James IV die at the Battle of Flodden

Tudor dynasty. Mary's son, James VI, was luckier, inheriting Elizabeth's throne in 1603, uniting the crowns and reigning until 1625 as James VI of Scotland and James I of England.

The Reformation in Scotland

The Reformation arrived during Mary, Queen of Scots' reign, creating a deep and long-lasting religious divide during which Catholicism was purged, albeit with revivals and impregnable strongholds in the Highlands and islands.
Scotland's most vociferous leader of the
Reformation was the preacher John Knox *(p83)*.

Open war between Scottish Presbyterians and King Charles I merged with England's Civil War, when Scots fought for both sides. Charles II, crowned at Scone after his father was deposed and beheaded in 1649, was driven into exile. Scotland became part of Cromwell's Commonwealth until Charles's restoration in 1660. Protestant Scots Covenanters resisted the Catholic-leaning Charles and his successor, James II, who was ousted in 1688 by the anti-Catholic Whig faction in favour of his daughter Mary II and her Dutch husband, Prince William of Orange.

THE JACOBITES

The first Jacobites were mainly Catholic Highlanders who supported James VII of Scotland (James II of England), deposed in 1688. Their desire to restore the Catholic throne led to uprisings in 1715 and 1745. Their failure led to the end of the clan system and suppression of Highland culture for at least a century.

1542
Mary, Queen of Scots, becomes Queen of Scotland when she is just six days old

1559
John Knox leads the Reformation

1603
James II of Scotland succeeds Elizabeth I to become King of both Scotland and England in the Union of the Crowns

1641
Cromwellian occupation of Scotland

1692
Clan Campbell murder 38 MacDonalds on the King's orders in the Glencoe Massacre

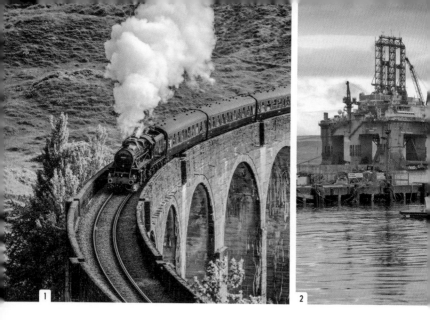

1

2

The Union with England

James VI had reigned for 36 years when he became heir to the English throne, but it was bankruptcy that finally forced Scotland into union with England in 1707. With this Act of Union came the dissolution of the Scottish Parliament. Eight years later the last Stuart monarch, Queen Anne, was succeeded by her cousin George, Duke of Hanover. Defeat at Culloden after Jacobite risings in 1715 and 1745 finally extinguished support for the exiled Stuarts. It was followed by brutal pacification of the Highlands. Peace, however, fostered a new mercantile economy. Trade with England's colonies enriched merchants whose capital eventually financed a steam-powered industrial revolution. Glasgow became a great manufacturing city, Edinburgh an intellectual powerhouse and Dundee a thriving centre of the textile industry.

The Road to Devolution

Scotland's newborn proletariat became a fertile recruiting ground for socialism and trade unionism. Glasgow's industrial heartland was nicknamed "Red Clydeside". Working-class areas like Fife and Dundee were also strongly left-wing. Industry

BONNIE PRINCE CHARLIE (1720-88)

The last of the Stuart claimants to the Crown, Bonnie Prince Charlie marched his army as far as Derby, only to be defeated at Culloden. Disguised as the loyal maidservant of a woman called Flora MacDonald, he fled to Skye and sailed back to France in 1746. He later died in Rome. Flora was buried in 1790 on Skye, wrapped in a bedsheet of the "bonnie" (handsome) prince.

Timeline of events

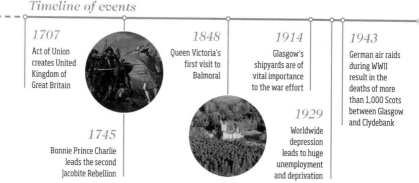

1707
Act of Union creates United Kingdom of Great Britain

1745
Bonnie Prince Charlie leads the second Jacobite Rebellion

1848
Queen Victoria's first visit to Balmoral

1914
Glasgow's shipyards are of vital importance to the war effort

1929
Worldwide depression leads to huge unemployment and deprivation

1943
German air raids during WWII result in the deaths of more than 1,000 Scots between Glasgow and Clydebank

suffered as the British Empire declined after World War II but discovery of North Sea oil in the mid-1970s boosted the economy. It was also a gift to the Scottish National Party, which adopted the slogan "It's Scotland's Oil". The majority of Scots voted in favour of the creation of a Scottish parliament in the Scottish devolution referendum in 1977.

Scotland Today

Scotland in the 21st century is a cosmopolitan society. Many Scots are descendants of 19th-century immigrants from Ireland and Italy. Others originate from Commonwealth countries, notably Pakistan, Bangladesh and India, or from EU countries. There are also substantial Turkish and Chinese communities.

The SNP has dominated politics since devolution, but their battle for independence was lost by a thin margin in the 2014 referendum. In the 2016 Brexit referendum, Scots voted to stay in the EU. England's vote to leave, however, means Scotland, as part of the UK, must follow against its will, which in turn has reignited calls for a second vote on independence. Whether this vibrant nation chooses to go its own way or stay within the UK is yet to be seen.

1 Jacobite Express on Glenfinnan Viaduct.

2 North Sea Oil Rig.

3 Campaigners during "Indyref", 2014.

4 Modern exterior of the Scottish Parliament in Edinburgh.

Did You Know?

The Scottish Parliament reconvened in Edinburgh almost 300 years after it was dissolved by the Act of Union in 1707.

1975
Exploitation of the newly discovered North Sea oilfields begins

1996
The Stone of Destiny is returned to Edinburgh Castle

1999
Scottish Parliament reinstated after 292 years

2014
Nicola Sturgeon becomes the first female First Minister of Scotland

2016
62% of Scots vote for Britain to remain in the EU referendum

2018
A fire destroys Glasgow School of Art and the V&A Dundee opens

EXPERIENCE

Cooper moving heavy whisky casks

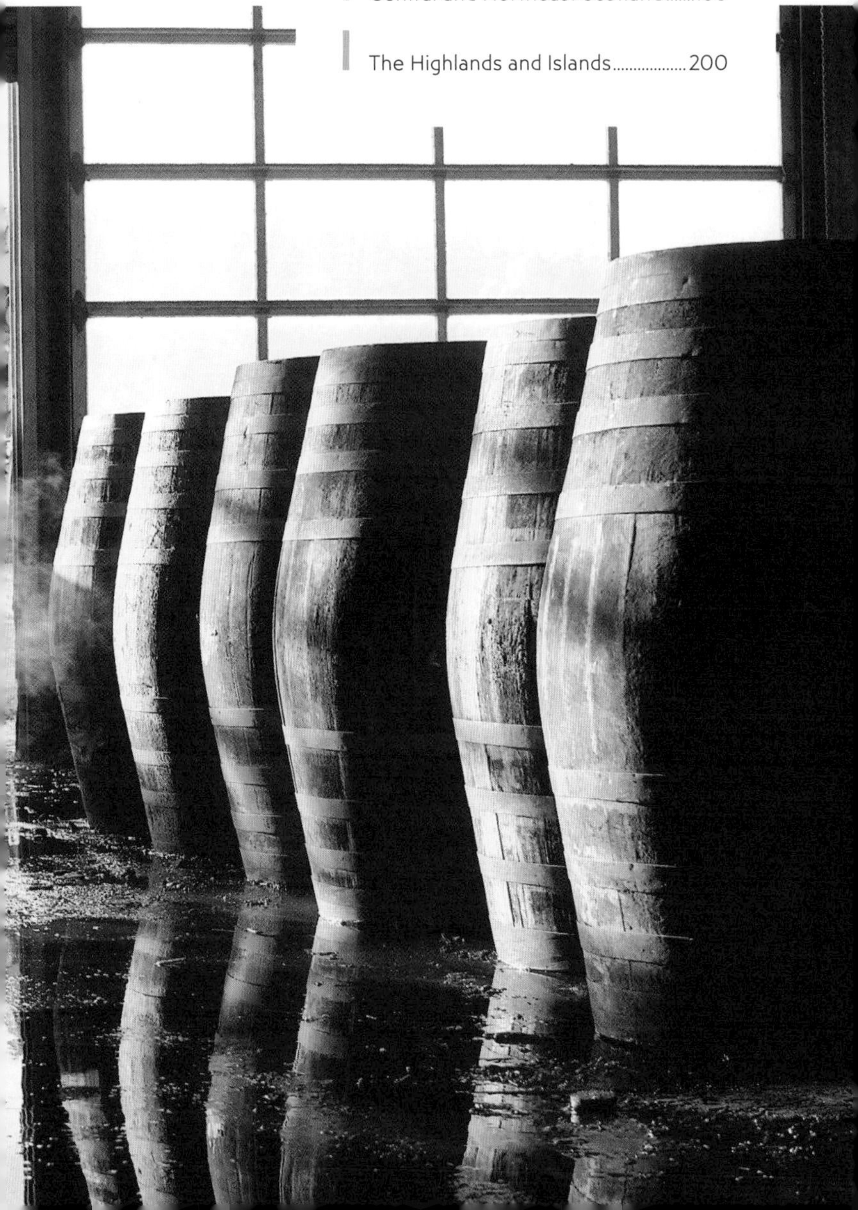

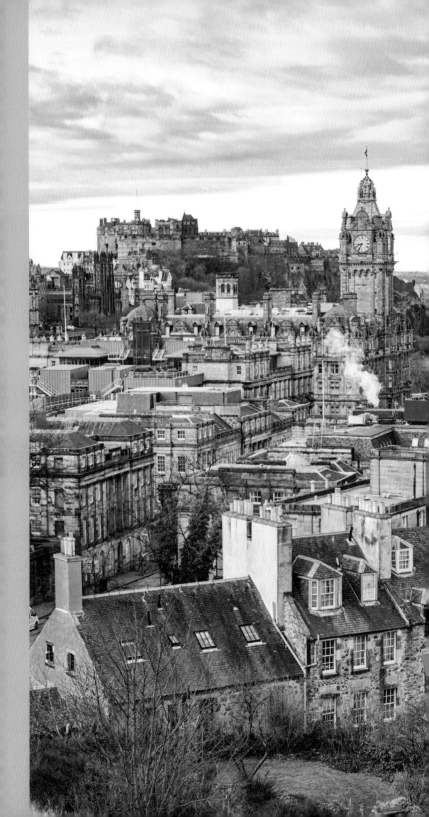

The city of Edinburgh as seen from Calton Hill

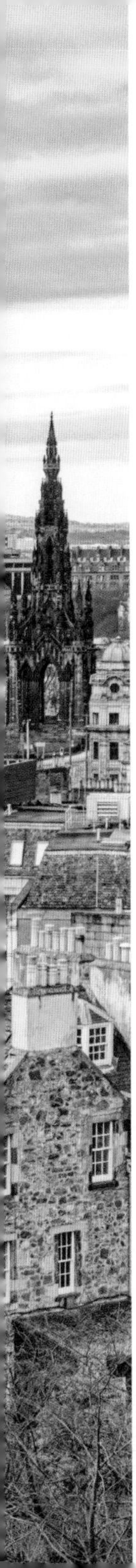

EDINBURGH

Edinburgh's uniquely intact medieval heritage makes it one of the world's most fascinating cities. The mighty Edinburgh Castle sits proudly atop Castle Rock, a clifftop crag which has been occupied since the Bronze Age thanks to its strategic position overlooking the Firth of Forth. Below it the Royal Mile slopes through the Old Town to the Palace of Holyroodhouse, home of monarchs since the 15th century. However, it was not until the reign of James IV (1488–1513) that the city of Edinburgh gained the status of Scotland's capital in 1498.

Over the years, overcrowding made Edinburgh's Old Town a dirty and difficult place to live, and sickness and disease was rife. In 1645, the city was ravaged by the bubonic plague, killing almost half of its population. A rather gruesome attempt to prevent further infection resulted in residents of vaults and closes being bricked into their homes and left to die, while new buildings were erected above this forgotten city. A Georgian New Town was constructed to the north in the late 1700s; its wide avenues and spacious private gardens gave the wealthy a welcome escape from the cramped conditions of the Old Town. With its elegant façades and broad streets, the area is still viewed today as a world-class example of Georgian urban architecture.

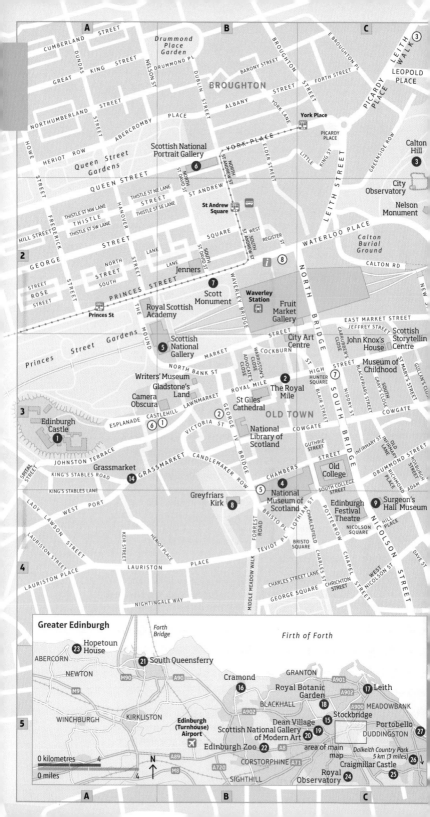

A
CUMBERLAND STREET
GREAT KING STREET
DUNDAS STREET
NELSON ST
Drummond Place Garden
DRUMMOND PL
NORTHUMBERLAND STREET
ABERCROMBY PLACE
HERIOT ROW
Queen Street Gardens
HOWE STREET
QUEEN STREET
FREDERICK STREET
HILL STREET
THISTLE STREET
THISTLE ST NW LANE
THISTLE ST NE LANE
THISTLE ST SE LANE
THISTLE ST SW LANE
HANOVER STREET
STREET
2
GEORGE STREET
ROSE STREET
NORTH ST DAVID ST
SOUTH ST DAVID ST
HANOVER STREET
SOUTH ST ANDREW ST
Jenners
PRINCES STREET
THE MOUND
Scott Monument ❼
Royal Scottish Academy
Princes St
Scottish National Gallery ❺
Princes Street Gardens

Scottish National Portrait Gallery ❻

B
Drummond Place Garden
BARONY STREET
BROUGHTON STREET
FORTH STREET
ALBANY STREET
DUBLIN STREET
YORK LANE
York Place
YORK PLACE
PICARDY PLACE
ELDER STREET
LITTLE KING ST
North St Andrew St
St Andrew Square
SOUTH ST ANDREW STREET
WEST REGISTER STREET
ⓘ ❽
Waverley Station
Fruit Market Gallery

C
LEITH WALK ❸
E BROUGHTON PL
BROUGHTON PL
LEOPOLD PLACE
PICARDY PLACE
GREENSIDE ROW
Calton Hill ❸
City Observatory
Nelson Monument
LEITH STREET
WATERLOO PLACE
Calton Burial Ground
CALTON RD
NEW ST
EAST MARKET STREET
JEFFREY STREET
Scottish Storytelling Centre
John Knox's House
Museum of Childhood
ST MARY'S STREET
GULLAN'S CLOSE
City Art Centre
MARKET STREET
COCKBURN STREET
NORTH BRIDGE
SOUTH BRIDGE
HIGH STREET
BLACKFRIARS STREET
SOUTH GRAY'S CLOSE
COWGATE
❼

3
Edinburgh Castle ❶
ESPLANADE
CASTLEHILL
Writers' Museum
Gladstone's Land
Camera Obscura ❻ ①
LAWNMARKET
Royal Mile ②
St Giles' Cathedral ②
The Royal Mile ❷
OLD TOWN
National Library of Scotland
VICTORIA ST
GEORGE IV BRIDGE
COWGATE
NORTH BANK ST
ADVOCATE'S CLOSE
WARRISTON'S CLOSE
BLAIR ST
HUNTER SQUARE
NIDDRY ST
HIGH STREET
GUTHRIE STREET
INFIRMARY ST
OLD INFIRMARY LANE
DRUMMOND STREET
ROXBURGH PLACE
RICHMOND PLACE
ADAM STREET

JOHNSTON TERRACE
SPITAL STREET
KING'S STABLES ROAD
KING'S STABLES LANE
Grassmarket ❶❹
GRASSMARKET
CANDLEMAKER ROW
CHAMBERS STREET
Greyfriars Kirk ❽
National Museum of Scotland ❹ ⑤
Old College
SOUTH COLLEGE STREET
Edinburgh Festival Theatre
Surgeon's Hall Museum ❾
CHARLESFIELD
POTTERROW
NICOLSON SQUARE
NICOLSON STREET
WEST NICOLSON STREET
HILL PLACE
DAVIE ST

4
LADY LAWSON STREET
LAURISTON STREET
KEIR STREET
HERIOT PLACE
WEST PORT
TEVIOT PL
BRISTO PL
LOTHIAN ST
FORREST ROAD
BRISTO SQUARE
LAURISTON PLACE
MIDDLE MEADOW WALK
CHARLES STREET LANE
CHARLES STREET
CHAPEL STREET
CRICHTON STREET
NIGHTINGALE WAY
GEORGE SQUARE

Greater Edinburgh

Forth Bridge
Firth of Forth

Hopetoun House ㉓
ABERCORN
NEWTON
South Queensferry ㉑
M90
A90
M9
WINCHBURGH
KIRKLISTON
Edinburgh (Turnhouse) Airport
A89
M8
Cramond ⑯
GRANTON
Royal Botanic Garden
BLACKHALL
A902
A90
A902
Scottish National Gallery of Modern Art
Dean Village ⑮
⑲ ⑳
Stockbridge
A901
Leith ⑰
A902
⑱
A900 MEADOWBANK
Portobello ㉗
DUDDINGSTON
area of main map
Edinburgh Zoo ㉒
A8
CORSTORPHINE A71
SIGHTHILL
A720
Royal Observatory ㉔
Craigmillar Castle ㉕
Dalkeith Country Park 5 km (3 miles) ㉖

0 kilometres 4
0 miles 4
N

A   **B**   **C**

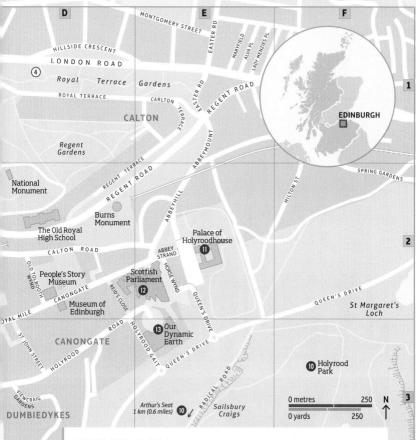

EDINBURGH

Must Sees

1. Edinburgh Castle
2. The Royal Mile
3. Calton Hill
4. National Museum of Scotland
5. Scottish National Gallery

Experience More

6. Scottish National Portrait Gallery
7. Scott Monument
8. Greyfriars Kirk
9. Surgeon's Hall Museum
10. Holyrood Park and Arthur's Seat
11. Palace of Holyroodhouse
12. Scottish Parliament
13. Our Dynamic Earth
14. Grassmarket
15. Stockbridge
16. Cramond
17. Leith
18. Royal Botanic Garden
19. Dean Village
20. Scottish National Gallery of Modern Art
21. South Queensferry
22. Edinburgh Zoo
23. Hopetoun House
24. Royal Observatory of Edinburgh
25. Craigmillar Castle
26. Dalkeith Country Park
27. Portobello

Eat

1. The Witchery by the Castle
2. Ondine
3. Valvona & Crolla
4. Gardener's Cottage
5. Tower Restaurant

Drink

6. The Scotch Whisky Experience

Stay

7. The Inn on the Mile
8. The Balmoral

←

1 St Stephen St, Stockbridge.

2 Intricate interior of The Dome, George Street.

3 Visitors admire tapestry, National Museum of Scotland.

4 Fine dining at 21212.

Edinburgh is marvellously compact, so in two leisurely days you can experience highlights such as the Royal Mile and Edinburgh Castle, then venture beyond the city centre to take in great galleries and enjoy the city's fresh air and greenery.

2 DAYS
in Edinburgh

Day 1

Morning Start exploring at Edinburgh Castle *(p76)*, the city's central landmark. The Stone of Destiny and Scotland's crown jewels are displayed in the 15th-century palace. From the Argyle Battery there's a fine view of the city. A block south of the Royal Mile *(p80)*, the treasures of the National Museum of Scotland *(p86)* include Highland silver, Pictish symbol stones, a Viking grave, a Roman treasure hoard and a huge Tyrannosaurus rex skeleton. The White Horse Oyster Bar *(266 Canongate)*, where the oldest inn on the Royal Mile stood, is a great spot for a lunch break.

Afternoon At the bottom of the Royal Mile, tour of the Palace of Holyroodhouse *(p96)* to discover royal treasures and portraits in the Throne Room, State Apartments and Queen's Gallery. A five-minute bus ride (hop off at St Andrew's House) takes you to Calton Hill *(p84)*, where the view from Nelson Monument encompasses the Firth of Forth and Fife across the water.

Evening Enjoy a sunset view and admire the frivolous National Monument before descending the steps to Royal Terrace, where you can dine at Paul Kitching's award-winning restaurant 21212. After dinner, head to The Stand comedy club on York Place for some late-night laughs. Choose your seats wisely – those in the front row are sure to be picked on.

Day 2

Morning St Giles' Cathedral *(p82)* is an unmistakable landmark from which to start a second day of discovery in Scotland's fine capital. It's downhill all the way to the Scottish National Gallery *(p90)*, where keynotes include Landseer's *Monarch of the Glen* and Raeburn's *Reverend Robert Walker Skating on Duddingston Loch*. Hop on the Gallery Bus to the Scottish National Gallery of Modern Art *(p100)* where sculptures adorn the grounds. Follow the Water of Leith Walkway to Stockbridge *(p86)*, which offers up a plethora of pubs and eateries.

Afternoon It's a short walk to the Royal Botanic Garden *(p100)*, a vast oasis of lawns, ponds, rhododendron walks and rock gardens. The palatial Victorian Palm Houses offer a refuge when weather is less than perfect.

Evening St Andrew Square, in the heart of the New Town, is home to Dishoom, which serves up superb, authentic Parsi Indian dishes alongside artisan Scottish ales. Its basement bar, the Permit Room, has a great cocktail list and stays open until late. Alternatively, take a stroll along George Street to The Dome. A favourite among Edinburgh's high-flyers, its Graeco-Roman façade and lavish interior make it a magnificent setting for after-dinner drinks. The street is lined with clubs and bars, should you wish to continue your evening into the wee hours.

EDINBURGH'S SUMMER FESTIVALS

First held in 1947, the Edinburgh International Festival has grown into the world's greatest celebration of art and culture. The more eclectic Festival Fringe developed in parallel with the official event, but soon exceeded it in terms of size, while the International Film Festival, Art Festival and Jazz & Blues Festival are also renowned in their own right. There really is something for everyone, with spin-off events of every genre including theatre, music, dance, cinema, comedy and street art taking place from June to September.

Edinburgh International Film Festival

Screenings of classic films, arthouse productions, world premieres and special events take place at artsy venues around the city during the Edinburgh International Film Festival (EIFF). With stars and directors taking part, it's a great opportunity for celeb-spotting.

Edinburgh Jazz & Blues Festival

Some of the hottest names in jazz, blues and funk perform in seriously intimate venues. Free events include open-air Mardi Gras performances in the Grassmarket (p98) and the spectacular Carnival in Princes Street Gardens.

Edinburgh International Festival

Combining performances by opera companies, ballet and contemporary dance ensembles, theatre groups and world premieres by the latest creative talents, this summer-long festival concludes with one of the world's biggest pyrotechnic displays, when more than 400,000 fireworks explode above Edinburgh Castle (p76), accompanied by a live symphony orchestra.

↑ Festival street entertainer performing on the Royal Mile

> 💬 INSIDER TIP
> **Book Ahead**
>
> Tickets for Edinburgh International Festival events go on sale at the beginning of the last week in March and they tend to sell out quickly. Buy online at eif.co.uk or call (0131) 473 2000.

← *Untitled*, 2016, by Jonathan Owen at Edinburgh Art Festival

Edinburgh Art Festival

The focus is on adventurous and challenging new work at this veritable feast for the eyes. Founded in 2004, Edinburgh Art Festival stages exhibitions at established galleries and at less conventional pop-ups in unexpected places, and most are free to visit.

Edinburgh Festival Fringe

The Festival Fringe is an open-access festival with no jury. It celebrates both amateur and world-famous performers offering comedy, musicals, drama, dance and mind-bending performance art. The Pleasance Courtyard is a major hub of the Festival Fringe, with several hundred venues hosting more than 3,000 shows most summers.

FREE FESTIVAL EXPERIENCES

There are more than 9,000 free comedy, cabaret, music, theatre and children's shows held each year, all run by the Free Fringe during the Edinburgh Festival Fringe. Audience members can make a donation at the end of a show if they wish. Some comedy clubs also run free shows thoughout the summer festivals, while the Royal Mile is packed with entertainers and musicians all summer long; they don't charge, but they do hope for a tip. Or why not head up Calton Hill (p84) and watch the dazzling pyrotechnics of the Festival's grand finale for free – and without being deafened.

← Fireworks above Edinburgh Castle at the close of the Edinburgh International Festival

Actor and director Stanley Tucci arriving at The Filmhouse for ↓ an event during EIFF

❶ 🖼️ 🅼 🍴 🖥️ 🛍️

EDINBURGH CASTLE

📍A3 🏛️Castlehill 🕐9:30am-6pm daily (Oct-Mar: to 5pm); last admission: 1 hour before closing 🔲edinburghcastle.scot

Dominating the city's skyline since the 12th century, Edinburgh Castle is a national icon and is, deservedly, Scotland's most popular visitor attraction.

Standing upon the basalt core of an extinct volcano, Edinburgh Castle is an assemblage of buildings dating from the 12th to the 20th century, reflecting its changing role as fortress, royal palace, military garrison and state prison. Though there is evidence of Bronze Age occupation of the site, the original fortress was built by the 6th-century Northumbrian king, Edwin, from whom the city takes its name. The castle was a favourite royal residence until the Union of the Crowns (p63) in 1603, after which the king resided in England. After the Union of Parliaments in 1707, the Scottish regalia were walled up in the palace for over a hundred years. The palace is now the zealous possessor of the so-called Stone of Destiny, a relic of ancient Scottish kings which was seized by the English and not returned to Scotland until 1996.

💬 INSIDER TIP
Festival Fireworks

Every night during the Edinburgh Festival, the Castle hosts a fireworks display to mark the end of the Military Tattoo (p205). Climb to the top of Calton Hill (p84) to watch this pyrotechnic spectacle for free.

Complete with Flemish-style crow-stepped gables, the Governor's House was constructed in 1742 and now serves as the Officers' Mess.

Military Prison

THE ONE O'CLOCK GUN

Resounding across the city at 1pm Mon-Sat, Edinburgh's One O'Clock Gun has been startling visitors since 1861. It was originally intended to help ships moored in the Firth of Forth to synchronize their chronometers to Greenwich Mean Time, essential for accurate navigation, but it has now become a time-honoured tradition. The first guns were muzzle-loading cannons, but since 2001 a more modern 105mm artillery piece has served.

Illustration of Edinburgh Castle, an ancient fortress on top of Castle Rock ↑

During the 18th and 19th centuries, the castle's prison vaults were used to hold French prisoners of war.

Edinburgh Castle dominates
the city's skyline *(above)*; castle
entrance gate *(inset)* ↑

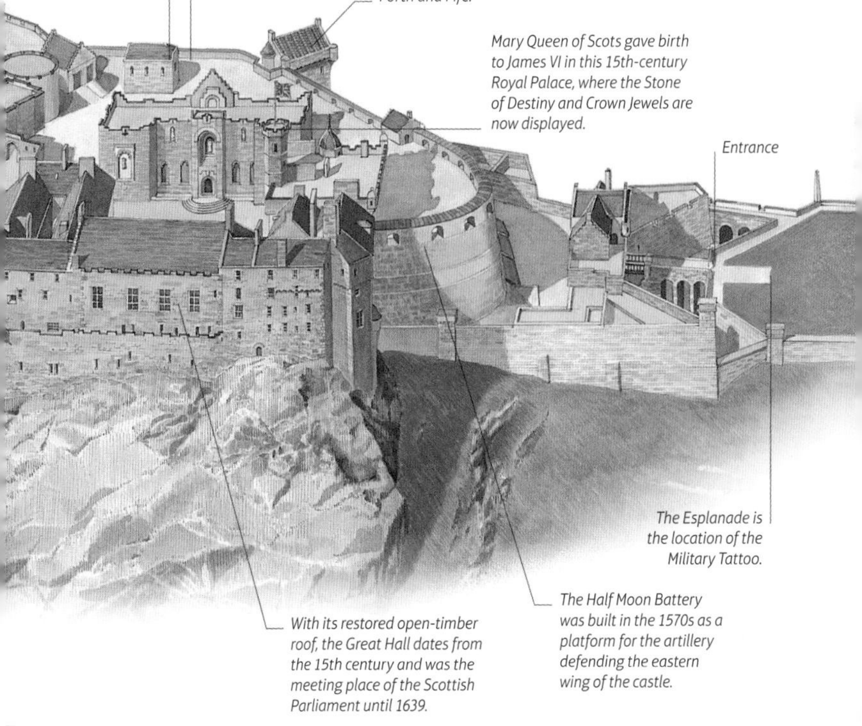

St Margaret's
Chapel is the oldest
surviving structure
from the medieval
castle. Built by
David I (1124–1153)
in honour of his
sanctified mother,
it is still used today.

Mons Meg, a giant six-
tonne seige gun. Built in
1449, it was cutting-
edge technology in the
Middle Ages.

Argyle Battery offers a panoramic
view north over Princes Street to
the city's New Town, the Firth of
Forth and Fife.

Mary Queen of Scots gave birth
to James VI in this 15th-century
Royal Palace, where the Stone
of Destiny and Crown Jewels are
now displayed.

Entrance

The Esplanade is
the location of the
Military Tattoo.

With its restored open-timber
roof, the Great Hall dates from
the 15th century and was the
meeting place of the Scottish
Parliament until 1639.

The Half Moon Battery
was built in the 1570s as a
platform for the artillery
defending the eastern
wing of the castle.

EXPLORING THE CASTLE

Standing guard over the city, Edinburgh Castle is always an impressive sight, but to best appreciate this fortress, explore the complex behind the imposing walls. From the entrance on the lower ward, over which looms the impressive Half Moon Battery, walk through the Middle Ward, with the Argyle Battery on the right and, a little further up, the famous One o'Clock Gun. Beyond the National War Museum is the Upper Ward, or Crown Square, location for the Great Hall and Royal Palace, the latter housing both the Stone of Destiny and Crown Jewels. Dominating the highest part of the complex is St Margaret's Chapel, which stands close to the iconic Mons Meg siege gun.

The Esplanade and Lower Ward

Fronting the castle entrance, the Esplanade is essentially one vast coach park, but is also traditionally used as the venue for the Edinburgh Military Tattoo, the famous military display hosted at the castle. This heritage explains the many memorials to members of the armed forces dotted around here. Seek out the monument to Field Marshal Earl Haig, who was an important figure on the Western Front of World War I.

Moving on, walk through the entrance to the castle. Beyond the gatehouse, head up through the Lower Ward to the Middle Ward and the Argyle Battery, which affords terrific views of the city, and the booming One o'Clock Gun *(p76)*. Try to time your visit with its firing if you can.

National War Museum and Royal Scots Dragoon Guards Museum

Tucked away behind the Governor's House, the superb National War Museum documents more than 400 years of Scottish military conflict, courtesy of dozens of cabinets packed with medals, uniforms and insignia, as well as paintings. One of the most curious exhibits is "Bob the Dog", the taxidermized pet of the Scots Fusilier Guards, 1st Battalion, in 1853–60, who stands complete with a shiny silver medal on his collar.

The equally illuminating Royal Scots Dragoon Guards Museum is located in the neighbouring New Barracks building; here you will find all kinds of memorabilia relating to the only Scottish cavalry regiment in the regular British Army.

Crown Square

The historic heart of the castle complex is Crown Square, whose south side is taken up by the Great Hall, a building notable for its magnificent hammer-beam roof designed by James IV and which was formerly the setting for the Scottish Parliament. Adjacent to the Great Hall stands the Renaissance-style Royal Palace, which harbours both the Stone of Destiny *(p174)* and the Honours of Scotland, more commonly known as the Crown Jewels – the most prominent exhibit is a richly bejewelled crown worn by James V. While you're still on the square, don't miss the Hall of Honour, housing the elegant Scottish National War Memorial, designed by Sir Robert Lorimer.

MONS MEG

Positioned outside St Margaret's Chapel, this six-tonne siege gun (or bombard) was made in Belgium in 1449 for the Duke of Burgundy, who gave it to his nephew, James II of Scotland. It was used by James against the Douglas family in their stronghold of Threave Castle *(p130)* in 1455, and later by James IV against Norham Castle in England. After exploding during a salute to the Duke of York in 1682, it was kept in the Tower of London until it was returned to Edinburgh in 1829.

Timeline

c 1130

▲ The first structure on Castle Rock is built by David I (c 1084-1153)

The imposing Great Hall, ↑
located on the south side of
Crown Square, and *(inset)*
the adjacent Royal Palace

1269
Edinburgh Castle
is captured by
Edward I (1239-
1307)

1650
▽ Oliver
Cromwell
besieges the
castle for
three months

1757
Edinburgh
Castle turned
into a prison

1356
David II (1324-
71) rebuilds
the castle

1573
△ Much of
the castle is
destroyed during
the Lang Siege
in the Civil War

1745
Bonnie Prince
Charlie
unsuccessfully
tries to take
the castle

1927
△ A section of the
castle is turned into
the Scottish National
War Memorial

79

2

THE ROYAL MILE

⚲ B3 🏠 Castlehill to Canongate

Thronged with street entertainers and lined with shops, pubs and restaurants, the lively Royal Mile is for many the first taste of Edinburgh, and for good reason: most of the city's top attractions are dotted along this ancient thoroughfare.

Redolent of the city's history, the Royal Mile is a stretch of four ancient streets (from Castlehill to Canongate) which formed the main thoroughfare of medieval Edinburgh, linking the ancient castle to the Palace of Holyroodhouse. Confined by the city wall, the "Old Town" grew upwards, with some tenements, or "lands", as they were known, rising 20 storeys above the dozens of dark, cobbled wynds and closes below.

↑ Visitors marvelling at the 18th-century pinhole camera at Camera Obscura

Timeline

_1124_
▲ St Giles' Cathedral founded either by King Alexander I or by King David I

_1688_
Holyrood Abbey ransacked by anti-Jacobite protesters

_1691_
Canongate Kirk built

_1745_
▽ Bonnie Prince Charlie proclaims his exiled father king at the Mercat Cross

_1856_
▲ Burgh of Canongate, founded 1143, becomes part of the City of Edinburgh

_2004_
New Scottish Parliament opens at Holyrood

←

Looking up Castlehill towards Edinburgh Castle at the top of the Royal Mile

life in the city centre as it happens. A marvel at the time, this feat of Victorian craftsmanship still astonishes visitors accustomed to 21st-century mobile devices, and it remains one of Edinburgh's most popular attractions.

② 🛍
Writers' Museum

🏠 Lady Stair's Close
🕐 10am-5pm daily
🌐 edinburghmuseums. org.uk

Celebrated Scottish authors Robert Burns *(p116)*, Sir Walter Scott *(p114)* and Robert Louis Stevenson are the stars of this museum, which is crammed with intriguing memorabilia, including a cast of Burns's skull, journals, manuscripts and belongings such as Stevenson's riding boots. It occupies Lady Stair's House, a gracious 17th-century building, constructed in 1622 on Makar's Court, where flagstones commemorate many more national treasures, such as Dame Muriel Spark, who lived by their pen.

① 🎨 Ⓜ 🛍
Camera Obscura

🏠 Castlehill 🕐 Times vary, check website 🌐 camera-obscura.co.uk

The lower floors of this building date from the early 17th century and were once the home of the Laird of Cockpen. In 1852, Maria Short added the upper floor, the viewing terrace and the Camera Obscura – a large pinhole camera that pictures

EAT & DRINK

The Witchery by the Castle

Excels at dishes with a rural flavour, like pheasant and venison terrine. Ask for a seat in the Secret Garden.

🏠 352 Castlehill
🌐 thewitchery.com

💷💷💷

Ondine

Classy outfit offering the city's finest seafood, from freshly chilled oysters to brown crab risotto.

🏠 2 George IV Bridge
🌐 ondinerestaurant. co.uk

💷💷💷

The Scotch Whisky Experience

Sample classic whiskies and new age malts at this centre for Scotland's national drink.

🏠 354 Castlehill
🌐 scotchwhisky experience.co.uk

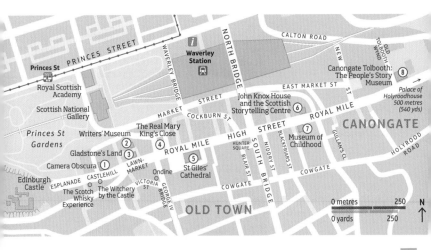

↑ Gladstone's Land, a surviving 17th-century high-tenement house in Old Town, Edinburgh

③ 🧭 Ⓜ 🏛 (NTS)

Gladstone's Land

🏠 477B Lawnmarket
🕐 Apr-Oct: 10am-5pm daily (Jul & Aug: to 6:30pm)
🌐 nts.org.uk

This restored 17th-century merchant's house provides a window on life in a typical Old Townhouse before overcrowding drove the rich inhabitants to the Georgian New Town. "Lands" were tall, narrow buildings on small plots of land. The six-storey Gladstone's Land was named after Thomas Gledstanes, the merchant who built it in 1617.

④ 🧭 Ⓜ 💻 🏛

The Real Mary King's Close

🏠 2 Warriston's Close
🕐 Tour times vary, check website 🌐 realmary-kingsclose.com

Until the 18th century most residents of Edinburgh lived along and beneath the Royal Mile and the Cowgate. The old abandoned cellars and basements, which lacked any proper water supply, daylight or ventilation, were once centres of domestic life and industry. Under these conditions, cholera, typhus and smallpox were common. Mary King's Close, under the City Chambers, is one of the most famous of these areas – its inhabitants were all killed by the plague in around 1645. In 2003 many of these closes were opened up for the first time and visits are now possible through The Real Mary King's Close, where costumed guides lead visitors in a walking tour of the Old Town's gruesome past.

⑤ Ⓜ 💻 🏛

St Giles' Cathedral

🏠 Royal Mile 🕐 10am-6pm Mon-Fri (to 5pm Sat)
🌐 stgilescathedral.org.uk

Properly known as the High Kirk (church) of Edinburgh, St Giles' is popularly known as a cathedral. Though it was twice the seat of a bishop in the 17th century, it was from here that John Knox directed the Scottish Reformation (p63), with its emphasis on individual worship freed from the authority of bishops. A tablet marks the place where Jenny Geddes, a local market stall-holder, scored a victory for the Covenanters in 1637 by hurling her stool at a preacher as he read from an English prayer book.

St Giles' Gothic exterior has a 15th-century tower, the only part to escape heavy renovation in the 1800s. Inside, the beautiful Thistle Chapel with its rib-vaulted ceiling and carved heraldic canopies, honours the knights of the Most Ancient and Most Noble Order of the Thistle. The royal pew in the Preston Aisle is

66

Alleys and closes lead off the Royal Mile, some to hidden courtyards.

reserved for Queen Elizabeth II during her visits to Edinburgh.

⑥ 🔧 Ⓜ️ 🖥️ 🛍️

John Knox House and the Scottish Storytelling Centre

🏠 43-45 High St ⏰10am-6pm Mon-Sat (Jul & Aug: also noon-6pm Sun) 🌐scottishstorytelling centre.com

This beautiful medieval building with its crow-step gables and overhanging upper storeys was home to the great patriarch of the Scottish Reformation. One of Edinburgh's oldest

← St Giles' Cathedral on the Royal Mile, Edinburgh

buildings it is well worth exploring for its many surviving decorative details. As a leader of the Protestant Reformation and minister at St Giles', John Knox (1513–72) was one of the most important figures in 16th-century Scotland. Ordained as a priest in 1536, Knox later became convinced of the need for religious change. He took part in the Protestant occupation of St Andrews Castle in 1547 and served two years as a galley slave in the French navy as punishment. On release, Knox went to London and Geneva to espouse the Protestant cause, returning to Edinburgh in 1559. It was in this townhouse on the Royal Mile that he spent the last few months of his life. Displays tell the story of Knox's life in the context of the political and religious upheavals of his time.

The building also incorporates the Scottish Storytelling Centre. This modern annex to the medieval John Knox House is a venue for local and visiting storytellers and other exponents of the spoken word, performing traditional tales and new work in English, Scots dialect and Gaelic.

⑦

Museum of Childhood

🏠42 High St ⏰10am-5pm daily 🌐edinburgh museums.org.uk

This is not merely a toy collection but an insight into childhood. Founded in 1955, it was the world's first museum of childhood. This wonderful exhibition includes books, games, costumes and dolls – the oldest item here is a Queen Anne doll from around 1740 – while a recent overhaul has seen the introduction of an interactive play space.

⑧

Canongate Tolbooth: The People's Story Museum

🏠163 Canongate ⏰10am-5pm daily 🌐edinburghmuseums. org.uk

Amid the Royal Mile's focus on monarchs and wealthy aristo-crats, the People's Story Museum emphasizes the lives of ordinary city dwellers from the 18th century to the present day. Oral histories and historic documents tell their stories, while the collection, ranging from photos and tableaux to the protest banners and regalia of workers' organizations, brings them to life. The museum is housed in the 16th-century Tolbooth, which until the mid-19th century was Edinburgh's courthouse, jail and council chamber.

> This is not merely a toy collection but an insight into childhood. Founded in 1955, it was the world's first museum of childhood.

↑ The Dugald Stewart Monument overlooking Edinburgh Old Town

❸

CALTON HILL

📍 C1 🏛 City centre east, via Waterloo Pl

Towering over the east end of Princes Street and crowned by an eclectic assortment of quirky Greek-style monuments, Calton Hill is the perfect place for a short stroll and summer picnic among sweet-scented gorse, complete with breathtaking views of the Old Town, Edinburgh Castle and the Firth of Forth.

①

National Monument

Calton Hill is home to one of Edinburgh's most memorable and baffling landmarks – a half-finished Greek-style Parthenon. Intended as a memorial to the Scottish soldiers and seamen of the French wars, construction of the National Monument began in 1822, only to run out of funding a few years later. The monument was never completed, and is now commonly referred to as "Edinburgh's Disgrace". A long-standing rumour has it that Glasgow City Council offered to pay for the monument's completion on the condition that it boldly display Glasgow City's official coat of arms. The offer was politely declined, and over the years public shame over its condition has given way to affection, and even a certain degree of pride.

②

Nelson Monument

🕐 10am-5pm daily (Oct-Mar: to 4pm) 🌐 edinburgh museums.org.uk

For the ultimate view of Edinburgh, climb the breathtaking spiral stair to the battlements of this slender, multi-tiered tower, designed to resemble a telescope standing on its end. Built between 1807 and 1815, it is 32 m (100 ft) high and commemorates Admiral Lord Horatio Nelson's victory at the Battle of Trafalgar. The bronze cannon near its foot is a trophy of Britain's 19th-century conquest of Burma (Myanmar).

③ 🏛🖼🏛🛍🍽

Collective Gallery

🏛 City Observatory & City Dome, 38 Calton Hill
🕐 10am-4pm Tue-Sun
🌐 collective-edinburgh.art

A quirky hybrid of mock-Gothic and Greek temple architecture, this distinctive dome was originally an astronomical observatory. In 2018, it reopened as Collective, an art gallery and

↑ Tourists climbing the half-finished National Monument

exhibition space, complete with a purpose-built restaurant. The free guided tours at 2pm on Saturdays are well worth attending.

---

④ Dugald Stewart Monument

This eight-columned Corinthian rotunda, designed by the ubiquitous William Henry Playfair as a homage to the Classical Monument of Lysicrates in Athens, is one of Edinburgh's most photographed icons, appearing in innumerable snaps looking westwards along Princes Street. Ironically, the philosopher Dugald Stewart (1753–1828) is far less well known than his memorial.

---

⑤ Burns Monument

It seems that every town and city in Scotland has its own memorial to the country's national bard. This modest mock-temple on the southern slope of Calton Hill, looking towards Arthur's Seat, is Edinburgh's. Begun in 1759, it was completed in 1796, the year of the poet's death. Originally it held a white marble bust of Robert Burns, which has since been removed and relocated to the Scottish National Portrait Gallery (p94).

---

⑥ The Old Royal High School

Also known as New Parliament House, The Royal High School was built during the 1820s on the Regent Road side of Calton Hill. Designed by Thomas Hamilton, it was based on the Temple of Theseus at Athens. Often cited as a possible home for a Scottish Parliament, the building was the focus for the Vigil for Scottish Democracy,

which campaigned from 1992 to 1997 for self government. A discreet cairn marking this effort stands a little way east of the National Monument on Calton Hill. The cairn contains several "gift" stones, including one from Auschwitz to commemorate a Scottish missionary who died there.

---

⑦ Calton Burial Ground

The obelisk of the Martyrs' Monument that towers over this ancient cemetery at the foot of Calton Hill was erected to honour members of the "Friends of the People", campaigners for democracy who were convicted of sedition in 1793 and exiled to the Botany Bay penal colony in Australia. Tombs and monuments around its foot include the grave of the philosopher David Hume (1711–1776), while a statue of Abraham Lincoln commemorates Scottish soldiers who gave their lives during the American Civil War.

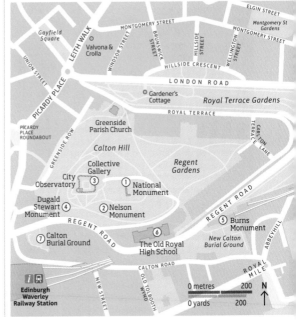

④ 🖎 🏍 🍴 💻 🛍

NATIONAL MUSEUM OF SCOTLAND

📍B3 🏛Chambers St 🕐10am–5pm daily 🌐nms.ac.uk

Everything you ever wanted to know about Scotland can be discovered at this palace of wonders, housed within two radically different buildings that stand side by side. The grand 19th-century gallery is complemented by a contemporary new wing that has become one of Edinburgh's most striking modern buildings.

Old Wing

In the older of these two buildings, human, scientific and natural marvels are brought to life in zones that highlight world cultures, evolution and the natural world, design and fashion, technology and the remarkable exploits of Scottish inventors, engineers and scientists through the ages. Look out for the animated masks, elaborate costumes and remarkable sculptures from Asia, Africa and South America on Level 3 and Level 4, and don't miss the late Dolly the Sheep, the world's first cloned mammal. The atrium of the Grand Gallery, a beautifully designed space filled with light, is also worth exploring. Here you'll find a kaleidoscopic range of treasures from across the world – making it a fitting introduction to the museum.

> 💬 INSIDER TIP
> **Guided Tours**
>
> Free, hour-long guided tours take place at 11am every day, and explore many of the museum's most interesting galleries and exhibits; the meeting point is the Entrance Hall on Level 0.

Grand Gallery, designed by Captain Francis Fowke and completed in 1888 ↓

1. The accessible Tower Entrance to the museum's contemporary wing can be found on Chambers Street.

2. Dolly the Sheep was the first mammal cloned from an adult cell in 1996.

3. The colourful Imagine Gallery is an inspiring and interactive space for children and families.

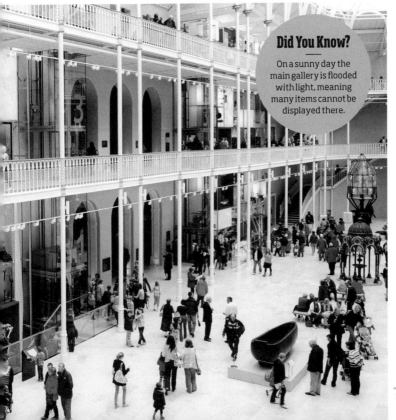

Did You Know?

On a sunny day the main gallery is flooded with light, meaning many items cannot be displayed there.

New Wing

The modern sandstone wing has been heralded as one of the most important constructs in postwar Scotland, and its exhibits are dedicated to the story of the country and its people. Begin your journey through the centuries with the superb Early People's exhibition down in the basement level -1. The next three levels are all occupied by the Kingdom of the Scots, which harbours some extraordinary medieval finds, not least the wonderful Lewis Chessmen. Level 3 has an exhibition entitled Scotland Transformed, with detailed insight into the Jacobite Rebellion and featuring Bonnie Prince Charlie's travelling canteen, while both Levels 4 and 5 focus on Scotland's role in industry and empire; among the many highlights is the beautiful steam locomotive, Ellesmere. The New Wing concludes up on Level 6 with modern-day Scotland; pride of place here is the Victoria Cross awarded to the famous Piper of Loos, Daniel Laidlaw, following his heroic actions in World War I.

↑ Ancient Pictish stones on display in the Scottish History and Archaeology galleries

Did You Know?

Architect Francis Fowke based his design for the museum on London's Crystal Palace.

EAT

Museum Brasserie and Balcony Café

Museum-goers can fuel up on open sandwiches, salads and hearty hot meals at the Museum Brasserie. For lighter bites and a coffee with a view, head to the Balcony Café on the second floor of the gallery. Kids' lunch boxes are also available for those on the go.

🕙 10am–5pm daily

£££

Arthur's Seat Coffins

▷ Undoubtedly the museum's most mysterious exhibit is a set of eight tiny wooden coffins, found on Arthur's Seat in 1836 by a group of young boys out rabbiting. Each coffin (there were 17 originally) contained an individually dressed carved figure, though the reason why they were placed there in the first place has never been fully understood; one theory has it that the coffins were lucky charms to be sold to sailors.

Viking Grave

This remarkable stone tomb chamber from Orkney contains the skeleton of a Viking chief, thought to be around 30 years of age at the time of burial. Buried alongside him were many of his possessions, including farming tools, weaponry and jewellery.

Tyrannosaurus Rex

▽ One of the museum's most popular exhibits, the 12-m- (40-ft-) long, 6-m- (20-ft-) high skeleton cast of a Tyrannosaurus rex with its fang-filled gaping jaws dominates the grand multi-level atrium of the Animal World gallery. Dwarfing the other animal exhibits, T-Rex - as it's more commonly known - is the second largest and, experts say, the most complete skeleton of its kind ever found. The original specimen, which is 85 per cent complete, was found in 1988 in Montana, USA.

Moby The Whale

This skull is from a 15-m- (40-ft-) long sperm whale that swam up the River Forth in 1997. Efforts to send Moby (as he subsequently became known) back out to sea failed, and he died after beaching on the foreshore at Airth - the first whale to stranded in the Forth for more than 200 years. In 2009, Moby received a different kind of accolade as he was the subject of Lucy Skaer's Turner Prize nominated work of art *Leviathan Edge* (2009).

Lewis Chessmen

▷ Found on a beach in Uig, Lewis in 1831, the Lewis Chessmen is a collection of early 13th-century chess pieces that are believed to have been made in Norway. Expertly hewn from walrus ivory, the 11 chess pieces on display in the Kingdom of the Scots section of the museum were actually part of a larger hoard found on the island. In July 2019, a piece was identified as a "warder", the equivalent of a castle or rook, and was sold for £735,000.

↑ A range of aeroplanes suspended in one of the many galleries

⑤ (M̃) (Ⓦ) (☐) (①)

SCOTTISH NATIONAL GALLERY

⊙ B3 **⌂ The Mound** **⊙ 10am–5pm daily (to 7pm Thu)** **Ⓦ nationalgalleries.org**

Home to one of the best collections of fine art in the world, this flagship gallery in the heart of the capital inspires and entrances with an international collection that spans over 500 years. It is also a place to see a uniquely rich concentration of works by Scottish masters from Ramsay and Raeburn to Wilkie and McTaggart.

Scottish society portraits by Allan Ramsay and Sir Henry Raeburn, including Raeburn's *Reverend Robert Walker Skating on Duddingston Loch*, and rural scenes and landscapes by David Wilkie and William McTaggart are among the highlights of the gallery's collections.

However, treasures are not limited to Scottish talents; the gallery is well worth visiting for its 15th- to 19th-century British and European paintings alone, though plenty more can be found to delight art lovers. An entire room is devoted to Nicolas Poussin's *The Seven Sacraments*, and Raphael's The *Bridgewater Madonna* appears alongside works by Titian, Tintoretto and Velazquez. Flemish and Dutch artists such as Rembrandt, Van Dyck and Rubens are also well represented. Paintings by Northern European Artists include Degas' *A Group of Dancers* and Van Gogh's *Olive Trees*, though the gallery's most treasured painting is Sir Edward Landseer's iconic image of a red deer stag, *The Monarch of the Glen*. Recently acquired, it takes pride of place in the refurbished gallery.

↑ Van Gogh's *Olive Trees,* one of many works by 19th-century European masters

> **Treasures are not limited to Scottish talents; the gallery is well worth visiting for its 15th- to 19th-century British and European paintings alone.**

↑ Neoclassical façade of the Scottish National Gallery, designed by William Henry Playfair

ROYAL SCOTTISH ACADEMY OF ART

This constantly growing treasury of almost 1,000 works by contemporary Scottish artists sits just next to the Scottish National Gallery, connected by an underground level. Don't miss the RSA's annual Open Exhibition in June and July each year. The event is a great opportunity for visitors to see and buy contemporary pieces by new Scottish talents at affordable prices.

Woman photographing the ↑
famous painting, *The Monarch of
the Glen* by Sir Edwin Landseer

Rooftops of Edinburgh Waverley Station

The Scott Monument towering over Princes Street Gardens

images of contemporary Scottish movers and shakers such as Scotland's current makar (poet laureate) Jackie Kay, playwright and painter John Byrne, musician Annie Lennox, and home-grown film stars including Sean Connery, Ewan McGregor, Robert Carlyle, Karen Gillan, James McAvoy and Katie Leung.

7

Scott Monument

📍B2 ⏰Princes St Gardens East ⏰10am-5pm daily (Oct-Mar: to 4pm) 🌐edin-burghmuseums.org.uk

Sir Walter Scott (p114) is one of the most important figures in Scottish literature. His works look back to a time of adventure, honour and chivalry, and did much to promote this image of Scotland abroad. After his death in 1832, the Scott Monument was constructed on the south side of Princes Street as a tribute to his life and work. This Gothic tower, designed by George

EXPERIENCE MORE

6

Scottish National Portrait Gallery

📍B1 ⏰1 Queen St ⏰10am-5pm daily 🌐nationalgalleries.org

This impressive sandstone gallery stands out from the austere Georgian façades of its New Town neighbours. Pause before entering to admire the statues that encrust its elaborate red sandstone exterior, including figures of philosopher David Hume and economist Adam Smith. A marble statue of Robert Burns presides over the atrium, surrounded by busts of such notables as Walter Scott, Robert Louis Stevenson and Scottish

Inventor James Watt. Upper galleries are dedicated to portraits of bewigged Stuart and Hanoverian grandees of the Enlightenment and the Victorian age. But it's not all about long-dead aristocrats and their literary figureheads. More vivid and engaging are the rooms dedicated to

> 💬 INSIDER TIP
> **Gallery Bus**
>
> The daily Gallery Bus circuit takes in the Scottish National Gallery, the National Portrait Gallery (drop-off only here) and the National Gallery of Modern Art, all for a reasonable £1 donation.

Meikle Kemp, and completed in 1840, has a statue of Sir Walter at its base, sculpted by Sir John Steell. Inside, 287 steps give access to the upper-most platform, which boasts impressive views.

8 (○) (○)

Greyfriars Kirk

(○) **B4** (○) **Greyfriars Pl**
(○) **Times vary, check website** (○) **greyfriars kirk.com**

Greyfriars Kirk occupies a key role in the history of Scotland. It was here that the National Covenant was signed in 1638, marking the Protestant stand against the imposition of an episcopal church by King Charles I. In the 17th century the kirkyard was used as a mass grave for executed Covenanters. It also served as a prison after the 1679 Battle of Bothwell Brig.

Greyfriars is perhaps best known for its association with a little dog called Bobby, who kept a vigil by his master's grave from 1858 until his own death in 1872. Bobby's statue stands outside the Kirk.

More recently, Greyfriar's has become a popular spot for fans of J K Rowling's *Harry Potter*

↑ Statue of the famous Greyfriars Bobby, a paragon of loyalty

books. Gravestones in the kirkyard inspired the names of many characters. The grave of Thomas Riddell, now better known to many as Lord Voldemort, is so popular that it is marked on Google Maps.

9 (○) (○)

Surgeon's Hall Museum

(○) **C4** (○) **Nicolson St**
(○) **10am-5pm daily**
(○) **museum.rcsed.ac.uk**

Housed in the former head-quarters of the Royal College of Surgeons and opened to the public in 1832, this rather

off-beat museum will almost certainly appeal to the morbidly curious. The collection reflects Edinburgh's status as a leading centre of medical research during the 18th and 19th centuries, with all manner of weird, wonderful and downright bizarre items on display, including an extensive assemblage of preserved organic tissue and bone, scientific instruments and a particularly gruesome array of anatomical and medical artifacts. The history of dentistry is also well documented here. If your thirst for all things gory still hasn't been sated, join the museum's Blood and Guts Edinburgh walking tour, which takes place every Saturday and Sunday at 2pm.

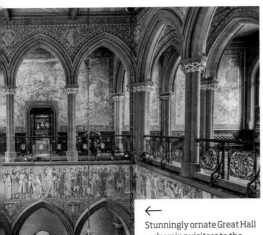

← Stunningly ornate Great Hall welcoming visitors to the National Portrait Gallery

10

Holyrood Park and Arthur's Seat

F3 **Main access via Holyrood Park Rd, Holyrood Rd and Meadowbank Terr**

Holyrood Park, adjacent to the Palace of Holyroodhouse, covers 2.6 sq km (1 sq mile) of varying terrain, topped by a rugged 250-m (820-ft) hill. Known as Arthur's Seat, the hill is actually a volcano that has been extinct for 350 million years. The area was a royal hunting ground since at least the time of King David I, who died in 1153, and a royal park since the 16th century.

The name Holyrood, which means "holy cross", comes from an episode in the life of David I when, in 1128, he was knocked down from his horse by a stag while out hunting. Legend has it that a cross appeared miraculously in his hands to ward off the animal and, in thanksgiving, the king founded the Abbey of the Holy Cross, Holyrood Abbey. The name Arthur's Seat is probably a corruption of Archer's Seat, a more prosaic explanation for the name than any link with the legendary King Arthur.

The park has three small lochs within its grounds. St Margaret's near the Palace is the most romantic, with its resident swans and position under the ruins of St Anthony's Chapel. Dunsapie Loch is the highest, sitting 112 m (367 ft) above sea level under Arthur's Seat. On the south side of the park, pretty Duddingston Loch is home to a number of swans, geese and wildfowl.

The Salisbury Crags are among the park's most striking features. Their dramatic profile, along with that of Arthur's Seat, can be seen from many kilometres away. The Crags form a parabola of dramatic red cliffs that sweep round and up a steep supporting hillside from the Palace of Holyroodhouse. A rough track, called the Radical Road, follows their base.

Did You Know?

Some ancient traces of habitation in Holyrood Park date back as far as 10,000 years.

11

Palace of Holyroodhouse

E2 **East end of the Royal Mile** **9:30am–6pm daily (Nov–Mar: to 4:30pm)** **rct.uk**

Known today as Queen Elizabeth II's official Scottish residence, the Palace of Holyroodhouse was built by James IV in the grounds of an abbey in 1498. It was later the home of James V and his wife, Mary of Guise, and was remodelled in the 1670s for Charles II. The Royal Apartments (including the Throne Room and Royal Dining Room) are used for investitures and for banquets whenever the Queen visits the palace. A chamber in the so-called James V tower is famously associated with the unhappy reign of Mary, Queen of Scots (p62). It was probably in this room, in 1566, that Mary saw the gruesome murder of her trusted Italian secretary, David Rizzio, authorized by her jealous husband, Lord Darnley. She was six months pregnant at the time of this attack.

↑ The Scottish Parliament building, designed by Enric Miralles

In the early stages of the Jacobite rising of 1745 *(p63)*, the last of the pretenders to the British throne, Charles Edward Stuart (Bonnie Prince Charlie) held court here, dazzling Edinburgh society with his magnificent parties.

Tours are given daily from April to October, or take an audio tour; both are included in the ticket price. The Queen's Gallery has works from the Royal Collection.

12

Scottish Parliament

📍 E2 🏠 Holyrood
🕐 10am–5pm Mon–Sat
🌐 parliament.scot

Following decades of Scottish calls for more political self-determination, a 1997 referendum on this issue resulted in a majority "yes" vote. Designed by the late Enric Miralles, known for his work on buildings at the 1992 Barcelona Olympics, the Parliament building was opened in 2004 by Queen Elizabeth II. It's well worth taking one of the regular tours (advance booking required) of this architecturally exciting public building.

13

Our Dynamic Earth

📍 E3 🏠 Holyrood Rd
🕐 Times vary, see website
🌐 dynamicearth.co.uk

In this permanent exhibition about the planet, visitors are taken on a journey from the earth's volcanic beginnings to the first appearance of life. Further displays cover the world's climatic zones and dramatic natural phenomena such as tidal waves and earthquakes. State-of-the-art lighting and interactive techniques, such as the immersive 360° Showdome and the new Mission Earth reality experience, make for a fabulous few hours' visit.

The exhibition building is fronted by a 1,000-seat stone amphitheatre designed by Sir Michael Hopkins. Situated beneath Salisbury Crags, the modern lines of Our Dynamic Earth contrast sharply with the natural landscape.

↑ Holyrood Park and Arthur's Seat, overlooking the city

💬 INSIDER TIP
Tide Times

Be sure to check the tide times when planning a trip across to Cramond Island. The causeway becomes submerged at high tide and walkers are often stranded. For information text CRAMOND to 81400.

14 Ⓜ 🏛

Grassmarket

📍 A3 🏛 Old Town

A stroll down colourful Victoria Street from George IV Bridge will bring you to the bustling Grassmarket. Lined by restored medieval buildings, restaurants, busy pubs and funky boutiques, it is a hive of activity, particularly during the arts, crafts and street-food market on Saturday. Its pubs were favoured by Robert Burns *(p116)* and the notorious 19th-century "resurrection men" Burke and Hare. The Last Drop pub is opposite the site where public hangings took place until 1784.

15 🏊 Ⓜ 🍽 🏛

Stockbridge

📍 C5

Nowhere else in Edinburgh is quite like Stockbridge. Despite gentrification, this urban village straddling the Water of Leith retains its boho vibe, with gastropubs, lively café-bars, and distinctive architecture in the Colonies, built for 19th-century artisans and their families. Vintage stores and small galleries cluster on St Stephen Street, and the Royal Botanic Garden *(p100)* is a short walk from Raeburn Place, Stockbridge's main thoroughfare.

Mouthwatering street-food aromas drift from **Stockbridge Market** every Sunday, when you can sample snacks from all over the world and shop for artsy accessories and other unusual trinkets.

Stockbridge Market
🏛 Saunders St ⏰ 10am–5pm Sun 🌐 stockbridgemarket.com

16

Cramond

📍 B3 🏛 Cramond Village

The Roman Empire once stretched as far as this pretty village of whitewashed houses on the east bank of the River Almond, and you can still see the foundations of a legionary fortress that dates from the 2nd century AD. At low tide you can cross the causeway to Cramond Island – an adventure involving a one-mile-walk to an uninhabited islet where cormorants and other waterfowl roost. From the island's shores there are views upriver to the three

Forth Bridges and across to Fife. World War II-era concrete bunkers are favourite targets for local graffiti artists.

17

Leith

📍 C5 🏛 Northeast of the city centre, linked by Leith Walk

Waterfront rejuvenation is the name of the game in Leith. Linked to the city centre by the broad thoroughfare of Leith Walk, which is peppered with international food shops, this former seaport has weathered hard times to gradually transform

The Shore in Leith, an attractive and bustling port

historic warehouses and merchants' houses dating from the 13th and 14th centuries. There was a great expansion of the docks in the 19th century, and many port buildings date from this period.

Shipbuilding and port activities have diminished, but there has been a renaissance in recent years in the form of conversions of warehouse buildings to offices, residences and, most notably, restaurants and bars. The Shore and Dock Place now has Edinburgh's most dense concentration of seafood bistros and varied restaurants.

The tourist attractions have been further boosted by the presence of the former **Royal Yacht Britannia**, the British royal family's vessel from 1953 to 1997. Self-guided tours take visitors to the Admiral's quarters and state apartments among other areas.

Royal Yacht Britannia
⊛ ⊕ ⊙ ⬜ Ocean Terminal, Leith Docks ⊙ Daily
🅦 royalyachtbritannia.co.uk

Did You Know?

Leith did not become part of Edinburgh until 1920. Before that it was an independent borough.

itself into one of Edinburgh's most vibrant multicultural communities, one that is proud of its roots but looks to the future. Its lively Saturday farmers' market is a delight for foodies.

Leith is a historic port town that has traded for centuries with Scandinavia, the Baltic States and the Netherlands, and has always been the main trading port for Edinburgh. Although fiercely proud of its independence, it was eventually incorporated into the city in 1920, and now forms a charming north-eastern suburb. The medieval core of narrow streets and quays includes a number of

←

World War II defences lining the Cramond causeway, visible at low tide

18 ♒ 🎿 🍴 🖥 🛍

Royal Botanic Garden

📍C5 🏠Inverleith Row
🕐10am-6pm daily (Feb &
Oct: to 5pm; Nov-Jan: to
4pm) 🌐rbge.org.uk

This magnificent garden lies a
short way to the north of the
New Town, across the Water of
Leith river. The garden was
founded by two doctors in
1670 as a Physic Garden, near
Holyroodhouse and moved to
its present location in 1820, to
be progressively enlarged and
developed. Access from the
east is well served by buses;
from the west there's better
parking. From its hillside site,
there are views across the city.

There is a rock garden in
the southeast corner and an
indoor exhibition and
interpretation display in the
northeast corner. Extensive
greenhouses in traditional
and modern architectural
styles offer fascinating
hideaways on rainy days.
Don't miss the alpine display
to the northwest of the
greenhouses, or the beautiful,
fragrant rhododendron walk.

19

Dean Village

📍C5 🏠Northwest of the
city centre

This interesting, tranquil area
lies in the valley of the Water
of Leith, just a short walk
northwest of the city centre
down Bell's Brae from
Randolph Crescent. A series
of water mills along the river
has been replaced by attractive buildings of all periods.

A pretty riverside walk *(p106)*
threads its way between the
historic buildings, crossing
the river on a series of
footbridges. Downstream,
the riverside walkway passes
under Thomas Telford's
magnificent high level bridge,
via St Bernard's Well before
continuing towards the Royal
Botanic Garden.

↑ Sculpture by Antony
Gormley at the National
Gallery of Modern Art

20 ♒ 🎿 🖥 🛍

Scottish National Gallery of Modern Art

📍C5 🏠75 Belford Rd
🚌Gallery bus (free, Mon-Fri
only) 🕐10am-5pm daily
🌐nationalgalleries.org

Since it opened its doors in
1960, the Scottish National
Gallery of Modern Art has
amassed some 5,000 pieces
dated from 1890 onwards.
Here you can find the work of
diverse figures such as Pablo
Picasso, Edvard Munch,
Charles Rennie Mackintosh
and the Pop Art trio of Richard
Hamilton, David Hockney and
Jake Tilson.

The gallery itself occupies
two buildings. Modern One is
housed in a Neo-Classical
building designed by William
Burn in 1825. The impressive
lawn and sculpture garden at
the entrance were designed
by Charles Jencks. The Pig
Rock Bothy was specially
commissioned by the Scottish
National Galleries as a
designated space for talks,
residences, performances and
special events. For exhibitions,
be sure to check out Modern
Two just opposite.

21

South Queensferry

📍A5 🚆Dalmeny, then taxi
🚌43, 63

The vast red-painted
framework of the Forth Rail
Bridge looms over the pretty,
old-fashioned town of South
Queensferry like a steam-age
colossus. This spectacular rail
bridge, the first major steel-
built bridge in the world, was
opened in 1890 and remains
one of the greatest

Iconic Forth Rail Bridge, ↑
named a UNESCO World
Heritage Site in 2015

achievements of the late Victorian era and was named as a UNESCO World Heritage Site in 2015.

You can get a good view of the rail bridge from the shore, or from the **Maid of the Forth** sightseeing boat, which sails from South Queensferry to Inchcolm Island, with its ruined medieval abbey. Look out for seals and puffins on the way.

The quaint **Queensferry Museum** has a fascinating collection that highlights the building of the Forth Bridges, the ferries that carried traffic across the Firth before the opening of the first road bridge, and local history and traditions like the annual Queensferry Fair and the New Year's Day "Loony Dook" where locals plunge into the chilly waters of the Forth.

Maid of the Forth
Hawes Pier, South Queensferry Scheduled sailings booked online maidoftheforth.co.uk

Queensferry Museum
53 High St, South Queensferry 10am–5pm daily (closed 1–2:15pm) edinburghmuseums. org.uk

---

 ②
Edinburgh Zoo

B5 134 Corstorphine Rd 12, 16, 26, 31 am–6pm daily (Mar & Oct: to 5pm; Nov–Feb: to 4pm) edinburghzoo.org.uk

The undoubted stars of Edinburgh Zoo are Tian Tian and Yang Guang, Britain's only giant pandas, but red pandas, meerkats, chimps, pelicans, penguins and hundreds of other mammal, bird and reptile species share the limelight.

Spreading across a vast hillside site south of the city centre, this non-profit zoo places a strong focus on conservation, education and research. Its spacious enclosures allow visitors to see animals in environments that imitate their natural habitat. Don't miss the Wee Beasties exhibition, where you can spot smaller creatures, such as the tiny and brilliantly coloured poison dart frog, or the many daily talks and events including the Penguin Parade.

 ㉓
Hopetoun House

A5 West Lothian Dalmeny Apr–Sep: 10:30am–5pm daily hopetoun.co.uk

Extensive grounds and gardens designed in the style of Versailles are the setting for one of Scotland's finest stately homes. The original house was completed in 1707, and its dignified, horseshoe-shaped plan and lavish interior represent Neo-Classical architecture at its best.

PICTURE PERFECT
The Forth Rail Bridge

For that stunning upward shot of the vast framework of the Forth Rail Bridge, walk to Hawes Pier, and stand right under its massive supports at the east end of Edinburgh Road.

EAT

Cavaliere

This long-standing, highly regarded Italian restaurant and wine bar makes for a decent evening's chow down after visiting the nearby country park. Take your pick from pizza and pasta as well as loads of meat and seafood dishes.

📍C5 🏠124-128 High St, Dalkeith
🌐thecavaliere.co.uk

£££

Skylark

Whether you're after breakfast, brunch, lunch or supper, this stylish Scottish-French fusion restaurant ticks all the right boxes. Try the slow-roasted garlic fennel pork shoulder with lemon potato and sautéed chard – a definite highlight of the supper menu.

📍C5 🏠241-243 Portobello High St
🌐theskylark.co.uk

£££

The Beach House

A buzzy beachside café-cum-bistro, The Beach House offers scrummy dishes, such as hot smoked salmon fishcakes, alongside tapas and sharing platters, and great homemade cakes. Many of the ingredients are harvested in its own garden.

📍C5 🏠57 Bath St, Portobello
🌐thebeachhousecafe.co.uk

£££

24

Royal Observatory of Edinburgh

📍C5 🏠Blackford Hill
🕐8am-midnight daily
🌐roe.ac.uk

A stargazer's haven atop Blackford Hill on the south side of the city, Edinburgh's Royal Observatory, finished in 1896, is easily identifiable by its two copper-covered rotatable domes. The visitor centre here sheds fascinating light on the work of the observatory, while the large Crawford collection, named after the eponymous Earl who was a distinguished amateur astronomer, displays a priceless collection of astronomical books and manuscripts, forming one of the largest astronomical libraries in the world. Its collections comprise many first editions of major books on astronomy, including works by Newton and Galileo. Look out, too, for the many special events and public astronomy evenings that take place here, though these are extremely popular so you'll need to book well in advance.

25

Craigmillar Castle

📍C5 🏠Castle Rd
🕐Apr-Sep: 9:30am-5:30pm daily; Oct-Mar: 10am-4pm daily (advance online booking required)
🌐historicenvironment.scot

In many ways Edinburgh's forgotten castle, the little-visited ruin of Craigmillar is well worth making the short trip from the city centre for, especially as you're likely to be one of the few people here. The oldest parts of Craigmillar are the remarkably intact Tower House, which dates from the late 14th century, and the Great Hall, complete with a rather splendid Gothic chimneypiece. Mary Queen of Scots sheltered in the castle in 1566 and it was originally considered as the royal castle

for Queen Victoria before she plumped for Balmoral. From the top floor there are splendid views across to Edinburgh in the distance, including Edinburgh Castle and Arthur's Seat. The neatly manicured lawns are ideal for a picnic after your visit.

26 ▣ 🏛

Dalkeith Country Park

▣ C5 🏠 Via King's Gate, Dalkeith 🕐 7am–7pm daily ⓦ dalkeithcountrypark. co.uk

Just 7 miles (10 km) southeast of the city centre, Dalkeith Country Park has much to offer both adults and kids, including a 700-year-old oak wood, farmland and some excellent waymarked walking and cycling trails. These activities aside, the park's

> **Did You Know?**
>
> The Royal Observatory of Edinburgh is a leading light in world astronomy.

main attraction is Fort Douglas (an entrance fee is payable for access to this part of the park), a superb turreted adventure park with exciting treehouses, climbing walls, zipwires, slides, bridges and much else. After an afternoon of adventure, retire to the appropriately named Restoration Yard nearby. Here you will find a fantastic restaurant with an outdoor terrace, a gift and homeware shop and a wellbeing lab, all quartered within the old eighteenth-century stables which have been beautifully restored. A varied calendar of events and activities take place here throughout the year, details of which can be found online.

27

Portobello

▣ C5

A genteel coastal suburb only 3 miles (5 km) east of

↑ Portobello beach, a popular destination for families in summer

Edinburgh city centre, Portobello was once a town in its own right. These days, it owes its popularity to its beach, a 2-mile-(3-km-) long stretch of golden sand set against a tidy promenade and a smattering of handsome Victorian buildings. Rammed with swimmers, sunbathers and surfers in the warmer summer months, it remains an attractive destination out of season too, popular with walkers out for a brisk afternoon stroll. Those who find the Scottish sea water just that little bit too chilly should make a beeline for the Victorian swimming pool and beautifully restored **Turkish Baths**, the ultimate relaxation therapy.

Away from the beach, the bustling High Street is lined with independent shops and cafés, while a popular market selling arts, crafts and local produce is held in nearby Brighton Park on the first Saturday of each month.

Turkish Baths

🏠 Portobello Swim Centre, 57 The Promenade 🕐 Times vary, check website ⓦ edinburghleisure.co.uk

← Royal Observatory of Edinburgh overlooking the city from Blackford Hill

A SHORT WALK
NEW TOWN

Distance 2 km (1 mile) **Time** 20 minutes

The first phase of Edinburgh's "New Town" was built in the 18th century to relieve the congested and unsanitary conditions of the medieval Old Town. Charlotte Square, at the western end, formed the climax of this initial phase, and its new architectural concepts were to influence all subsequent phases. Of these, the most magnificent is the Moray Estate, where a linked series of very large houses forms a crescent, an oval and a twelve-sided circus. The walk shown here explores this area of monumental Georgian town planning and architecture.

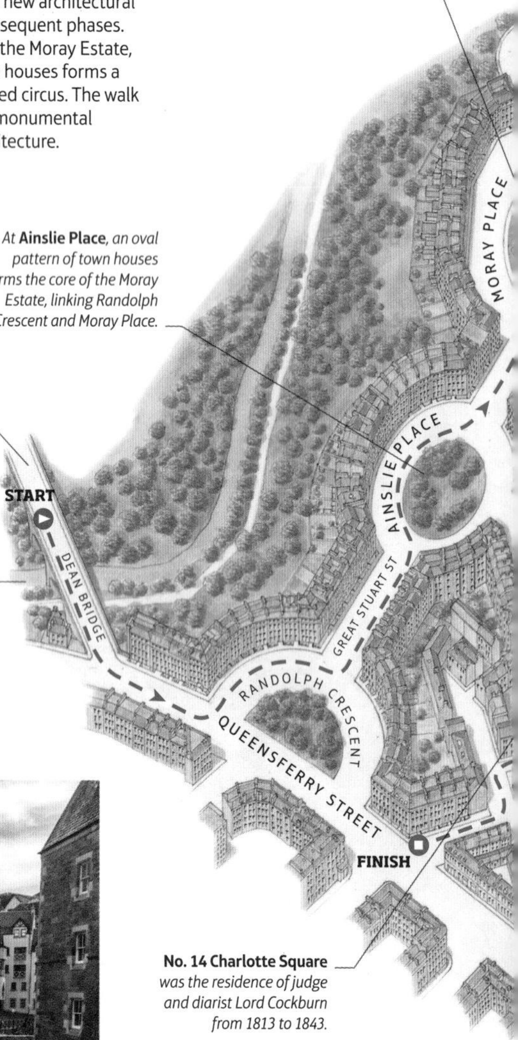

*The crowning glory of the Moray Estate, **Moray Place** consists of a series of immense houses and apartments, many of which are still inhabited.*

*At **Ainslie Place**, an oval pattern of town houses forms the core of the Moray Estate, linking Randolph Crescent and Moray Place.*

Dean Bridge, *built in 1829 to the design of Thomas Telford, offers views down to the Water of Leith and upstream to the weirs and old mills of Dean Village (p100).*

The Water of Leith *is a small river running through a gorge below Dean Bridge. There is a riverside walkway (p106) to Stockbridge (p98).*

MORAY PLACE

AINSLIE PLACE

START

DEAN BRIDGE

GREAT STUART ST

RANDOLPH CRESCENT

QUEENSFERRY STREET

FINISH

0 metres 100
0 yards 100
N ↑

No. 14 Charlotte Square *was the residence of judge and diarist Lord Cockburn from 1813 to 1843.*

←

The Water of Leith flowing through picturesque Dean Village

New Town

Locator Map

↑ The Georgian House and other grand
period buildings on Charlotte Square

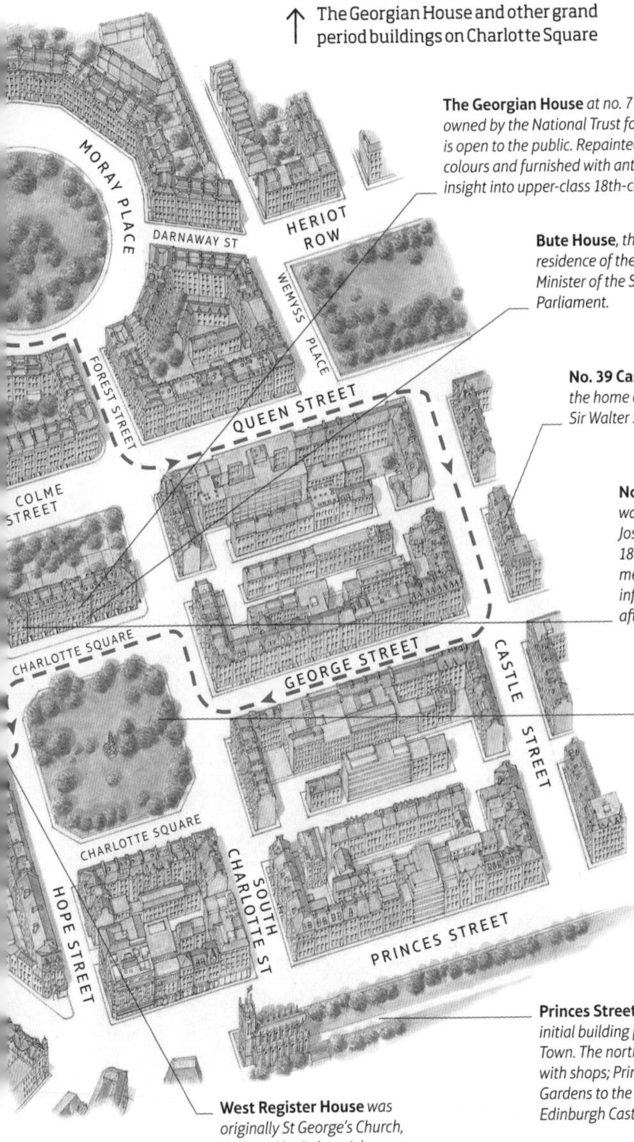

The Georgian House *at no. 7 Charlotte Sq is
owned by the National Trust for Scotland and
is open to the public. Repainted in its original
colours and furnished with antiques, it is an
insight into upper-class 18th-century Edinburgh.*

Bute House, *the official
residence of the First
Minister of the Scottish
Parliament.*

No. 39 Castle Street *was
the home of the writer
Sir Walter Scott (p114).*

No. 9 Charlotte Square
*was the home of surgeon
Joseph Lister from 1870 to
1877. He developed
methods of preventing
infection both during and
after surgery.*

Charlotte Square
*was built between
1792 and 1811 to
provide a series of
lavish town houses
for the most
successful city
merchants. Most of
the buildings are now
used as offices.*

MORAY PLACE

DARNAWAY ST

HERIOT ROW

WEMYSS PLACE

FOREST STREET

QUEEN STREET

COLME STREET

CHARLOTTE SQUARE

GEORGE STREET

CASTLE STREET

CHARLOTTE SQUARE

HOPE STREET

SOUTH CHARLOTTE ST

PRINCES STREET

Princes Street *was part of the
initial building phase of the New
Town. The north side is lined
with shops; Princes Street
Gardens to the south lie below
Edinburgh Castle.*

West Register House *was
originally St George's Church,
designed by Robert Adam.*

A LONG WALK

WATER OF LEITH WALKWAY

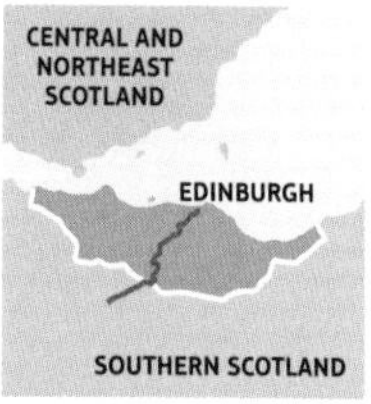

Distance 20.5 km (13 miles) **Walking Time** 4.5 hours
Terrain Well-maintained path, mostly paved with some sections stony and unsurfaced. **Nearest Bus** Lothian Bus number 44 from Shandwick Place to Balerno.

The tea-coloured Water of Leith rises in the Pentland Hills and flows for 40 km (24 miles) through Edinburgh to meet the Firth of Forth at Leith. On the way it passes through attractive urban villages, parks and woodland. Old weirs and former watermills hint at its history as a source of power for local industries. The Water of Leith Walkway, following the river for around half its length, forms part of the coast-to-coast John Muir Trail.

Locator Map
For more detail see p70

CENTRAL AND NORTHEAST SCOTLAND

EDINBURGH

SOUTHERN SCOTLAND

Water of Leith Walkway as it passes below an aqueduct carrying the Union canal

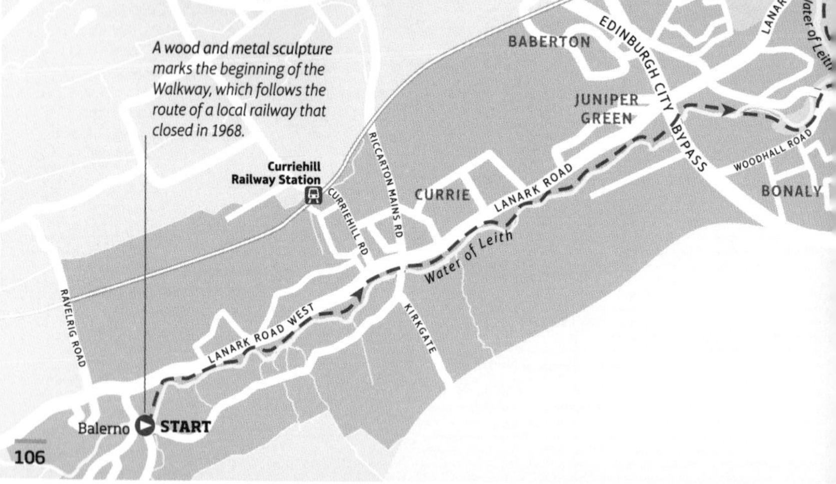

A wood and metal sculpture marks the beginning of the Walkway, which follows the route of a local railway that closed in 1968.

Curriehill Railway Station

STENHOUSE DR

CALDER RD

CALDER ROAD

LONGSTON

SIGHTHILL

MURRAYBURN ROAD

Kingsknowe Railway Station

KINGSKNOWE

Kingsknowe Golf Club

LANARK ROAD

BABERTON

EDINBURGH CITY BYPASS

JUNIPER GREEN

Water of Leith

WOODHALL ROAD

BONALY

RICCARTON MAINS RD

CURRIEHILL RD

CURRIE

LANARK ROAD

Water of Leith

RAVELRIG ROAD

KIRKGATE

LANARK ROAD WEST

Balerno ▶ START

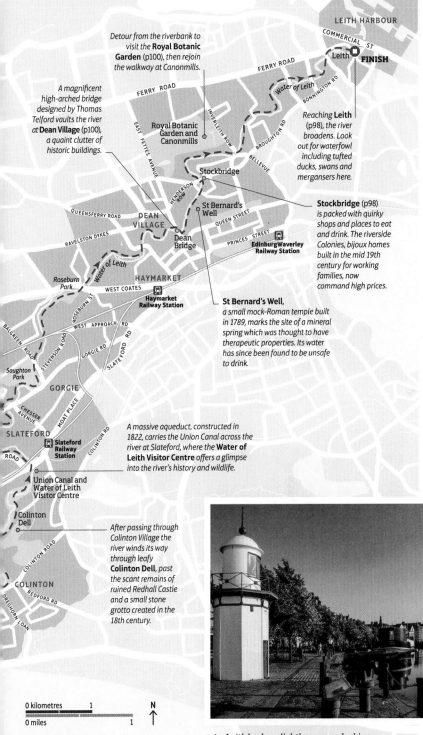

LEITH HARBOUR

Detour from the riverbank to visit the **Royal Botanic Garden** (p100), then rejoin the walkway at Canonmills.

A magnificent high-arched bridge designed by Thomas Telford vaults the river at **Dean Village** (p100), a quaint clutter of historic buildings.

COMMERCIAL ST

Leith **FINISH**

FERRY ROAD

Water of Leith

BONNINGTON RD

FERRY ROAD

Royal Botanic Garden and Canonmills

EAST FETTES AVENUE

INVERLEITH ROW

BROUGHTON RD

BELLEVUE

Reaching **Leith** (p98), the river broadens. Look out for waterfowl including tufted ducks, swans and mergansers here.

QUEENSFERRY ROAD

HENDERSON ROW

Stockbridge

St Bernard's Well

QUEEN STREET

DEAN VILLAGE

RAVELSTON DYKES

Dean Bridge

PRINCES STREET

Edinburgh Waverley Railway Station

Stockbridge (p98) is packed with quirky shops and places to eat and drink. The riverside Colonies, bijoux homes built in the mid 19th century for working families, now command high prices.

Roseburn Park

Water of Leith

HAYMARKET

WEST COATES

ROSEBURN ST

Haymarket Railway Station

BALGREEN ROAD

STEVENSON ROAD

WEST APPROACH RD

GORGIE RD

SLATEFORD RD

St Bernard's Well, a small mock-Roman temple built in 1789, marks the site of a mineral spring which was thought to have therapeutic properties. Its water has since been found to be unsafe to drink.

Saughton Park

CHESSER AVENUE

GORGIE

MOAT PLACE

COLINTON RD

SLATEFORD

ROAD

Slateford Railway Station

A massive aqueduct, constructed in 1822, carries the Union Canal across the river at Slateford, where the **Water of Leith Visitor Centre** offers a glimpse into the river's history and wildlife.

Union Canal and Water of Leith Visitor Centre

Colinton Dell

COLINTON ROAD

After passing through Colinton Village the river winds its way through leafy **Colinton Dell**, past the scant remains of ruined Redhall Castle and a small stone grotto created in the 18th century.

COLINTON

REDFORD RD

DREGHORN LOAN

0 kilometres 1
0 miles 1

N
↑

↑ Leith harbour lighthouse overlooking the water on a sunny evening

SOUTHERN SCOTLAND

In 1296 Scotland committed itself to the Wars of Independence against the English, and it was Southern Scotland that suffered the most. The strife caused by the many battles fought here lasted for three centuries, as first, Scottish self-determination and then alliances with France led to strained relations between Scotland and its southernmost neighbour.

The virtual independence of the southern Borders district brought further conflict. Powerful families had operated under local laws set in place since the mid-12th century, and when Scottish kings were not fighting the English, they led raids into the Border country to try to bring it back under central control.

Over the centuries, some of the great dramas of Scottish history have been played out in Southern Scotland. Robert the Bruce's guerrilla army defeated an English force at Glen Trool in 1307, but Flodden, near Coldstream, was the scene of the country's worst military reverse in 1513, when King James IV of Scotland and thousands of his men fell in battle. Today, the quiet countryside around the Borders market towns and the striking mountain vistas of Dumfries and Galloway belie their violent history. The area is now known for its manufacturing of textiles and for its literary associations. But it is the ruins of the great Border abbeys, castles and battlegrounds that serve as a reminder of Southern Scotland's turbulent past.

SOUTHERN SCOTLAND

Must Sees

1. Culzean Castle and Country Park
2. Abbotsford
3. Burns Heritage Trail

Experience More

4. East Lothian Coast
5. North Berwick
6. Tantallon Castle
7. Direlton Castle
8. Haddington
9. National Museum of Flight
10. St Abb's Head
11. Pentland Hills
12. Rosslyn Chapel
13. Linlithgow Palace
14. Kelso
15. Peebles
16. Drumlanrig Castle
17. Traquair House
18. Jedburgh
19. Eildon Hills
20. Melrose Abbey
21. New Lanark
22. Dumfries
23. Wigtown
24. Sweetheart Abbey
25. Dawyck Botanic Garden
26. Colvend Coast
27. Kirkcudbright
28. Caerlaverock Castle
29. Threave Castle
30. Whithorn
31. Dumfries House
32. Firth of Clyde
33. Scottish Maritime Museum
34. Galloway Forest Park
35. The Rhinns of Galloway

1 ⊘ Ⓜ ⊡ 🏠 (NTS)

CULZEAN CASTLE AND COUNTRY PARK

🅰C6 🏠6 km (4 miles) west of Maybole, Ayrshire 🚆Ayr, then bus 🕐Castle: Apr–Oct: 10:30am–4:30pm (last entry 4pm); grounds: 9am–dusk daily year-round 🌐nts.org.uk

Standing on a cliff's edge in an extensive parkland estate, the late-16th-century keep of Culzean (pronounced Cullayn) is a masterpiece in a land full of magnificent castles, with a glorious estate to match.

Formerly a crumbling fortified tower house, Culzean Castle was transformed by the great Scots architect Robert Adam into a mansion of sumptuous proportions and elegance. Work began in 1777 and lasted almost 20 years, with no expense spared in the decoration and craftsmanship of this breathtaking clifftop fortress. Culzean was fully restored and gifted to the nation in the 1970s.

The Castle Grounds

The castle's magnificent grounds became Scotland's first public country park in 1969 and, with farming flourishing alongside ornamental formal gardens, they reflect both the leisure and everyday activities of life on a great country estate. Free tours depart from the Home Farm visitor centre, or you can go it alone – the views across the Firth of Clyde waters to the mountains of Arran are glorious from the clifftop and delightful shoreline trails.

ORANGES AND LEMONS

Camellia House, Culzean's elegant stone-framed orangery, was restored in 2018 and replanted with clementine, lime, lemon and orange trees. Built in around 1840, it was designed by John Patterson, a disciple of Robert Adam. Orangeries in this style, built in emulation of those created for 17th-century monarchs like Louis XIV of France, were enviable status symbols for wealthy 19th-century notables.

The clock tower was originally the family coach house and stables.

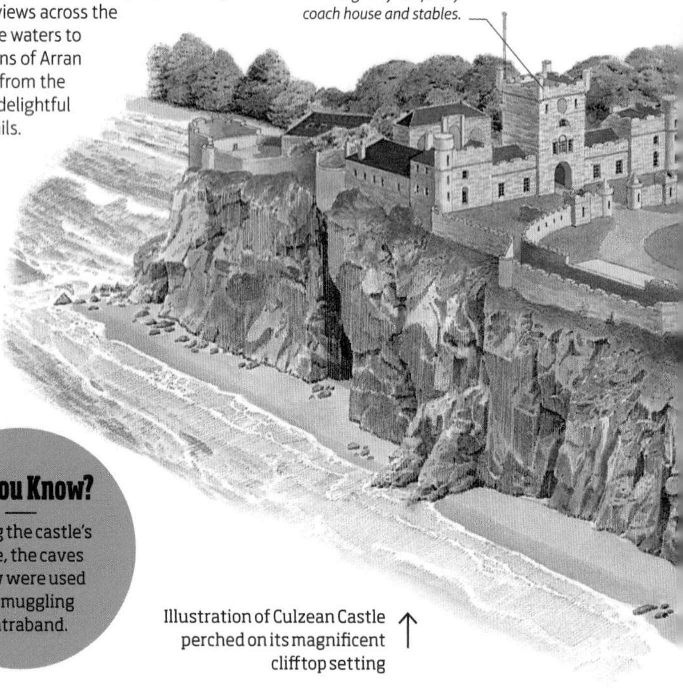

Did You Know?

During the castle's prime, the caves below were used for smuggling contraband.

Illustration of Culzean Castle perched on its magnificent clifftop setting ↑

Culzean Castle's iconic turrets
as seen from the beach below ↑

→

Culzean's oval
staircase, an
architectural triumph

*The elegantly restored
18th-century Round
Drawing Room perches
on the cliff's edge
46 m (150 ft) above
the Firth of Clyde.*

*Illuminated by an overarching
skylight, the Oval staircase is
considered one of Adam's
finest design achievements.*

*The Armoury houses a
collection of 18th- and 19th-
century weaponry purchased
from the Tower of London.*

*State Bedroom
and Dressing
Rooms*

*Fountain Court
sunken garden
is a good place
to begin a tour
of the grounds
to the east.*

*The Eisenhower
Apartment was a gift to
the US president for his
support in World War II.
It is now a small hotel.*

ABBOTSFORD

E6 🚶 **Tweedbank, Melrose** 🚆 **Tweedbank** 🚌 **X62, 72, Abbotsford Minibus from Tweedbank Station** 🕐 **Mar & Nov: 10am-4pm; Apr-Oct: 10am-5pm** 🌐 **scottsabbotsford.com**

Few houses bear the stamp of their creator so intimately as Abbotsford House, the home of Georgian Scotland's greatest author, Sir Walter Scott, for the final 20 years of his life. The house is adorned with arms and armour and Scott spared no expense in converting what was a humble farmhouse by the Tweed into this fabulous baronial home, complete with towers, turrets and grand halls.

Walter Scott bought a farm here in 1811, known as *Clarteyhole* ("dirty hole" in Borders Scots), though he soon renamed it Abbotsford, in memory of the monks of Melrose Abbey. He demolished the house to make way for the turreted building we see today, its construction funded by the sales of his novels.

Rob Roy's claymore is among the prized mementoes displayed in Scott's majestic home, where suits of armour and fearsome weaponry decorate the Great Hall. A treasury of rare books and memorabilia reflects his passion for a romanticized version of Scotland's history, showcasing relics of the Stuarts including a richly adorned crucifix owned by Mary, Queen of Scots, and a lock of Prince Charles Edward Stuart's hair. The study where Scott wrote many of his novels is a shrine to his prodigious literary output. Surrounding the house, the 120-acre Abbotsford Estate was laid out by Scott himself, and now boasts an award-winning visitor centre, beautiful formal gardens, extensive forest trails and family-friendly activity areas for all ages.

↑ Impressive interior of the celebrated Abbotsford Library

← Medieval jousting Armour, one of the many relics displayed at Abbotsford

SIR WALTER SCOTT

Sir Walter Scott (1771–1832) penned around 30 novels, 20 histories and biographies, and a dozen anthologies of verse, starting with *Waverley* in 1814. A heartfelt royalist, he stage-managed George IV's tour of Scotland in 1822 and was rewarded with a knighthood. His novels inspired other creative spirits, such as Donizetti, who turned one of Scott's tales into the opera *Lucia di Lammermoor*. Today, he's best remembered for *Rob Roy*, his swashbuckling saga of a Highland outlaw.

9,000
—
The number of
rare books that fill the
shelves of the library
at Abbotsford
House.

↑ Abbotsford House
surrounded by beautiful
floral gardens

Modern wooden exterior of
the Robert Burns Birthplace
Museum in Alloway ↑

3

BURNS HERITAGE TRAIL

🅰C6 🅰South Ayrshire, Dumfries & Galloway

Robert Burns (1759–96) is Scotland's most beloved writer, whose remarkable body of work ranges from satirical poetry to tender love songs. An official Burns Heritage Trail takes visitors on a tour of various sights in southwest Scotland where he lived and worked.

The real centre of the Burns Trail is the village of Alloway, where the excellent **Robert Burns Birthplace Museum** displays a wealth of manuscripts, memorabilia and personal effects. Close by, and part of the museum, is Burns Cottage, the poet's birthplace and home for the first seven years of his life. The atmospheric ruins of Alloway Kirk – where Burns' father, William, is buried – and the iconic 13th-century Brig o'Doon bridge – which was the setting for one of Burns' most famous poems – are also near here.

In Dumfries, the **Robert Burns Centre** has further exhibits on display, including a slice of bark from a tree felled at Ellisland Farm into which Burns carved his name. Also on show is a scale model of the town from the 1790s and a collection of original manuscripts. The lively centre transforms into a small film theatre in the evenings. A short stroll across the river is **Burns House**, where the poet lived for the last three years of his life and wrote many of his best-known poems. The house features first editions and photographs. Burns is buried in a Greek-style mausoleum in nearby St Michael's churchyard.

> **A short stroll across the river is Burns House, where the poet lived for the last three years of his life and wrote many of his best-known poems.**

→

Viewing the scale model of
the town of Dumfries at the
Robert Burns Centre

Real Burn's fanatics venture to the remote
Ellisland Farm, which is located some 18 km
(11 miles) east of Ayr. Burns built this peaceful
place for his wife Jean Armour in 1788.
Idyllically located near the River Nith,
it's a tranquil spot for a wander and offers
a glimpse into the Bard's family life.

Robert Burns Birthplace Museum
⊛⊛ⓝⓢ ⬛ Alloway ⏱ 10am-5pm daily
🅦 nts.org.uk

Robert Burns Centre
⊛ ⬛ Mill Rd, Dumfries ⏱ Times vary, check
website 🅦 rbcft.co.uk

Burns House
⬛ Burns Street, Dumfries ☎ (01387) 255
297 ⏱ Apr-Sep: 10am-5pm Mon-Sat,
2-5pm Sun; Oct-Mar: 10am-1pm & 2-5pm
Tue-Sat

Ellisland Farm
⊛⊛ ⬛ Holywood Rd, Auldgirth ⏱ Apr-Sep:
10am-5pm Mon-Sat, 2-5pm Sun; Oct-Nov
& Jan-Mar: Mon-Wed & Sat 10am-5pm
🅦 ellislandfarm.co.uk

CELEBRATING BURNS NIGHT
The birthday of Burns is celebrated with
much pomp. A Burns Supper opens with
the reading of Burns's Selkirk Grace,
before the ceremonious piping in of the
haggis, the event's main dish. The
Address to the Haggis, the poet's homage
to the "great chieftain o' the pudding-
race", and other readings
follow, along with the
patronizing Toast to
the Lassies, usually
met with a sar-
castic riposte
from a female
guest. The
event ends
with Auld
Lang Syne.

→
Sea Cliff's sandstone
harbour with Tantallon
Castle in the distance

EXPERIENCE MORE

4

East Lothian Coast

E5 **East Lothian**
Edinburgh Lothians
(0845) 225 5121

Stretching east from Mussel-
burgh for some 65 km (40
miles), the coast of East
Lothian offers opportunities
for beach activities, golf,
windsurfing, viewing seabirds
and coastal walks. It has a
pleasant mixture of beaches,
low cliffs, woodland and some
farmland. Although the A198
and A1 are adjacent to the
coast for only short distances,
they give easy access to a
series of public car parks

> **INSIDER TIP**
> **East Lothian
> Coastal Walk**
>
> For a long scenic coast
> walk, take the coastal
> footpath from Gullane
> Bay to North Berwick,
> across grassy heath-
> land between sandy
> bays and low rocky
> headlands, with views
> of the coast of Fife to
> the north.

(a small charge is made in
summer) close to the shore.
Among these is Gullane,
perhaps the best beach for
seaside sports and activities.
Yellowcraig, near Dirleton, is a
lovely bay, lying about 400 m
(440 yds) from the car park.
Limetree Walk, near Tyning-
hame, has the long, east-
facing beach of Ravensheugh
Sands (a ten-minute walk
along a woodland track).
Belhaven Bay, just west of
Dunbar, is a large beach with
walks along the Tyne estuary.
Barns Ness, east of Dunbar,
offers a geological nature trail
and an impressive lighthouse.
There is another delightful
beach at Seacliff, reached by a
private toll road that leaves
the A198 about 3 km (2 miles)
east of North Berwick.

5

North Berwick

E5 **North Berwick**
X5, X24

A charming seaside town,
North Berwick has plenty to
keep visitors entertained,
including boat trips, coastal
walks, putting greens and golf

courses, plus quirky shops,
coffee houses and ice-cream
parlours. During the summer
regular boat trips leave the
picturesque harbour for a
breezy tour of nearby islands
and Bass Rock, home to
Britain's largest gannet colony.
Learn more about the area's
birdlife at the **Scottish
Seabird Centre**, where you
can control cameras for live
coverage of the birds without
disturbing them. After a day of
exploring, enjoy fish and chips
on the beachfront. For golf,
head to North Berwick, The
Glen or Muirfield Links.

Scottish Seabird Centre
Times vary, see
website **seabird.org**

6

Tantallon Castle

E5 **East Lothian**
North Berwick **120**
**Apr-Sep: 9:30am-5:30pm
daily; Oct-Mar: 10am-4pm
daily** **historic
environment.scot**

For a magnificently snappable
stop on a day trip from
Edinburgh, Tantallon is hard to

with space for 1,000 roosts, stands in the impressive castle grounds, which are home to the world's longest herbaceous border.

8

Haddington

**⚑E6 ⚑East Lothian
🛈Edinburgh & Lothians
(0845) 225 5121**

This attractive county town, about 24 km (15 miles) east of Edinburgh, was destroyed during the Wars of Independence in the 13th–14th centuries, and again in the 16th century. The agricultural revolution brought prosperity, giving Haddington many historic houses, churches, and other public buildings, and a programme of restoration has helped to retain the town's character. The River Tyne encloses the town, and there are a number of attractive

riverside walks as well as parkland. ("A Walk Around Haddington" guide is available from most newsagents).

The parish church of St Mary's, southeast of the town centre, dates back to 1462 and is one of the largest churches in the area. Parts of the church have been refurbished and rebuilt in later years, having been destroyed in the famous siege of Haddington in 1548.

beat. Its 15-m (50-ft-) tall and 4-m (12-ft-) thick battered red sandstone walls overlook the North Sea and the Bass Rock, and it's easy to see why the Red Douglases, among the mightiest families of medieval Scotland, chose it as their seat.

---

7 (symbols)

Dirleton Castle

**⚑E5 ⚑Dirleton ⚑X5
⚑Apr-Sept 9:30am–5:30pm
daily; Oct-Mar: 10am–4pm
daily 🖥historic
environment.scot**

A short bus ride from Edinburgh city centre, Dirleton Castle makes for a fun day out. Its De Vaux towers, built in the early 13th century, are among the oldest in Scotland and served a succession of aristocratic families, among them the Earl of Gowrie, executed in 1585 for plotting against James VI. Beneath the three-storey keep is a pit wherein languished prisoners of its noble owners. A huge dovecot (pronounced *doocot* in the Scots vernacular),

→
St Mary's Collegiate Church on the banks of the Tyne in Haddington

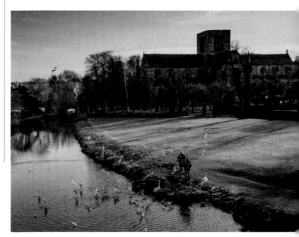

9 (icons)

National Museum of Flight

⚠E6 ⚑East Fortune Airfield, EH39 5LF 🚌X5, change at Haddington for 121 to Museum of Flight, East Fortune 🚉Drem, change for 121 bus towards North Berwick 🕐Apr–Oct: 10am–5pm daily; Nov–Mar: 10am–4pm Sat & Sun 🌐nms.ac.uk

Scotland's only Concorde is the star of the show at this former military airfield, with a supporting cast that includes civil aircraft and warbirds like the bizarre Weir W-2 auto-gyro, the iconic Spitfire, the

↑ Spitfire at National Museum of Flight

> During the May to June breeding season, St Abbs Head National Nature Reserve becomes an important site for more than 50,000 cliff-nesting seabirds.

supersonic English Electric Lightning and the ominous nuclear bomber, the Avro Vulcan. The Concorde Experience reveals the history of supersonic aviation, and the free Airfield Explorer means that you can easily get around the hangars and outdoor exhibits.

10 (NTS)

St Abb's Head

⚠E6 ⚑The Scottish Borders 📞(01890) 771443 🚉Berwick-upon-Tweed 🚌From Edinburgh 🕐Nature Centre: Apr–Oct: 10am–5pm daily 🌐nts.org.uk

The jagged cliffs of St Abb's Head, rising 91 m (300 ft) from the North Sea, offer visitors a spectacular view of thousands of seabirds wheeling and diving below. During the May to June breeding season, St Abbs Head National Nature Reserve becomes an important site for more than 50,000 cliff-nesting seabirds, including fulmars, guillemots, kittiwakes and puffins. St Abb's village

has one of the few unspoiled working harbours on Scotland's east coast. A cliff-top trail begins at the visitor centre, where displays include identification boards and a touch table where young visitors can get to grips with wings and feathers.

11

Pentland Hills

⚠D6 ⚑The Lothians 🚆Edinburgh, then bus ℹHarlaw House Visitor Centre: 10:30am–3:30pm daily; www.pentland hills.org

The wilds of the Pentland Hills stretch for 26 km (16 miles) southwest of Edinburgh, and offer some of the best hill-walking country in Southern Scotland. Walkers can saunter along the many signposted footpaths, while the more adventurous can climb the 493-m (1,617-ft-) peak of Allermuir. Even more ambitious is the classic scenic route along the ridge from Caerketton to West Kip. Those

The clifftop village of St Abbs and *(inset)* a couple of resident guillemots ↑

who would like a helping hand in order to reach the higher ground can take the chairlift at **Midlothian Snowsports Centre**, which is home to Britain's largest artificial ski slope.

Midlothian Snowsports Centre

🏠 Biggar Rd, Hillend, Midlothian 🕐 9:30am-9pm Mon-Fri (to 7pm Sat & Sun) 🌐 midlothian.gov.uk

---

12

Rosslyn Chapel

🗺 D6 🚌 37, 140 🚆 Eskbank 🕐 9:30am-5pm Mon-Sat (Jun-Aug: to 6pm), noon-4:45pm Sun 🌐 rosslynchapel.com

To the east of the A703, in the lee of the Pentland Hills, stands the exquisite and ornate 15th-century Rosslyn Chapel, which famously features in *The Da Vinci Code*, Dan Brown's bestselling novel and the 2006 film adaptation of the same name.

The building was originally intended as a church, but after the death of its founder, William Sinclair, it was used as a burial ground for his descendants. It has remained the property of the family since 1446, and the chapel continues to be used as a place of worship to this day.

The delicately wreathed Apprentice Pillar recalls the legend of the talented apprentice carver who was killed by the master stone mason in a fit of jealous rage when he discovered his pupil's superior skill. Photography and video recording are not permitted within the chapel.

DRINK

Glenkinchie Distillery

For a whisky experience that doesn't involve a long journey into the Highlands, head to Glenkinchie Distillery near the village of Pencaitland. Informative tours include a visit to the exhibition and a viewing of the distillery itself, before ending with the obligatory tasting.

🗺 E6 🏠 Pencaitland, Tranent 🕐 10am-5pm daily (Nov-Feb: to 4pm) 🌐 malts.com

←
Rosslyn Chapel, still owned by descendants of its founder

13 (icons)

Linlithgow Palace

📍D5 🚩Kirk Gate, Linlithgow 🚆Linlithgow 🚌From Edinburgh 🕐9:30am-5:30pm daily (Oct-Mar: 10am-4pm) 🌐historic-environment.scot

Standing on the edge of Linlithgow Loch, amid lovely gardens, the former royal palace of Linlithgow is one of the country's most-visited ruins. It dates back largely to the building commissioned by James I in 1425, though some sections date from the 14th century. The vast scale of the building is best seen in the 28-m- (94-ft-) long Great Hall, with its huge fireplace and windows. The restored fountain in the courtyard, which can be seen in operation on Sundays in July and August, was a wedding present in 1538 from James V to his wife, Mary of Guise. His daughter, Mary, Queen of Scots (p62), was born at Linlithgow in 1542.

The adjacent Church of St Michael is Scotland's largest pre-Reformation church and a fine example of the Scottish Decorated style. Consecrated in the 13th century, the church was damaged by the fire of 1424 and largely rebuilt.

14

Kelso

📍E6 🚩The Scottish Borders 🚌From Edinburgh

At the confluence of the rivers Teviot and Tweed, Kelso has a charming centre, with a cobbled square surrounded by Georgian and Victorian buildings. The focus of the town is the ruin of the 12th-century abbey. This was the oldest and wealthiest of the four Border Abbeys founded by David I, but it suffered from wars with England and was severely damaged in 1545. **Floors Castle** on the northern edge of Kelso was designed by William Adam in the 1720s, and reworked by William Playfair after 1837. A short drive away is **Mellerstain House**, a stunning stately home built by the Adam brothers. There are formal gardens, and the grounds include the Borders Sculpture Park which showcases the work of contemporary artists.

Floors Castle

(icons) 🏠 Roxburghshire 🕐May-Sep: daily 🌐floorscastle.com

Mellerstain House

(icons) 🏠Gordon 🕐May-Sep: Fri-Mon 🌐mellerstain.com

15

Peebles

📍D6 🚩The Scottish Borders 🚌From Edinburgh

Set on the banks of the River Tweed, this charming Borders town is home to the **Tweeddale Museum and Gallery**, which houses full-scale plaster casts of part of the Parthenon Frieze, and casts of a frieze depicting the entry of Alexander the Great into Babylon. The walled **Kailzie Gardens** attract many day-trippers, especially for its ospreys (April to August), while **Glentress Forest**, which lies on the fringes of town, is popular with hikers and mountain bikers.

Tweeddale Museum and Gallery

🏠Chambers Institution, High St 📞(01721) 724820 🕐10:30am-4pm Mon-Fri, 9:30am-12:30pm Sat

Kailzie Gardens

(icons) 🏠Kailzie, Peebles 🕐Apr-Oct: 10am-5pm daily 🌐kailziegardens.com

Glentress Forest

(icons) 🕐Daily 🌐forestryandland.gov.scot

↑ The River Tweed flowing through Peebles town centre

← Kelso Abbey, a soaring medieval ruin

the relics recalling the period of the Highland rebellions. Following a vow made by the fifth Earl, Traquair's Bear Gates (the "Steekit Yetts"), which closed after Bonnie Prince Charlie's visit in 1745, will not reopen until a Stuart reascends the throne. A secret stairway leads to the Priest's Room, which, with its clerical vestments that could be disguised as bedspreads, attests to the problems faced by Catholic families until Catholicism was legalized in 1829.

One wing of the house now contains the Traquair House Brewery, which dates back to the 18th century and still uses the original equipment and 200-year-old oak barrels.

The grounds are home to the impressive Traquair Maze. Planted in 1981 with over 1,500 Leylandi Cyprus trees, it is now the largest hedged maze in Scotland. An annual Easter Egg hunt is held here on Easter Sunday. Each May, the grounds also play host to Scotland's only authentic Medieval Fayre.

Did You Know?

The Fountain at Linlithgow Palace flowed with wine to welcome Bonnie Prince Charlie.

16 Drumlanrig Castle

D6 Thornhill, Dumfries & Galloway ⛴🚌 Dumfries, then bus ⏰ Grounds: Apr-Sep: 10am-5pm daily; Castle: Easter, Jul & Aug only: 11am-4pm daily 🌐 drumlanrigcastle.co.uk

Rising squarely from a grassy platform, the massive fortress-palace of Drumlanrig Castle was built from pink sandstone between 1679 and 1691 on the site of a 15th-century Douglas stronghold. The castle's multi-turreted, formidable exterior conceals a priceless collection of art and Jacobite treasures.

Hanging on the walls of oak-panelled rooms are paintings by Thomas Gainsborough, Sir Joshua Reynolds, Allan Ramsay and Rembrandt, whose *Old Lady Reading* takes pride of place. The emblem of a crowned, winged heart recalls the famous Douglas ancestor "The Good Sir James". Legend has it he bore Robert the Bruce's heart on crusade against the Moors in Spain.

17 Traquair House

D6 Peebles, The Scottish Borders 🚌 From Peebles ⏰ Apr-Jun & Sep: 11am-5pm daily; Jul & Aug: 10am-5pm daily; Oct: 11am-4pm daily; Nov: 11am-3pm Sat & Sun 🌐 traquair.co.uk

Scotland's oldest continuously inhabited house has deep roots in Scottish religious and political history stretching back over 900 years. Evolving from a fortified tower to a 17th-century mansion, the house was a Catholic Stuart stronghold for 500 years. Mary, Queen of Scots was among the many monarchs to have stayed here: her crucifix is kept in the house and her bed is covered by a counter-pane that she made herself. Family letters and engraved Jacobite drinking glasses are among

STAY

Cringletie House

Set in beautiful private grounds, this grand house boasts traditional and deluxe rooms with modern amenities. Its award-winning restaurant offers a seasonal dinner menu and delightful afternoon teas.

D6 Edinburgh Rd, Peebles 🌐 cringletie.com

£££

Winter view of Linlithgow Palace

18

Jedburgh

⚑E6 ⬚The Scottish Borders 🚌 ℹMurray's Green; (01835) 863170

This historic Borders town is home to the impressive mock-medieval **Jedburgh Castle, Jail and Museum**. Built during the 1820s and once functioning as the local jail, it now serves as a local museum, with some interesting displays on the area's history and the grim reality of life in a 19th-century Scottish prison.

Built around 1500, the **Mary, Queen of Scots' Visitor Centre** is so called due to a visit paid by Mary, Queen of Scots in 1566. The house itself was converted into a museum in the 1930s, and in 1987 (on the 400th anniversary of Mary's execution) it became a centre dedicated to telling her life story. Exhibits include a fine collection of paintings, objects, and a copy of her death mask.

Nearby, **Jedburgh Abbey** is one of the great quartet of 12th-century Border Abbeys, along with Dryburgh, Kelso and Melrose.

Jedburgh Castle, Jail and Museum

⊛ 📞(01835) 864750
🕐Apr-Oct: daily

Mary, Queen of Scots' Visitor Centre

⊛ 📞(01835) 863331
🕐Mar-Nov: 10am-3pm daily

Jedburgh Abbey

⊛🅿 🕐Apr-Sep: 9:30am-5:30pm daily; Oct-Mar: 10am-4pm daily 🌐historic-environment.scot

---

19

Eildon Hills

⚑E6 ⬚The Scottish Borders 🚌From Melrose

The three peaks of the Eildon Hills dominate the central Borders landscape. Mid Hill is the tallest at 422 m (1,385 ft), while North Hill once had a Bronze Age hill fort dating from before 500 BC, and later it became home to a major Roman military complex strategically placed between Hadrian's Wall and the Antonine Wall (p191) to guard the crossing of the River Tweed at

Newstead in the 2nd century AD. In summer, guided walks through Melrose's medieval centre to historic sights depart from the **Trimontium Museum of Roman Scotland**. The centre contains aerial photography of the Trimontium site, ancient artifacts and Roman treasures. The most celebrated name hereabouts is Sir Walter Scott (p114), who had a particular affection for these hills. A panorama of the Eildon Hills called Scott's View lies just east of Melrose, near Dryburgh Abbey. This is the best location to see the hills as they rise above the Tweed.

Trimontium Museum of Roman Scotland

⊛ ⬚The Ormiston, Market Square, Melrose 🕐Apr-Oct: 10:30am-4:30pm Mon-Sat 🌐trimontium.co.uk

---

20 ⊛ 🅿

Melrose Abbey

⚑E6 ⬚Melrose, The Scottish Borders 🕐Apr-Sep: 9:30am-5:30pm daily; Oct-Mar: 10am-4pm daily 🌐historicenvironment.scot

The ruins of this Border Abbey bear witness to the devastation of English invasions. Built by David I in 1136 for Cistercian monks, and also to replace a 7th-century monastery, Melrose was repeatedly ransacked by English armies, most notably in 1322 and 1385. The final blow came in 1545, when Henry VIII of England implemented his destructive Scottish policy known as the "Rough Wooing". This resulted from the failure of the Scots to ratify a marriage treaty between Henry VIII's son and the infant Mary, Queen of Scots. What remains of the abbey are the outlines of

←

Elaborate tomb in the light-filled mausoleum at Jedburgh Abbey

cloisters, the kitchen, monastic buildings and the shell of the church. The south exterior wall includes a gargoyle shaped like a pig playing the bagpipes. An embalmed heart, found here in 1920, is probably that of Robert the Bruce, the abbey's chief benefactor, who had decreed that his heart be taken on a crusade to the Holy Land. It was returned here after its bearer, Sir James Douglas, was killed in Spain.

㉑
New Lanark

🅰D6 🚆Lanark, Clyde Valley 🚌🚌Lanark 🌐newlanark.org

By the beautiful Falls of Clyde, the village of New Lanark was founded in 1785 by the industrial entrepreneur David Dale. Ideally located for its water-driven mills, the village became the largest producer of cotton in Britain by 1800. Cotton manufacturing continued here until the 1960s.

The **New Lanark Visitor Centre** has exhibits illustrating the World Heritage Site's significance as a window to the realities of working life in the early 19th century. A ticket here gives entry to many of the town's historical buildings.

24 km (15 miles) north, the town of Blantyre has a memorial to the Clyde Valley's most famous son, the explorer David Livingstone.

New Lanark Visitor Centre
🚭🚫☺ 🄲(01555) 661345 🄾Apr-Oct: 10am-5pm daily; Nov-Mar: 11am-4pm daily

㉒
Dumfries

🅰D7 🚆Dumfries & Galloway 🛈64 Whitesands; (01387) 253862

By some distance the largest town in southwest Scotland, Dumfries is associated, above all, with the famous Scottish

> ### Did You Know?
> The town of New Lanark was once the UK's largest cotton-spinning mill complex.

↑ Autumnal colours at the three-tiered Falls of Clyde, New Lanark

poet and lyricist Robert Burns, and while **Robert Burns Centre** (p116) is the reason most people visit, there's a lot more to see here. A good place to start is the **Dumfries Museum**; housed in an 18th-century windmill it also features the world's oldest working camera obscura, one of just three in Scotland. A short walk along the riverbank, and perched on one end of the six-arched Devorgilla Bridge, is the **Old Bridge House Museum**; reputedly the town's oldest building, it was once also an inn (and where Burns most likely drank), but today has a few small rooms, each one pertaining to a different theme.

Dumfries Museum
🄰Rotchell Rd 🄾Easter-Sep: 10am-5pm Mon-Sat, 2-5pm Sun; Oct-Easter: 10-5pm Tue-Sat 🌐dgculture.co.uk

Old Bridge House Museum
🄰Mill Rd 🄾Easter-Sep: 10am-5pm Mon-Sat, 2-5pm Sun 🌐dgculture.co.uk

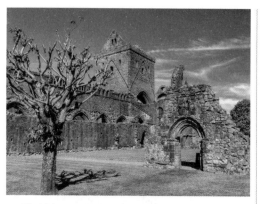

↑ The 13th-century ruins of Sweetheart Abbey in the village of New Abbey

SHOP

A book-lover's paradise, Wigtown has many, mostly secondhand, bookshops where you can be sure to pick up a bargain on just about any topic.

Beltie Books

An eccentric shop crammed to the brim with all manner of dusty volumes. It also has an excellent little café.

⚑C7 ◯6 Bank St
Ⓦbeltiebooks.co.uk

The Bookshop

Wigtown's oldest, and Scotland's largest, secondhand bookshop.

⚑C7 ◯17 North Main St
Ⓦthe-bookshop.com

Foggie Toddle Books

A dedicated children's bookshop with both new and secondhand editions, plus toys and games.

⚑C7 ◯18 North Main St
Ⓦfoggietoddlebooks.
co.uk

㉓
Wigtown

⚑C7 ◯Dumfries & Galloway
Ⓦwigtown-booktown.co.uk

Designated Scotland's book capital in 1998, Wigtown has in excess of a dozen bookshops, and many more book-related businesses. Literary fever sweeps through this small town in late September during the ten-day Wigtown Book Festival, which pulls in some of the biggest names from the world of publishing. It's also worth ambling through the main square, little changed since medieval times and today the setting for a lively market each Saturday from Easter to September.

㉔ ⊘ (NTS)
Sweetheart Abbey

◯D7 ◯New Abbey ➡From Dumfries ◯Apr-Sep: 9:30am-5:30pm daily; Oct-Mar: 10am-4pm Sat-Wed
Ⓦhistoricenvironment.scot

Founded by the Cistercian order in 1273, the evocatively

titled Sweetheart Abbey takes its name from its founder, Lady Devorgilla de Balliol, who had it built in memory of her husband John Balliol, of Oxford College fame; legend supposes that she carried Balliol's embalmed heart around with her for the remaining twenty-two years of her life, and it is here that she is buried, along with a casket containing his heart. The now roofless abbey is a magnificent red sand-stone structure – largely intact and betraying some superb tracery in the windows and corbelling around the massive central tower. Note that at the time of writing, part of the abbey was enveloped in scaffolding and off limits pending some important restoration work.

㉕ ⊘ ▭ 🛍
Dawyck Botanic Garden

⚑D6 ◯Stobo ➡From from Peebles ◯10am-6pm daily (Mar & Oct: to 5pm; Nov-Feb: to 4pm) Ⓦrbge.org.uk

Tucked away in the picturesque Borders region, the lovely Dawyck Botanic Garden – a satellite of the Royal Botanic Garden in Edinburgh (p100) – is regarded as one of the world's finest arboreta.

→
The pretty town of Kirkcudbright seen from the Kirkcudbright Bridge

Enjoying a continental climate in which plants flourish, its seasonal highlights include snowdrops in February, blue poppies in June, and the wildly colourful Azalea Terrace in May and June, while more than 300 years of tree planting are manifest in some of the tallest and oldest trees in Britain dating back to 1680. Visitors can walk among towering Giant Sierra redwoods, magnificent European Silver and Douglas firs, and fountain-like Brewer's weeping spruce.

Dawyck is also home to the world's first cryptogamic reserve, where mosses, lichens, fungi and suchlike are on display. Among all this there are some fabulous woodland walks and themed trails, while a smart, modern visitor centre rounds off a wonderful day out.

> **Dawyck Botanic Garden has some fabulous woodland walks and themed trails, while a smart, modern visitor centre rounds off a wonderful day out.**

Benefiting from the warm air of the Gulf Stream, it is for the most part a largely indented shoreline characterized by dramatic cliffs, shallow coves and sheltered small bays, and interspersed with comely estuary villages such as Sandyhills, with its golden beaches and expansive views across the mud flats to the Solway Firth. There's also picturesque Rockcliffe village, from where there's a bracing wooded coastal walk to Kippford, a small yachting centre on a narrow cove, with some agreeable places to stay and eat.

from the early 1600s, is now the **Tolbooth Art Centre**, and exhibits a large range of work by Kirkcudbright artists from 1880 to the present day. The most celebrated of these was Edward Hornel (1864–1933), one of the Glasgow Boys, who painted striking images of Japanese women. Some of his work is displayed in his former home, Broughton House, on the High Street.

The impressive **MacLellan's Castle** in the town centre was built in 1582 by the then Provost of Kirkcudbright, while outside, the ruins of Dundrennan Abbey date from the 12th century. Mary, Queen of Scots spent her last night there before fleeing to England in May 1568.

26
Colvend Coast

D7 **Dumfries & Galloway**

Around 32 km (20 miles) southwest of Dumfries, and somewhat optimistically dubbed the "Scottish Riviera", the Colvend coast is nevertheless a lovely stretch of coastline, with enough to rate a day's leisurely exploration.

27
Kirkcudbright

D7 **Dumfries & Galloway** **Harbour Sq; (01557) 330494** **kirkcudbright.town**

Situated by the mouth of the River Dee, at the head of Kirkcudbright Bay, this lively fishing port has an artistic heritage. The Tolbooth, a former debtor's prison dating

Tolbooth Art Centre
✏️🕐 **High St**
☎ (01557) 331556
🕐 11am–4pm Mon–Sat (also 1–4pm Sun mid-Apr–Sep)

MacLellan's Castle
✏️ **Kirkcudbright town centre** 🕐 Apr–Sep: 9:30am–5:30pm daily **historic environment.scot**

↑ Threave Castle sitting on an island in the River Dee, Kirkcudbrightshire

A giant menacing tower, this 14th-century Black Douglas stronghold on an island in the River Dee commands the most complete medieval riverside harbour in Scotland.

㉙ ⊘ 🏛

Threave Castle

🅰D7 🅰Castle Douglas, Dumfries & Galloway 🚆Dumfries 🕐Apr-Sep: 10am-4:30pm daily (Oct: to 3:30pm) 🆆historic-environment.scot

A giant menacing tower, this 14th-century Black Douglas stronghold on an island in the River Dee commands the most complete medieval riverside harbour in Scotland. Douglas's struggles against the early Stuart kings resulted in his surrender here after a two-month siege in 1455. Threave was dismantled after Protestant Covenanters defeated its Catholic defenders in 1640. Only the shell of the kitchen, great hall and domestic levels remain.

Arguably an even bigger attraction than the castle itself these days is a pair of peregrine falcons, who occupy the upper two floors, which does mean that these areas are off limits between the months of April and July.

㉘ ⊘ 💻 🏛

Caerlaverock Castle

🅰D7 🅰Dumfries & Galloway 🕐9:30am-5:30pm daily (Oct-Mar: 10am-4pm) 🆆historic-environment.scot

This impressive, three-sided, red stone structure, with its distinctive moat, is southwest Scotland's finest example of a medieval castle. Built in around 1270 some 14 km (9 miles) south of Dumfries, Caerlaverock Castle came to prominence in 1300, during the Wars of Independence, when it was besieged by Edward I, king of England, setting a precedent for more than three centuries of strife that was to follow. Chronicles of Edward's endeavours describe the castle much as it stands today, despite being partially razed and rebuilt after violent clashes with the English during the 14th and 16th centuries.

Though the subject of dispute for centuries, the castle remained the stronghold of the Maxwell family, and their crest and motto can still be seen over the door to this day. It was the struggle between Robert Maxwell, a staunch supporter of Charles I, and a Covenanter army that caused the castle's eventual fall to ruin in 1640.

Today Caerlaverock remains the epitome of a medieval stronghold, and it's a popular destination for family days out. Young visitors might enjoy Historic Environment Scotland's entertaining free app, Caerlaverock Castle Quest, an augmented reality game that brings the castle's history to life. Players can meet the members of the Caerlaverock household after the seige of 1300 as they explore the castle grounds in real life. The app is available to download for Android and iOS devices.

→

Opulent exterior of Dumfries House and its beautiful landscaped gardens

Surrounding the castle, Threave Garden and Estate is one of Scotland's most biodiverse nature reserves, with a variety of wildlife, flora and fauna. Getting to the castle from here is an adventure in itself, involving a ten-minute walk from the visitor centre to the banks of River Dee, whereupon you ring a brass bell and a boat comes to take you to the island.

---

③⓪
Whithorn

📍 C7 🚉 Dumfries & Galloway 🚂 Stranraer ℹ️ 45–47 George St 🌐 withorn.com

The earliest site of continuous Christian worship in Scotland, Whithorn (meaning white house) takes its name from the white chapel built by St Ninian in 397. Though only ruins remain, a guided tour of the archaeological dig reveals evidence of Northumbrian,

💬 INSIDER TIP
Make It Mondays

On the first Monday of each month Dumfries House hosts evening craft classes, including gardening, sewing, cooking, baking and stone carving. For more information, visit www. dumfries-house.org.uk/ blog/2/whats-on.

Viking and Scottish settlements ranging from the 5th to the 19th centuries. **The Whithorn Story** provides audio-visual information on the excavations, and contains fascinating ancient carved stone artifacts.

The Whithorn Story

♿😊🔊🍴 📍 45–47 George St 🕐 Easter–Oct: 10:30am–5pm daily 🌐 whithorn.com

---

③① ♿🚫🐕💻🛍️
Dumfries House

📍 C6 🚗 Cumnock, Ayrshire 🕐 Dawn to dusk daily (Nov–Mar: Sat & Sun only) 🌐 dumfries-house.org.uk

This wonderful Palladian villa is off the beaten track, but worth the detour. Sitting in sweeping parkland, the grand symmetrical villa was built for the fifth Earl of Dumfries, William Crichton Dalrymple. Designed to lure a wife, it was decorated in fashionable Rococo style between 1756 and 1760.

More recently, and in a much publicized case, the house and all its contents were put up for sale, before a consortium, headed by Prince Charles, intervened and bought the estate. On a guided tour of the house, you are led through a dozen or so rooms where there's much to admire, not least a priceless collection of Chippendale furniture which includes a stunning rosewood bookcase said to be valued at around £20 million.

STAY

Dumfries House Lodge

Spacious rooms decorated in the traditional style offer all the conveniences of a modern hotel. For those wanting extra living space, there are also cottages available nearby.

📍 C6 🏨 Dumfries House Estate, Cumnock

💷💷💷

Keep your eyes peeled out for a rare, 18th-century Grand Orrery, a captivating mechanical model of the solar system.

The gardens, too, are well worth exploring. Crossing the beautiful Avenue Bridge, take a stroll through the arboretum, abundant with woodland flowers and shrubs; beyond here lies the recently restored Queen Elizabeth walled garden, with its neatly ordered rows of flower beds, herb and vegetable plots, and glasshouses. Close by stands the superbly restored 17th-century dovecote. There are plenty of woodland strolls to be had too, while there's an adventure playground and a maze for kids. Fuel up at the onsite Woodlands Restaurant (advance booking required).

32

Firth of Clyde

🅰 B7, C7 🅽 Numerous counties west of Glasgow 🚆 Helensburgh & Dumbarton in the north; Troon & Ayr in the south 🚢 From Largs to Great Cumbrae; from Gourock to Dunoon

As might be expected of a waterway that leads from Glasgow, a former economic powerhouse of the British Empire to the Irish Sea and the Atlantic, the Firth of Clyde has many reminders of its industrial past.

Greenock, some 40 km (25 miles) west of Glasgow, was once a shipbuilding centre. Few come here for the town's beauty, but the **McLean Museum and Art Gallery**, with its exhibits and information on the engineer James Watt, a native of Greenock, is worth a visit. Princes Pier is a departure point for cruises on the Clyde.

Dumbarton, 24 km (15 miles) from Glasgow on the northern bank, dates from the 5th century AD. Its ancient castle perches on a rock overlooking the rest of the town.

The Firth itself is L-shaped, heading northwest as it opens up beyond the Erskine Bridge.

Did You Know?

Ireland and the Isle of Man are visible from the Mull of Galloway, Scotland's most southerly point

On reaching Gourock, just west of Greenock, the Firth branches south to more open water. Kip Marina at nearby Inverkip is a major yachting centre, while many towns on the Ayrshire coast have served as holiday resorts for Glaswegian holidaymakers since Victorian times.

The largest of these is Largs, site of the clash between Scots and Vikings in 1263, and which has an exhibition about Vikings in Scotland, as well as a modern monument to the battle. From here, a ferry service operates to Great Cumbrae, just off the coast, and whose main town, Millport, nestles around a picturesque bay.

The western side of the Firth of Clyde is much less developed, and is bordered by the Cowal Peninsula with its hills and lochs. The only town of note in this wild country is Dunoon. Also once a Victorian holiday resort, it still relies on tourism for its income. For many years there was a strong American influence in Dunoon due to the US nuclear submarine base at Holy Loch, but that is now closed.

McLean Museum and Art Gallery

🏠 15 Kelly St, Greenock
📞 (01475) 715624
🕐 10am–2pm Wed–Fri

33

Scottish Maritime Museum

🅰 X9 🅽 6 Gotties Rd, Irvine 🕐 10am–5pm daily 🌐 scottishmaritime museum.org

Once the principal port for trade between Scotland and Ireland, the somewhat downat-heel town of Irvine is home to the outstanding Scottish Maritime Museum. Situated within the old engine shed, you could quite easily spend a few hours here poring over its fine collection of vessels, like the *Uffa Fox*, an ingenious parachuted airborne lifeboat, and the *Bass Conqueror*, a glass-fibre dinghy that was

↑ Picturesque Loch Trool in Galloway Forest Park, Dumfries & Galloway

discovered near Stavanger in Norway several months after setting sail, but without its skipper, Kenneth Kerr, who was never found. A short walk away, on Harbour Street, you can board a couple more vessels, including the coaster *MV Kyles*, and the *SY Carola*, the oldest seagoing steam yacht in the country.

---

34 🖵 🏛

Galloway Forest Park

🗺 C7 🏠 Dumfries & Galloway 🚆 Stranraer 🛈 Clatteringshaws, Glen Trool, Kirroughtree 🌐 gallowayforestpark.com

This is the wildest stretch of country in Southern Scotland, with many points of historical interest as well as great beauty. The park extends to 670 sq km (260 sq miles) just north of Newton Stewart. The principal focal point is Loch Trool. By Caldons Wood, west of the loch, the Martyrs'

←

Equipment and vessels on display at the Scottish Maritime Museum

Monument marks the spot where six Covenanters were killed at prayer in 1685. Bruce's Stone, above the north shore, commemorates an occasion in 1307 when Robert the Bruce routed English forces. To the north of Loch Trool are several hills; Bennan stands at 562 m (1,844 ft) and Benyellary at 719 m (2,359 ft), while Merrick, at 843 m (2,766 ft), is the tallest mountain in Southern Scotland. The area is great for mountain biking and is home to the famous 7stanes route. It is also the UK's first Dark Sky park, with information panels mapping the night sky.

35

The Rhinns of Galloway

🗺 C7 🏠 Dumfries & Galloway 🚆 Stranraer 🚌 Stranraer, Portpatrick ⛴ Cairnryan 🛈 28 Harbour St, Stranraer; (01776) 702595

In the extreme southwest, this peninsula is almost separated from the mainland by Loch Ryan and Luce Bay. At the **Logan Botanic Garden**, subtropical species thrive. Stranraer is 10 km (6 miles) from Cairnryan, the ferry port for Northern Ireland. Nearby Portpatrick is prettier, with a

ruined 17th-century church and the remains of 16th-century Dunskey Castle.

Logan Botanic Garden
🌀 🕙 🖵 🏠 Near Port Logan, Stranraer 🕙 Mar–mid-Nov: 10am–5pm daily (Feb: Sun only) 🌐 rbg.org.uk

---

EAT

The Waterside
This restaurant and bar on the water's edge uses the freshest of local ingredients.

🗺 C6 🏠 Ardrossan Rd, West Kilbride 🌐 waterside ayrshire.com

£ £ £

Braidwoods
Ayrshire's only Michelin-starred restaurant serves stunning plates such as roast loin of rabbit stuffed with mushrooms and caper *jus*.

🗺 C6 🏠 Drumcastle Mill Cottage, Dalry 🌐 braidwoods.co.uk

£ £ £

A DRIVING TOUR
TOUR OF THE BORDER ABBEYS

Length 50 km (32 miles) **Stopping-off points** Dryburgh Abbey for a short walk along the banks of the River Tweed.

The Scottish Borders are scattered with the ruins of ancient buildings destroyed in conflicts between England and Scotland. Most poignant of all are the Border Abbeys, whose magnificent architecture bears witness to their former spiritual and political power. Founded during the 12th-century reign of David I, the abbeys were destroyed by Henry VIII in 1545. This tour takes in the abbeys and some other sights.

Scott's View was Sir Walter Scott's favourite view of the Borders. During his funeral, the hearse stopped here briefly as Scott had done so often in life.

Melrose Abbey (p126) was one of the richest abbeys in Scotland. It is here that Robert the Bruce's heart is said to be buried.

Also set on the bank of the Tweed, **Dryburgh Abbey** is considered the most evocative monastic ruin in Scotland. Sir Walter Scott is buried here.

Redpath
Leaderfoot
Melrose Abbey
FINISH Melrose
Newstead
Old Melrose
Scott's View
Bemersyde
A68
Clintmains
River Tweed
Newtown St Boswells
Dryburgh Abbey
St Boswells
Broomhill
A699
Maxton
Hiltonshill
Thronielaw
Morridgeha
Muirhouselaw
Longnewton
A68
Bellsbutts
Ancrum

← A walker stops to admire Scott's View looking west towards Melrose and the Eildon Hills

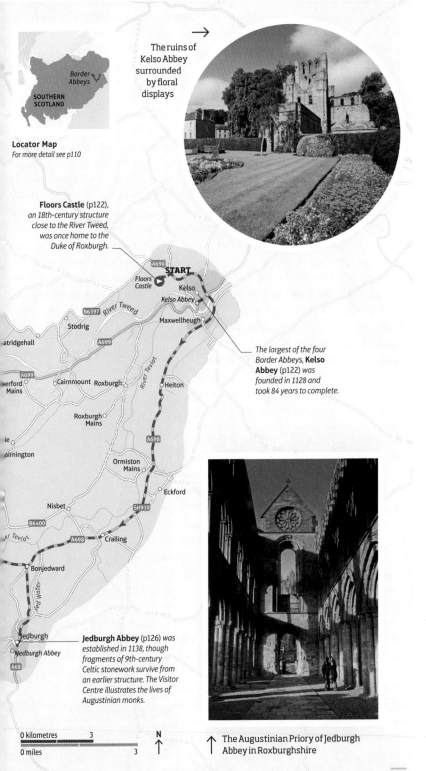

The ruins of Kelso Abbey surrounded by floral displays

Locator Map
For more detail see p110

SOUTHERN SCOTLAND
Border Abbeys

Floors Castle (p122), an 18th-century structure close to the River Tweed, was once home to the Duke of Roxburgh.

START

Floors Castle

Kelso

Kelso Abbey

Maxwellheugh

The largest of the four Border Abbeys, **Kelso Abbey** (p122) was founded in 1128 and took 84 years to complete.

River Tweed

Stodrig

atridgehall

erford Mains

Cairnmount   Roxburgh

Heiton

Roxburgh Mains

ie

airnington

River Teviot

Ormiston Mains

Nisbet

Eckford

er Tevio

Cralling

Bonjedward

edburgh

Jedburgh Abbey

Jedburgh Abbey (p126) was established in 1138, though fragments of 9th-century Celtic stonework survive from an earlier structure. The Visitor Centre illustrates the lives of Augustinian monks.

0 kilometres   3
0 miles   3

N

↑ The Augustinian Priory of Jedburgh Abbey in Roxburghshire

GLASGOW

Glasgow's city centre, on the north bank of the River Clyde, has been occupied since ancient times. The Romans already had a presence in the area some 2,000 years ago, and there was a religious community here from the 6th century. Records show Glasgow's growing importance as a merchant town from the 12th century onwards.

Historic buildings such as Provand's Lordship, a 15th-century townhouse, remind visitors of its pre-industrial roots, but modern Glasgow grew from the riches of the British Empire and the Industrial Revolution. In the 18th century Glasgow imported rum, sugar and tobacco from the colonies, while in the 19th century it reinvented itself as a cotton-manufacturing centre. It then became a site for shipbuilding and heavy engineering works, attracting many incomers from poverty-stricken districts in the Scottish Highlands and islands and Ireland in the process.

Between the 1780s and the 1880s the population exploded from around 40,000 to over 500,000. The city boundaries expanded exponentially and, despite an economic slump between the two world wars, Glasgow clung to its status as an industrial giant until the 1970s, when its traditional skills were no longer needed. The city has since bounced back; it was named European Capital of Sport in 2003 and hosted the 2014 Commonwealth Games, while a £500 million project at Glasgow Harbour has transformed the city's old shipyards and dockland into a hub for commercial, residential and leisure usage.

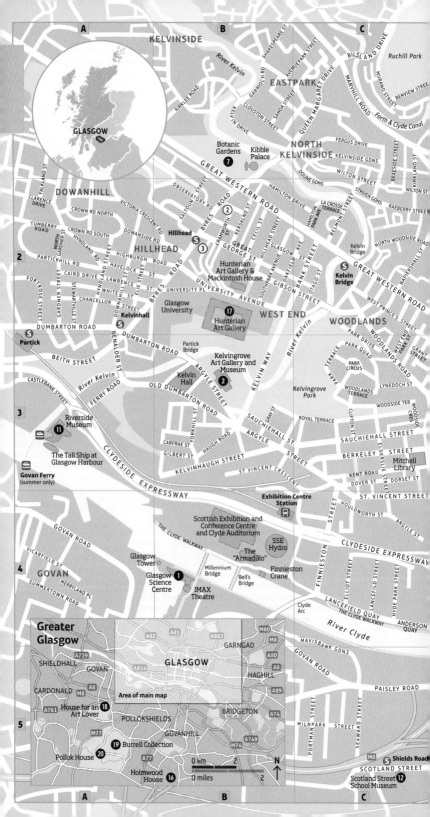

KELVINSIDE

River Kelvin

EASTPARK

Ruchill Park

BILSLAND DRIVE

MURANO STREET

BENVIEW STREE

SHAKESPEARE ST

AVENUEPARK STREET

GARRIOCH RD

KIRKLEE ROAD

KELVIN DRIVE

CLOUSTON STREET

SANDA STREET

QUEEN MARGARET DRIVE

MARYHILL ROAD

Forth & Clyde Canal

Botanic
Gardens **7**

Kibble
Palace

NORTH
KELVINSIDE

FERGUS DRIVE

BRAESIDE STREET

KIRKLAND ST

WILTON ST

GREAT WESTERN ROAD

KELVINSIDE GDNS

DOUNE GDNS

WILTON STREET

STRIVEN GDNS

RAEBERRY STREET

DOWANHILL

FALKLAND ST

CLARENCE
DRIVE

VICTORIA CRESCENT RD

CROWN RD NORTH

DOWANSIDE RD

OBSERVATORY RD

SALTOUN STREET

BYRES ROAD

HAMILTON DRIVE

CRANWORTH

KERSLAND ST

GREAT
GEORGE ST

CECIL ST

LA CROSSE
TERRACE

BELMONT ST

HAMILTON PARK AVE

NORTH WOODSIDE RD

Kelvin
Bridge

S

2

Hillhead
S
3

GLASGOW ST

HILLHEAD DRIVE

HILLHEAD

HIGHBURGH ROAD

BYRES ROAD

HAVELOCK ST

HILLHEAD ST

GIBSON STREET

BANK ST

OTAGO ST

GREAT WESTERN ROAD

S
Kelvin
Bridge

NAPIERSHALL ST

WEST PRINCE'S STREET

TUMBERRY
ROAD

NORTH
GARDNER ST

HYNDLAND RD

DOWANHILL STREET

CROWN RD SOUTH

CAIRD DRIVE

STEWARTVILLE ST

LAWRENCE
ST

WHITE ST

HYNDLAND STREET

ELIE STREET

UNIVERSITY PL.

SOUTHPARK AVENUE

OAKFIELD AVE

Hunterian
Art Gallery &
Mackintosh House

WEST END

WOODLANDS

WOODLANDS ROAD

WEST END PARK ST

GRANT
STREET

PARTICKHILL RD

2

FORTROSE STREET

GARDNER STREET

CHANCELLOR
ST

BENALDER ST

UNIVERSITY AVENUE

Glasgow
University

17
Hunterian
Art Gallery

PARK DRIVE

PARK QUAD

PARK
CIRCUS

WOODSIDE
TERRACE

WOODLANDS
TERRACE

LYNEDOCH ST

WOODSIDE TER

WOODSIDE
CRES

Kelvinhall
S

Partick
S

DUMBARTON ROAD

BEITH STREET

Partick
Bridge

River Kelvin

Kelvin
Hall

OLD DUMBARTON ROAD

ARGYLE STREET

Kelvingrove
Art Gallery and
Museum

2

KELVIN WAY

River Kelvin

Kelvingrove
Park

CLIFTON ST

ROYAL TERRACE

SAUCHIEHALL STREET

CASTLEBANK STREET

3

Riverside
Museum

11

FERRY ROAD

CLYDESIDE EXPRESSWAY

CARFRAE ST

YORKHILL ST

HAUGH ROAD

GILBERT ST

KELVINHAUGH STREET

ARGYLE
STREET

DERBY ST

SAUCHIEHALL ST

BERKELEY
STREET

Mitchell
Library

KENT ROAD

ELDERSLIE STREET

DORSET ST

The Tall Ship at
Glasgow Harbour

Govan Ferry
(summer only)

ST VINCENT CRESCENT

DOVER ST

ST. VINCENT STREET

HOULDWORTH ST

ARGYLE ST

GOVAN ROAD

4

GOVAN

VICARFIELD ST

SUMMERTOWN ROAD

MERRYLAND PL

THE CLYDE WALKWAY

Glasgow
Tower

Glasgow
Science
Centre

1

IMAX
Theatre

Scottish Exhibition and
Conference Centre
and Clyde Auditorium

SSE
Hydro

The
"Armadillo"

Millennium
Bridge

Bell's
Bridge

Finnieston
Crane

Exhibition Centre
Station
S

FINNIESTON
STREET

CLYDESIDE EXPRESSWAY

ELLIOT STREET

LANCEFIELD STREET

HYDE PARK STREET

FINNIESTON
STREET

LANCEFIELD QUAY
THE CLYDE WALKWAY

Clyde
Arc

River Clyde

ANDERSON
QUAY

MAVISBANK GDNS

GOVAN ROAD

PAISLEY ROAD

PORTMAN
STREET

STREET

MILNPARK STREET

SEAWARD STREET

M8
S Shields Road

SCOTLAND STREET

S Scotland Street
School Museum **12**

**Greater
Glasgow**

A739

A82   A81   A803

M80

GARNGAD

SHIELDHALL

GOVAN

A814

GLASGOW

M8

A80

A8

HAGHILL

CARDONALD

A8

M8

Area of main map

A89

PAISLEY ROAD

A761   House for an
Art Lover **18**

POLLOKSHIELDS

BRIDGETON

A74

M77

19 Burrell Collection

GOVANHILL

A749

M74

Pollok House

20

A77

Holmwood
House **16**

0 km   2

0 miles   2

N

A   B   C

GLASGOW

Must Sees

1. Glasgow Science Centre
2. Kelvingrove Art Gallery and Museum

Experience More

3. George Square
4. Gallery of Modern Art
5. Glasgow School of Art
6. St Mungo Museum of Religious Life and Art
7. Botanic Gardens
8. Tenement House
9. Glasgow Cathedral and Necropolis
10. Provand's Lordship
11. Riverside Museum
12. Scotland Street School Museum
13. People's Palace
14. National Piping Centre
15. The Lighthouse
16. Holmwood House
17. Hunterian Art Gallery
18. House for an Art Lover
19. Burrell Collection
20. Pollok House

Eat & Drink

1. Mackintosh at the Willow
2. Hillhead Bookclub
3. Ubiquitous Chip

Shop

4. The Barras
5. Princes Square
6. Argyll Arcade

Stay

7. Grasshoppers
8. Z Hotel

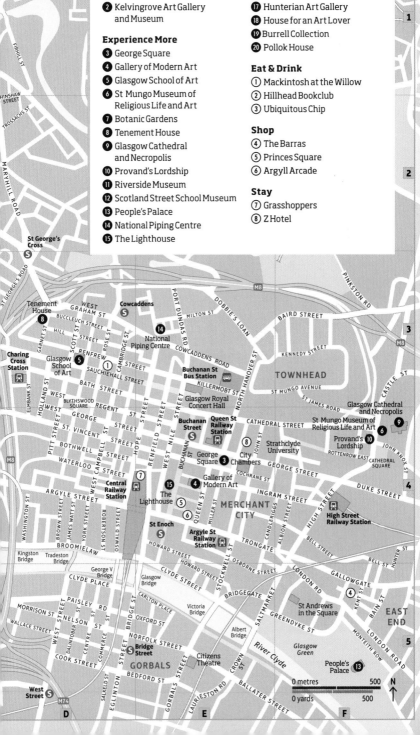

←

1 Pretty fairy lights illuminate Ashton Lane.

2 Vintage shopping at The Barras indoor market.

3 Botanical Gardens.

4 Street art by Rogue-One on Glasgow City Centre Mural Trail.

In just two experience-packed days in Glasgow you can travel in time from a 13th-century cathedral to a tenement time capsule, admire the ingenuity of Victorian engineers, and tip your hat to classical painters and 21st-century street artists.

2 DAYS
in Glasgow

Day 1

Morning Start the day by meandering through Glasgow's Botanic Gardens (p152), where palms and tropical blossoms flourish in vast, airy glasshouses. From there, stroll through the beautifully lush Kelvingrove Park to Kelvingrove Art Gallery and Museum (p146) where the work of the Scottish Colourists, Charles Rennie Mackintosh, and the "Glasgow Boys" take pride of place.

Afternoon Take your pick of pubs on nearby Argyle Street for lunch then walk to the Riverside Museum (p153) to spend a nostalgic afternoon admiring vintage vehicles and locomotives inside architect Zaha Hadid's impressive glass and metal building. The equally impressive Clyde-built sailing ship Glenlee is berthed alongside, and another historic vessel, the Clyde steamer Queen Mary II, is undergoing restoration nearby.

Evening Finish your day of exploration in style by boarding a speedboat for a high-speed evening cruise with a view of the Clyde and its bridges and brand new waterfront district from the river. Once back on dry land, choose from a stylish and eclectic range of dishes at Oran Mor's Brasserie Restaurant. The fun doesn't stop there; this legendary venue in a former church also hosts live music, comedy and club nights (www.oran-mor.co.uk).

Day 2

Morning Start the day with a peek into everyday life in Glasgow's not-so-distant past at the Tenement House (p152). Find more insights into the lives of ordinary Glaswegians at the People's Palace (p154), then walk across Glasgow Green to stop for lunch at The Winged Ox Bar and Kitchen at St Luke's and browse vintage stalls at The Barras (p151).

Afternoon Pay your respects to St Mungo, the city's patron saint, at his tomb in the crypt of 13th-century Glasgow Cathedral (p152), then join a guided walk around the hilly Necropolis, which is filled with grandiose monuments to the city's great and wealthy. Back at street level, take in street art along the Glasgow City Centre Mural Trail (p42) on your way to the Gallery of Modern Art (p150), a growing collection of cutting-edge work by Glasgow-based artists.

Evening For a change of cultural pace, enjoy an evening at the Theatre Royal, home of Scottish Opera. For after-show dinner and drinks, book a table at late-night restaurant Ubiquitous Chip on Ashton Lane in Glasgow's West End. Don't be fooled by its seemingly casual vibe – its innovative menu features regional Scottish produce such as venison haggis, champit tatties and neep cream, and the wine list is a cut above the rest.

Clydebank Colossus

The towering giant steel structure of the Titan Crane is Glasgow's gritty answer to the Eiffel Tower. Built in 1906 to hoist massive loads on to ships for export worldwide, visitors can now enjoy awesome views from the top-level viewing platform, or swing, bungee-jump and abseil from its giant boom 50 m (164 ft) above the river.

Did You Know?
———
Glasgow was a hub for manufacturing ships and armaments during the First and Second world wars.

→

Colossal Titan Crane and thrillseekers bungee jumping from the top *(inset)*

GLASGOW'S
INDUSTRIAL
HERITAGE

Coal, iron and steam turned Glasgow from a prosperous merchant city into the British Empire's greatest industrial centre. Although heavy industry declined in the 20th century, its legacy is still a source of pride.

All Aboard Glenlee

Glenlee is one of the last great Clyde-built sailing ships. Meet volunteers in period costume and imagine what life was like as a voyager aboard this three-masted seafaring vessel more than a century ago. Launched in 1896, she circumnavigated the globe four times before being rescued from dereliction in 1992. The ship is now moored next to the futuristic Riverside Museum *(p153)*.

←

Three masts of the Tall Ship *Glenlee* looming high above the Clyde

A Steam Cruise on the Clyde

Take a cruise aboard the Waverley paddle steamer to experience the age of steam first-hand. Built on the Clyde in 1947, the last seagoing paddle steamer in the world once carried Glasgow folk to ports like Ayr, Campbeltown, Rothesay and Helensburgh along the Firth of Clyde (p132).

SLAVES, SUGAR AND TOBACCO

Glasgow has only recently started to come to terms with the unsavoury sources of its early wealth. Much of the sugar and tobacco that enriched the city's 18th-century merchants came from slave plantations in America and the Caribbean. When slavery was finally abolished in 1833, plantation owners reinvested their windfall in the new industrial economy.

$\rightarrow$
Waverley paddle steamer moored at Pacific Quay on the River Clyde

Futuristic structures of Glasgow Science Centre reflected in the River Clyde ↑

❶ 🏛️ Ⓜ️ 🖥️ 🛍️

GLASGOW SCIENCE CENTRE

📍 B4 🚌 50 Pacific Quay Ⓢ Cessnock 🚌 X19, 90, 23, 26 🕐 Apr-Oct: 10am-5pm daily; Nov-Mar: 10am-3pm Wed-Fri (to 5pm Sat & Sun) 🌐 glasgow sciencecentre.org

The gleaming tower and metallic dome of Glasgow Science Centre are unmistakable landmarks on the city's skyline. Inside is a feast of inspiring and innovative exhibits to fascinate visitors of all ages.

Opened by Queen Elizabeth II in 2001, Glasgow Science Centre's titanium-clad futuristic structures are designed to mimic the hull of a ship, a homage to the Clyde's maritime and industrial heritage. The buildings are linked by a teflon fabric roof and a "discovery" tunnel.

Inside, the three-storey Science Mall uses interactive exhibits, laboratories and multimedia tools to take visitors of all ages on a journey through the inner workings of cutting-edge applied science, from solar power to artificial intelligence and the latest advancements in quantum physics.

Next door, Scotland's only IMAX Theatre projects breathtaking images from the natural and scientific world on to its 24-m (80-ft) by 18-m (60-ft) screen. Other exhibits include a lab where you can examine your hair and skin, and a spectacular planetarium featuring a state-of-the-art full-dome digital projection system.

↑ Children enjoying the many interactive exhibits in the busy Science Mall

---

UNMISSABLE EXHIBITS

Bodyworks
Research capsules in the Science Mall's Bodyworks section showcase the latest developments in medical science, while a giant hamster wheel, a virtual autopsy and the "snot barrier" are perfect for curious kids.

Planetarium
State-of-the-art digital imagery takes audiences on a virtual journey around our solar system, with live narration by an expert team of astronomers, rocket scientists and astronauts.

The Space Zone
The Space Zone lets visitors walk among the planets of the solar system, from tiny Mercury to the moons of Jupiter and beyond.

Quantum Technologies
Guaranteed to amaze, this interactive exhibition aims to make the invisible visible, untangling the weird and still unexplored frontiers of quantum physics.

Powering the Future
This exhibit shows young visitors where the energy that heats and lights their homes, schools and cities comes from, with interactive features on climate change and alternative energy sources.

↑ A Question of Perception, an exhibit where nothing is quite as it seems

Did You Know?

In 1996 a number of works were stolen from the collection and sold on the black market.

② 🛇 🍴 🖵 🏛

KELVINGROVE ART GALLERY AND MUSEUM

📍B3 🏠Argyle St, Kelvingrove 🆂Partick 🚌2, 3, 11 🕙10am-5pm Mon-Thu & Sat, 11am-5pm Fri & Sun 🌐glasgowlife.org.uk/museums

Housed in a grand Spanish Baroque building in Glasgow's West End, the Kelvingrove Art Gallery and Museum is deservedly Scotland's most popular civic art collection.

Kelvingrove's 8,000-item-collection includes many pieces of international significance. Among these are 19th-century British artists including Turner and Constable, a painting by Salvador Dali widely acknowledged to be one of his finest, and French Impressionist and Dutch Renaissance painters. Scottish art and design is well represented with rooms dedicated to the Scottish Colourists and the Glasgow Style.

Elsewhere within its 22 galleries, the museum offers insight into Glasgow's evolution from its medieval beginnings to its 19th- and 20th-century economic and cultural transformation. Among the museum's signature exhibits are a Spitfire, suspended high above the vast West Court, and an Asian elephant by the name of Sir Roger.

> 💬 INSIDER TIP
> **Organ Recital**
>
> Don't miss the daily organ recital which takes place at 1pm, or 3pm on Sundays, in the Centre Hall. The magnificent giant organ has been in the hall since 1902 and many eminent artists have played on it.

↑ Spitfire hanging dramatically from the ceiling of the West Court of the museum

① Animal exhibits can be found in the West Wing of the Natural History Gallery.

② Kelvingrove Art Gallery and Museum is housed in an imposing red sandstone building.

③ Classical paintings can be found in the art gallery.

Exploring Kelvingrove

Within the Kelvingrove Art Gallery and Museum's distinctive sandstone façade, an impressive galleried main hall runs the entire length of the building, which in turn gives way to a series of upper balconies, with small interlinked galleries connecting throughout.

The displays themselves are arranged under two main themes: Life, which is located in the western half of the building showcases archaeology – including pieces from Ancient Egypt – local history, and Scottish culture and wildlife; Expression, sited on the opposite, eastern side, focuses almost exclusively on art and design. It is a truly world-class collection, with many paintings by celebrated European Masters such as Rembrandt, Van Gogh and Dalí, as well as works by the much-loved Scottish Colourists, who feature prominently. Here, too, on the ground floor, is an exhibition devoted to local Glasgow legend Charles Rennie Mackintosh *(p158)*, something no fan of the celebrated architect and designer should miss.

CHRIST OF ST JOHN OF THE CROSS

The museum's most famous painting is Salvador Dali's *Christ of St John of the Cross*, which is located in its own room up on the south balcony. Acquired by the museum in 1952, this mesmerizing piece depicts Christ on the Cross floating over water and looking down upon a boat full of fishermen.

8,000

The number of items in Kelvingrove's collection today.

↑ Prints on display at the *Mackintosh: Making the Glasgow Style* exhibition

The Dutch Gallery

Rembrandt's *Man in Armour* sets the tone for Kelvingrove's collection of 17th-century Dutch and Flemish masters, which is recognized as one of the UK's finest. Other paintings worth seeking out include Benjamin Gerritszoon Cuyp's *The Quack Doctor*, and a supporting cast of works by Nicolaes Pieterszoon Berchem, Daniel de Blieck, and Abraham van Beyeren.

The French Gallery

Van Gogh's portrait of the red-headed, red-bearded Alexander Reid makes the Glasgow-born art dealer, a friend of the artist, look almost like Vincent's twin brother. Raoul Dufy's *The Jetties of Trouville-Deauville* is another stand-out work in a stellar portfolio of paintings by 19th- and 20th-century greats including Braque, Gauguin, Monet, Pissarro and Renoir.

The Scottish Colourists

◀ Though they are more closely associated with Edinburgh than with Glasgow, the Scottish Colourists are well represented at Kelvingrove. Cadell's elegantly poised *A Lady in Black* and Peploe's *Roses* are outstanding examples of each artist's style. Hunter's *A Summer Day, Largo* and Fergusson's *On the Beach at Tangier* are variations on the classic maritime themes that both these painters loved.

The Glasgow Boys

James Guthrie's *Old Willie; The Village Worthy*, a sympathetic portrait of an elderly man, contrasts strongly here with the colourful, almost psychedelic mysticism of *The Druids: Bringing in the Mistletoe* by George Henry and E A Hornel, illustrating the breadth of vision of this celebrated group of painters. The Kelvingrove collection is the world's leading portfolio of works by the dynamic "Glasgow Boys".

Mackintosh and the Glasgow Style

Woodwork and gesso panels, stylish furniture, beautifully detailed light fittings and other decorative elements that are hallmarks of Charles Rennie Mackintosh's distinctive style have pride of place in the reconstructed Ingram Street Tearooms, designed by Mackintosh working together with his wife Margaret Macdonald between 1900 and 1912. Tearooms were the first dining establishments to allow unaccompanied women, and the elegant Ladies Luncheon Room is the epitome of Edwardian elegance.

↑ An array of medieval armour on display at the Kelvingrove Art Gallery and Museum

EXPERIENCE MORE

3

George Square

📍 E4

George Square was laid out in the late 18th century as a residential area, but Victorian redevelopment conferred its enduring status as the city's focal point. The only building not to be affected by the later 19th-century makeover is the Millennium Hotel (1807) on the north side of the Square.

The 1870s saw a building boom, with the construction of the former Post Office (1876) at the southeast corner, and the Merchants House (1877) to the west side. The latter is home to Glasgow's Chamber of Commerce, founded in 1781 and the UK's oldest organization of its kind. The dominant structure, however, is the **City Chambers** on the east side. Designed by William Young in Italian Renaissance style, the imposing building was opened in 1888 by Queen Victoria. With its elegant interior, decorated in marble and mosaic, the opulence of this building makes it the most impressive of its type in Scotland.

City Chambers

♿🕎 🏠 82 George St
🕐 Guided tours only: 10:30am & 2:30pm Mon-Fri

4

Gallery of Modern Art

📍 E4 🏠 Royal Exchange Sq
🕐 10am-5pm Mon-Wed & Sat, 10am-8pm Thu, 11am-5pm Fri & Sun 🌐 glasgow life.org.uk/museums

Once the home of Glasgow's Royal Exchange (the city's centre for trade), this building dates from 1829 and also incorporates a late-18th-century mansion that formerly occupied the site. The local authority took over the Exchange just after World War II, and for many years it served as a library. It finally opened its doors as the Gallery of Modern Art in 1996. One of the largest contemporary art galleries outside London, the GoMA is constantly building on its collection of work by Glasgow-based artists. Accordingly, most of the gallery is home to a lively and thought-provoking programme of temporary exhibitions featuring work by Scottish and international artists.

Many of these focus on contemporary and social issues, often featuring groups that are marginalized in today's society.

5

Glasgow School of Art

📍 D3 🏠 167 Renfrew St 🕐 For renovation 🌐 gsa.ac.uk

Widely regarded as Charles Rennie Mackintosh's masterpiece, Glasgow School of Art is a well-loved Glasgow institution. Erected between 1897 and 1909, it was noted for the ground-breaking style of the exterior and high level of attention that Mackintosh devoted to every detail within, from decorative woodwork and windows to door handles and light switches. The interior was damaged by fire in 2014 and was due to reopen in 2019 after meticulous restoration. Tragically, a second and more severe fire in 2018 virtually destroyed the building, raising doubts over whether it could, or should, be rebuilt at all.

← Monument to Sir Walter Scott rising above the City Chambers on George Square

← Gallery of Modern Art, in the Royal Exchange building, surrounded by fairy lights

⑥ Ⓜ️ ▭ ⛶

St Mungo Museum of Religious Life and Art

📍F4 🏠2 Castle St
🕐10am–5pm Tue–Thu & Sat, 11am–5pm Fri & Sun; tours by appointment only
🌐glasgowlife.org.uk/museums

Glasgow has strong religious roots, and the settlement that grew to become today's city started with a monastery founded in the 6th century AD by a priest called Mungo. He died in the early years of the 7th century, and his body lies buried underneath Glasgow Cathedral. The building itself dates from the 12th century, and stands on ground blessed by St Ninian as long ago as AD 397. The ever-growing numbers of visitors to the cathedral eventually prompted plans for an interpretive centre. Despite the efforts of the Society of Friends of Glasgow Cathedral, however, sufficient funds could not be raised. The local

authority decided to step in with money, and with the idea for a more extensive project – a museum of religious life and art. The site chosen was adjacent to the cathedral, where the 13th-century Castle of the Bishops of Glasgow once stood. The museum has the appearance of a centuries-old fortified house, despite the fact that it was completed in 1993. The top floor describes the story of the country's religion from a non-denominational perspective. Both Protestant and Catholic versions of Christianity are represented, as well as the other faiths of modern Scotland. The many, varied displays touch on the lives of communities as extensive as Glasgow's Muslims, who have had their own Mosque in the city since 1984, as well as local followers of the Baha'i faith. The other floors are given over to works of art – among them is Craigie Aitchison's *Crucifixion VII*, which sits alongside religious artifacts and artworks such as burial discs from Neolithic China (2000 BC), contemporary paintings by Aboriginal Australians, and some excellent Scottish stained glass from the early part of the 20th century. Further displays examine the issues that are of fundamental concern to people of all religions – war, persecution, death and the afterlife – and exhibits from

Did You Know?

Glasgow's name comes from the Gaelic phrase meaning green valley or dear green place.

SHOP

The Barras
This most Glaswegian of markets is a glorious mix of stalls selling everything under the sun. The Glasgow Vintage and Flea Market is a regular weekend fixture.

📍F5 🏠244 Gallowgate
🌐theglasgowbarras.com

Princes Square
This five-storey atrium beneath a Victorian glass cupola is a paradise for fans of big-name fashion, with brands such as Vivienne Westwood, Kurt Geiger and Kate Spade.

📍E4 🏠48 Buchanan St
🌐princessquare.co.uk

Argyll Arcade
Glasgow's glittering emporium of bling gleams with new and pre-loved goods, from luxury watches to diamond rings and vintage jewellery.

📍E4 🏠Argyll St
🌐argyll-arcade.com

cultures as far afield as West Africa and Mexico. In the grounds surrounding the building, there is a permanent Zen Garden, which was created by Japanese garden designer Yasutaro Tanaka. Such gardens have been a traditional aid to contemplation in Japanese Buddhist temples since the beginning of the 16th century.

↑ *Eve*, by Scipione Tadolini, in a glasshouse, Glasgow Botanic Gardens

Botanic Gardens

☉ B1 ☉ Great Western Rd ☉ Byres Road ☻ 6, 6A ☉ 7am–dusk; glasshouses: 10am–6pm (till 4:15pm in winter) ☷ glasgow botanicgardens.com

These gardens form a peaceful space in the heart of the city's West End, by the River Kelvin. Originally founded at another site in 1817, they were moved to the current location in 1839 and opened to the public three years later. Aside from the main range of greenhouses, with displays including palm trees and tropical crops, one of the most interesting features is the wrought-iron framed Kibble Palace. Built at Loch Long in the Highlands by John Kibble,

> **GREAT VIEW**
> **Glasgow Necropolis**
>
> Glasgow Cathedral's hauntingly beautiful necropolis boasts great views over the city's rooftops. Modelled on the Père Lachaise cemetery in Paris, it's a welcome escape from the busy streets below.

More a time capsule than a museum, the Tenement House is an almost undisturbed record of life as it was in a modest Glasgow tenement flat in the early 20th century.

---

the beautiful glass palace was moved to its present site in the early 1870s. It houses a collection of carnivorous plants, tropical orchids and tree ferns.

Tenement House

☉ D3 ☉ 145 Buccleuch St ☏ (0141) 333 0183 ☉ Mar–Oct: 10am–5pm daily; Nov–Feb: 11am–4pm Fri–Mon ☷ nts.org.uk

More a time capsule than a museum, the Tenement House is an almost undisturbed record of life as it was in a modest Glasgow tenement flat on a tenement estate in the early 20th century. Glasgow owed much of its vitality and neighbourliness to tenement life, though in later years many of these Victorian and Edwardian apartments were to earn a bad name due to increased poverty and extreme overcrowding.

The Tenement House was the home of Miss Agnes Toward, who lived here from 1911 until 1965. It remained largely unaltered during that time and, since Agnes threw very little away, the house has become a treasure-trove of social history. In the parlour, which would have been used only on formal occasions, afternoon tea is laid out on a white lace cloth. The kitchen, with its coal-fired range and

box bed, is filled with the tools of a vanished era, such as a goffering-iron for ironing lace, a washboard and a stone hot-water bottle.

Agnes's lavender water and medicines are still arranged in the bathroom as though she stepped out of the house 70 years ago and forgot to return.

Glasgow Cathedral and Necropolis

☉ F4 ☉ Cathedral Sq ☉ Cathedral: Apr–Sep: 9:30am–5pm Mon–Sat, 1–4:30pm Sun; Oct–Mar: 10am–3:30pm Mon–Sat, 1–3:30pm Sun; Necropolis: 24hrs daily ☷ glasgowcathedral.org

One of the few churches to survive the Reformation *(p63)* by adapting itself to Protestant worship, Glasgow Cathedral is a rare example of an original 13th-century church. It was built on the site of a chapel founded by the city's patron saint, St Mungo. According to legend, Mungo placed the body of a holy man on a cart yoked to two wild bulls, telling them to take it to the place ordained by God. There he built his church.

The crypt contains the intricate tomb of St Mungo. The Blacader Aisle is reputed to have been built over an existing cemetery that was blessed by St Ninian.

→

Iconic jagged structure of the Riverside Museum on the Clyde waterfront

Behind the cathedral, a likeness of John Knox (p83) overlooks the necropolis containing monuments to the dead of Glasgow's wealthy.

10
Provand's Lordship

F4 3 Castle St
10am–5pm Tue–Thu & Sat, 11am–5pm Fri & Sun
glasgowlife.org.uk/museums

Built as a canon's house in 1471, Provand's Lordship is now Glasgow's oldest surviving house. Its low ceilings and wooden furniture create a vivid impression of life in a wealthy 15th-century household. Mary, Queen of Scots (p62) may have stayed here when she visited Glasgow in 1566 to see her cousin, and husband, Lord Darnley.

11
Riverside Museum

A3 100 Pointhouse Place Partick 59
10am–5pm Mon–Thu & Sat, 11am–5pm Fri & Sun
glasgowlife.org.uk/museums

This landmark attraction sits on the Clyde in a dramatic zinc-panelled building designed by the late architect Zaha Hadid.

Formerly the Museum of Transport and Travel, this outstanding collection features just about every aspect of transport, including trams and trains, boats and bikes, cars and even skateboards. The museum also examines the social impact of transport advancements in Glasgow.

Train buffs will be in their element inspecting the large assemblage of locomotives, not least a magnificent South African Class 15F model built by the North British Locomotive Company here in Glasgow in the 1940s. Visitors can also get a glimpse into the future of rail transport courtesy of the fully interactive Nova 2 TransPenine Express train cab.

Petrolheads, meanwhile, will love the cleverly designed Wall of Cars, and fans of two wheels can indulge their passion in the Velodrome section; the bike that Graham Obee broke the one-hour world record on is stationed here.

Did You Know?

The 2,500-tonne roof of the Riverside Museum is one of the UK's most complex structures.

Other highlights to look out for include the motor-bike ridden by the actor Ewan McGregor on his epic long-distance road trip in 2004, as featured in the documentary Long Way Round, and an exquisite collection of model ships. Elsewhere there are walk-through streets, with shops, cafés and restaurants (displaying their original interiors) offering fascinating insight into the city's social fabric of the time. Berthed alongside the museum is the Tall Ship Glenlee, which circumnavigated the globe four times before finally retiring on the banks of the River Clyde.

12 🎿 Ⓜ 🏛

Scotland Street School Museum

📍 C5 🚇 225 Scotland St, Ⓢ Shields Road ⏰ 10am–5pm Tue–Thu & Sat, 11am–5pm Fri & Sun 🌐 glasgow life.org.uk/museums

The Scotland Street School, which operated between 1906 and 1979, was the second Charles Rennie Mackintosh commission for the Scottish School Board, and the last building he designed in Glasgow. It has the great architect's stamp all over it, from the colourful, geometrically-patterned columns in the Drill Hall to the thick, leaded pane windows.

As well as being a design and architectural gem, it's now a charming museum, with a series of reconstructed and restored classrooms designed to reflect developments in the education system from the Victorian era through to the 1970s. You can read and hear recollections of former pupils covering topics such as classroom discipline, evacuation and World War II, school attire and playground games. One room has various objects, such as books, photos and gas masks, while another displays some of Mackintosh's original designs for the school. As you'd expect, the museum is very child-friendly, so look out for one of the many fun events held here, where kids can experience what it was like to be taught by a stern Victorian teacher back in the day.

13 Ⓜ 🖥

People's Palace

📍 F5 🚇 Glasgow Green ⏰ 10am–5pm Mon–Thu & Sat, 11am–5pm Fri & Sun 🌐 glasgowlife.org.uk/museums

Built in 1898 as a cultural museum for the people of Glasgow's East End, the handsome, red-sandstone People's Palace offers an illuminating trawl through

> The one exhibit that grabs the most attention is a pair of bright yellow banana-shaped boots belonging to local comedian Billy Connolly.

the city's social history, from the 12th century right up to the present day. Different rooms pertain to different themes, for example crime and punishment, where you'll find the bell that once rang at the notorious Duke Street prison to serve notice of a hanging; politics, featuring the campaigning desk used by the revolutionary socialist leader John MacClean; and alcohol, where there's a Drunk's Barrow on show. Another room on dancing and entertainment displays, among other things, posters from the much loved Barrowland Ballroom located just a few streets away. The one exhibit that grabs the most attention is a pair of bright yellow banana-shaped boots belonging to local comedian Billy Connolly. Tacked on to the back of the palace is the Victorian glass-house, which conceals the

delightful Winter Gardens, complete with a range of exotic flowers and shrubs as well as a super little café. The glasshouse is, however, currently closed pending restoration work.

National Piping Centre

🔵E3 ⓐ30-34 McPhater St Ⓢ Cowcaddens ⏰9am-7pm Mon-Thu (to 5pm Fri, to noon Sat) Ⓦ thepiping centre.co.uk

The National Piping Centre, which is housed in a refurbished church, aims to promote the study and history of piping in Scotland. It offers in-person and online tuition at all levels, and also houses the National Museum of Piping, which traces the development of this iconic instrument. Displays show that bagpipes were introduced to Scotland as early as the 14th century, although the golden age of piping was between the 17th and 18th centuries. This was the era of the MacCrimmons of Skye (hereditary pipers to the chiefs of Clan MacLeod), when complex, extended tunes (ceol mor, or "the big music") were written for clan gatherings, battles and in the form of laments.

↑ Visitors admiring some of Mackintosh's work on display in The Lighthouse

The Lighthouse

🔵E4 ⓐ11 Mitchell Lane 🚆Glasgow Central ⏰10:30am-5pm Mon-Sat, noon-5pm Sun Ⓦ thelight house.co.uk

A conversion of the former offices of the *Glasgow Herald* newspaper, the Mackintosh-designed Lighthouse has functioned as the Centre for Design and Architecture since 1999, when Glasgow was nominated the UK's City of Architecture and Design. At the heart of this spectacular, light-filled building is the Mackintosh Interpretation Centre. This area, up on the third floor, is home to some of the celebrated architect's work such as plans, photos and models, as well as some original items like a cabinet commissioned for a former director of the *Glasgow Herald*. The Lighthouse also houses a shop, visitor centre and a temporary exhibition space. After perusing the design work on display, head up to the sixth (top) floor viewing platform for a wonderful vista of the city. Guided tours are also on offer.

←

The ornate Doulton Fountain standing in front of the People's Palace

Holmwood House

🔵 ⓐ61-63 Netherlee Rd 🚆Muirend 🚌374 ⏰Times vary, check website Ⓦnts.org.uk

This Victorian villa is located some 4 miles (6 km) south of the city centre in the leafy suburb of Cathcart. The impressive work of Alexander "Greek" Thompson, Holmwood House was designed in 1858 for local paper manufacturer James Couper. The exterior betrays classic elements of Grecian design, notably its cupolas and columns, while the richly designed interior offers the opportunity to view several rooms which retain their original decor. The most impressive room in the house is the dining room, which features a magnificent frieze covering all four walls and comprising scenes from Homer's *Iliad*. The standout aspect upstairs is a stunning white Italian marble chimney-piece in the drawing room.

Once you're done exploring the house, there are some lovely riverside walks to be had and the verdant lawns surrounding the complex are an ideal spot for a picnic. Holmwood also has a small café offering tea and scones, among other snacks, as well as a gift shop.

Spiral staircase inside the Lighthouse in Glasgow

17 ⌁ ⌁

Hunterian Art Gallery

📍 B2 🏠 82 Hillhead St
🚇 Hillhead 🚌 4, 4A
🕐 10am-5pm Tue-Sat,
11am-4pm Sun. 🌐 gla.ac.
uk/hunterian

Built specifically to house a number of paintings bequeathed to Glasgow University by an ex-student and physician, Dr William Hunter (1718–83), the Hunterian contains Scotland's largest print collection, with works by many major European artists dating from the 16th century.

A collection of work by celebrated Glasgow designer Charles Rennie Mackintosh, often cited as the father of the famous "Glasgow School", known as the "Glasgow Boys", a group of painters that came to fame at the beginning of the 20th century, is supplemented by a reconstruction of his home at No 6 Florentine Terrace, where he lived from 1906 to 1914.

The building also houses a major collection of 19th- and 20th-century Scottish art, but by far the most famous collection is that containing works by the Paris-trained American painter James McNeill Whistler (1834–1903), who influenced so many of the Glasgow School painters.

CHARLES RENNIE MACKINTOSH

Glasgow's most celebrated designer (1868-1928) entered Glasgow School of Art at the age of 16. After his success with the Willow Tea Room, he became a leading figure in the Art Nouveau movement. His characteristic straight lines and flowing detail are the hallmark of early 20th-century style.

18 ⌁ ⌁ 🖥 🏠

House for an Art Lover

📍 A5 🏠 Bellahouston Park,
10 Dumbreck Rd 🚇 Ibrox
🕐 10am-5pm daily
🔒 Regularly for functions
🌐 houseforanartlover.
co.uk

Plans for the House for an Art Lover were submitted by Charles Rennie Mackintosh and his partner Margaret Macdonald in response to a competition in a German magazine in the summer of 1900. The competition brief was to create a country retreat for someone of elegance and taste who loved the arts. As it was a theoretical exercise, the couple were unrestrained by logistics or budget and won a special prize for their efforts. The plans lay unused for over 80 years until consulting engineer Graham Roxburgh, who had been involved in the refurbishment of other Mackintosh interiors in Glasgow, decided to build the House for an Art Lover. Construction began in 1989 and was completed in 1996. The House is host to a digital design studio and postgraduate study centre for students at the Glasgow School of Art. The rooms on the main floor give a real insight into the vision of Mackintosh and the artistic talent of Macdonald. The Oval Room is a beautifully proportioned space in a single light colour, designed to be a tranquil retreat for ladies,

Sun shining through medieval stained glass at the Burrell Collection ↓

while the Music Room and its centrepiece piano (enclosed within a four-poster bed) that is played to add to the atmosphere, is also bright and inspiring. The Main Hall leads into the Dining Room, which contains a long table, sideboard and relief stone fireplace. The great attention to detail demonstrated throughout the House, in the panelling, light fixtures and other elements, is enormously impressive. The exterior of the building is also an extraordinary achievement in art and design.

Grand exterior of Pollok House surrounded by lush parkland ↑

Burrell Collection

📍A5 🏠200 Pollokshaws Rd 🚇Pollokshaws West 🕐For refurbishment until 2022 🌐glasgowlife.org.uk/museums

Given to the city in 1944 by Sir William Burrell (1861–1958), a wealthy shipping owner, this internationally acclaimed collection is the gem in Glasgow's crown, but it is closed for refurbishment until 2022. The 9,000-piece collection features over 600 medieval stained-glass panels, 150 tapestries, a collection of ancient Middle Eastern, Greek and Roman treasures, Chinese ceramics and superb Oriental embroideries and carpets, and even celebrated works by Old Masters such as Rembrandt's *Self Portrait* (1632). Additional displays will be unveiled when the collection reopens.

> **The Hunterian contains Scotland's largest print collection, with works by many major European artists dating from the 16th century.**

Pollok House

📍A5 🏠2060 Pollokshaws Rd 🚇Pollokshaws West 🕐10am–5pm daily 🌐nts.org.uk

Glasgow's finest 18th-century domestic building boasts one of Britain's best collections of Spanish paintings. The Neo-Classical central block of Pollok House was finished in 1750, the sobriety of its exterior contrasting with the exuberant plasterwork within.

The Maxwells have lived at Pollok since the mid-13th century, but the male line ended with Sir John Maxwell, who added the entrance hall and designed the terraced gardens and parkland.

Hanging above the family silver, porcelain, hand-painted Chinese wallpaper and Jacobean glass, are William Blake's *Sir Geoffrey Chaucer and the Nine and Twenty Pilgrims* (1745) as well as William Hogarth's portrait of James Thomson, who wrote the words to *Rule Britannia*. El Greco's *Lady in a Fur Wrap* (1541) and works by Francisco de Goya and Esteban Murillo adorn the library and drawing room.

In 1966 Anne Maxwell Macdonald gave the house and parkland, containing the Burrell Collection, to the City of Glasgow.

EAT & DRINK

Mackintosh at the Willow

A Glasgow institution, with a menu that includes gluten-free and vegetarian options.

📍E3 🏠215-17 Sauchiehall St 🌐mackintoshat thewillow.com

£££

Hillhead Bookclub

This trendy bar and eatery has a dazzling portfolio of craft beers and cocktails.

📍B2 🏠17 Vinicombe St 🌐hillheadbookclub.co.uk

£££

Ubiquitous Chip

At this champion of Scottish produce and experimental cuisine, the casual vibe belies its fine-dining menu.

📍B2 🏠12 Ashton Lane 🌐ubiquitouschip.co.uk

£££

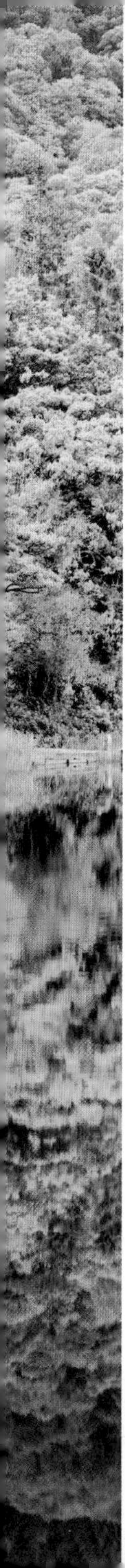

Autumnal colours at Loch Ard, the Trossachs

CENTRAL AND NORTHEAST SCOTLAND

Central and Northeast Scotland is a contrast of picturesque countryside and major urban centres, where a modern industrialized country meets an older and wilder landscape. Historically, it was here that the English-speaking Lowlands bordered the Gaelic Highlands, and there is still a strong sense of transition for anyone travelling north.

The Highland Boundary Fault runs through Central Scotland from Arran in the southwest to Stonehaven on the northeast coast. For hundreds of years this line was a border between two very different cultures. To the north and west was a Gaelic-speaking people, who felt loyalty to their local clan chiefs. This way of life was marginalized in the late 18th century, as the more Anglicized Lowlands established their dominance.

In the Lowlands, Scotland's industry developed, drawing on coal reserves in districts such as Lanarkshire and the Lothians, while the Highlands were depopulated and eventually set aside for sporting estates and sheep farming. The country's first coal-run ironworks was built at Carron in 1759, very close to Falkirk, where Bonnie Prince Charlie had enjoyed one of his last military successes as claimant to the British throne 13 years earlier, while Perth and Dundee were important centres of commerce just a short distance from the relative wildness of the southern Highlands.

CENTRAL AND NORTHEAST SCOTLAND

Must Sees

1. Aberdeen
2. Dundee
3. St Andrews
4. Scone Palace
5. Loch Lomond and the Trossachs National Park
6. Stirling Castle

Experience more

7. Stirling
8. Stonehaven
9. Dunnottar Castle
10. Pennan
11. Forvie National Nature Reserve
12. Duff House
13. Balmoral Castle and Royal Deeside
14. Ballater
15. Braemar
16. Alford
17. Findhorn
18. Elgin
19. Castle Fraser Garden and Estate
20. Doune Castle
21. The Malt Whisky Trail®
22. Loch Leven Castle and Heritage Trail
23. Perth
24. Glamis Castle
25. Dunkeld
26. Dunfermline
27. Culross
28. Falkirk Wheel
29. The Helix
30. Antonine Wall
31. Falkland Palace
32. East Neuk
33. Dunblane
34. Kirriemuir
35. Pitlochry
36. Tay Forest Park
37. Aberfeldy
38. Meigle Sculptured Stone Museum

Moray Firth

Lossiemouth
urghead   Portknockie   Cullen   PENNAN
17 **FINDHORN** Portsoy Macduff Crovie **10** Rosehearty Fraserburgh
18 **ELGIN**   Banff **12** **DUFF HOUSE**   Inverallochy
Forres   Lhanbryde   Cornhill   A98   Rathen
Dallas Dhu Fochabers Aberchirder New Pitsligo Strichen Crimond
Distillery   A95   Turriff New Deer   A952 Mintlaw
Rothes   Keith   Deveron   Peterhead
Archiestown Craigellachie   A96   Huntly Methlick Clola A90 Cruden Bay
Cardhu Aberlour Macallan Fyvie **FORVIE NATIONAL**
Distillery **21** Dufftown Colpy Oldmeldrum Ellon **NATURE RESERVE**
Lettoch **THE MALT WHISKY** Insch A920   Newburgh **11**
ntown- Glenfarclas **TRAIL®** Rhynie Pitcaple Inverurie
Spey Glenlivet Cabrach The Buck A96 Newmachar
Cromdale 721 m (2,365 ft)   Kintore A947 Balmedie
Knockandhu Kildrummy **CASTLE FRASER** Buchburn
Tomintoul Castle **GARDEN AND ESTATE** **19** Don
Colnabaichin A97 **16** Echt **ABERDEEN** **1**
Morven Craigievar **ALFORD** Drum Peterculter
Monadhliath 871 m (2,858 ft) Castle Castle The Den And Glen
Mountains Logie Torphins Crathes Netherley
Crathie Coldstone Castle Cammachmore
RAEMAR **14** **BALLATER** Aboyne A93 Banchory
15 **13** **BALMORAL CASTLE** Dee Strachan A957
nverey **AND ROYAL DEESIDE** **8** **STONEHAVEN**
Lochnagar **9** **DUNNOTTAR CASTLE**
1,154 m (3,786 ft)
he Cairnwell Braedownie North Esk A90 Inverbervie
m (3,061 ft) Spittal of Fettercairn A92
Glenshee Clova Edzell Laurencekirk Johnshaven
A93 Marykirk St Cyrus
Kirkmichael Cortachy A90 A937 Brechin Montrose
allinluig Kirkton of South Esk Montrose Basin
Bridge of Kingoldrum **34** **KIRRIEMUIR** Friockheim Wildlife Centre
Cally Alyth **GLAMIS** Forfar A92 Inverkeilor **North Sea**
Blairgowrie **CASTLE** **24** Glamis A933 Auchmithie
25 **DUNKELD** Isla **38** **MEIGLE SCULPTURED** Arbroath
ankfoot Coupar **STONE MUSEUM**
A9 A93 Angus A90 A92 Carnoustie
Guildtown **DUNDEE** **2** Monifieth
ethven Balbeggie Firth of Tay Tayport
4 **SCONE** Newport-on-Tay
PERTH **23** **PALACE** A92 Leuchars
Bridge Newburgh Dairsie
of Earn A91 Cupar **3** **ST ANDREWS**
tevin Strathmiglo Pitscottie Boarhills
A91 Hill of Tarvit Mansion
FALKLAND **31** Ladybank **EAST NEUK** Crail
PALACE A913 **32** Anstruther
Kinross **22** Glenrothes Leven Pittenweem
LOCH LEVEN CASTLE Earlsferry Elie
AND HERITAGE TRAIL Buckhaven
Kirkcaldy
26 **DUNFERMLINE** Firth of Forth
7 Rosyth North
ULROSS Berwick
A198
EDINBURGH Dunbar
p68 A1 East Linton
Edinburgh Cockburnspath
SOUTHERN Dalkeith Haddington
SCOTLAND Gifford Grantshouse A1 Eyemouth
p108 Penicuik Cranshaws
A702 A703 A7 A68

0 kilometres   20
0 miles   20

N
↑

↑ Granite buildings of Union Street, Aberdeen's main thoroughfare

①

ABERDEEN

▲E4 ⊞Grampian ✈13km (8 miles) NW of Aberdeen
⊟⊞ Union Sq 🚉23 Union St; www.visitabdn.com

Nicknamed the "Granite City" for its distinctive, hard-edged architecture, Aberdeen is Scotland's third-largest city. After the discovery of oil beneath the North Sea in the 1970s, it became Europe's offshore oil capital and, despite some decline in recent years, its harbour still bustles with commercial shipping. At the east end of Union Street modern redevelopments surround the ornate granite walls of Marischal College. North of the centre, Old Aberdeen is a late medieval enclave of historic buildings nestled around one of the UK's oldest universites.

①
Marischal College

⊞Broad St (just off Union St)

The world's second-largest granite building (narrowly losing out to the Escorial in Spain), Marischal College was founded in 1593 by the fifth Earl Marischal of Scotland as a Protestant alternative to King's College. It's austere façade has become a symbol of the "Granite City", and rather fittingly the college houses Aberdeenshire Council's headquarters.

②
St Nicholas Kirk

⊞Union St ⊙Jun-Sep: noon-3pm Mon-Fri; 9:30am-1pm Sun ⊞kirk-of-st-nicholas-org.uk

Founded in the 12th century, St Nicholas Kirk – also known as "The Mither Kirk" – claims to be Scotland's largest parish church. During the reformation, it was divided into the East and West church, separated by the transepts – it is actually two churches in one. The West church was designed by James Gibbs, of St Martin's

in the Field (London) fame. The East Church contains ancient relics, including iron rings once used to secure women accused of witchcraft in the 17th century.

③
Tolbooth Museum

Castle St ⊙Jul-Sep 10am-4pm Tue-Sat, 12:30-3:30pm Sun ⊞aagm.co.uk

Within the old city jail is the Tolbooth museum, whose focus is on the history of crime and punishment. The granite and sandstone building retains its chilly 17th- and 18th-century cells, original doors, barred windows and 17th-century guillotine blade.

④
St Andrew's Cathedral

⊞King St ⊙Times vary, check website ⊞standrewscathedral aberdeen.org.uk

The Mother Church of the Episcopal Church in the United States, St Andrew's has a memorial to Samuel Seabury, the first Episcopalian bishop in the US, who was consecrated in Aberdeen in 1784. Coats of arms representing the American states and Jacobite families adorn the interior.

---

⑤

King's College

🏛 College Bounds
🕐 Daily (chapel: 10am-3:30pm Mon-Fri)

Founded in 1495 by Bishop Elphinstone, King's College was the city's first college building and the fifth in all of Britain. The college remains the focal point of the Old Town campus, sitting at the heart of the quadrangle. The most striking aspects of the interior are the chapel with its distinctive lantern tower, a ribbed arch wooden ceiling, and a pulpit dating from 1540. Douglas Strachan's stained-glass windows add a modern touch. The visitor centre has an illuminating display on the history of the college.

↑ Student cycling along cobbled lanes of King's College campus

⑥ 🏍

St Machar's Cathedral

🏛 The Chanonry
🕐 9:30am-4:30pm daily (Nov-Mar: 10am-4pm)
🌐 stmachar.com

The twin granite towers of this 15th-century cathedral, dedicated to Aberdeen's patron saint, rise above the Old Aberdeen to pinpoint St Machar's Cathedral. Stained-glass windows light the interior, depicting the 6th-century saint and the cathedral's earliest bishops, but it's the stunning heraldic ceiling that steals the show.

EAT

Wild Ginger

Arguably the city's best Indian restaurant, offering delish plates like tandoori garlic chilli chicken.

🏛 367 Union St
🌐 wildginger unionstreet.co.uk

£££

Moonfish

Imaginative bites precede delightful mains at this hideaway restaurant off Union Street.

🏛 9 Connection Wynd
🌐 moonfishcafe.co.uk
🕐 Sun & Mon

£££

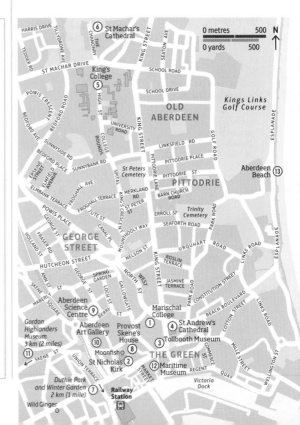

↑ The Cactus House at Duthie Park and Winter Garden

⑦
Duthie Park and Winter Garden

🏠 Polmuir Rd 🕐 9:30am-4:30pm daily (to 7:30pm May-Aug)

Nestled up against the banks of the River Dee, a 20-minute walk from the city centre, Duthie Park was gifted to the city by Lady Elizabeth Combe Duthie in 1880 and has remained a much loved destination for Aberdonians ever since. It's a wonderful place to explore at any time of year, but it really comes into its own in summer when the Rose Garden is in full bloom. The highlight for many though is the Winter Garden, with its exceptional collection of bromeliads and giant cactuses. There's also a boating pond with boats and kayaks for hire.

⑧
Provost Skene's House

🏠 Guestrow 🕐 10am-5pm Mon-Sat 🖥 aagm.co.uk

The city's oldest private residence, this grand 16th-century house was so named after George Skene, a 17th-century Scottish merchant who was also provost (mayor) of the city between 1676 and 1685. Recently refurbished, it now houses an enlightening and eclectic museum, with rooms furnished in the style of the 17th to 18th centuries and comprising everything from archaeological treasures and local history to period costumes. The undoubted highlight, however, is the Painted Gallery, featuring a series of boldly coloured tempera paintings depicting scenes from the life of Christ.

⑨
Aberdeen Science Centre

🏠 107 George St 🕐 10am-5pm daily 🖥 aberdeen sciencecentre.org

Scotland's first Science and Discovery Centre, Aberdeen Science Centre is yet another of the city's institutions that has recently been renovated. Now a sparkling, state-of-the-art facility, the Science Centre, formerly Aberdeen's old tram depot, offers a range of fun, mostly hands-on, exhibits for all ages, as well as themed live shows and captivating demonstrations.

↓ Illustration of Provost Skene's House

The 18th-century Parlour was the informal room in which the family would have tea.

The Regency Room typifies early 19th-century elegance.

The Painted Gallery has one of Scotland's most important cycles of religious art.

Provost Skene's coat of arms hangs above the fireplace in the Great Hall

The Georgian Dining Room has its original flagstone floor.

Entrance

The main hall of the newly re-opened Aberdeen Art Gallery ↑

(10) 🖥 📷

Aberdeen Art Gallery

📍Schoolhill ⏰10am–5pm Mon–Sat; 11am–4pm Sun
🌐aagm.co.uk

Totally transformed after an extensive renovation programme, the city's landmark art gallery is home to a fine collection of works by both British and European artists and designers. Representing the home shores are the likes of Raeburn, Reynolds, Hogarth, Paul Nash, Stanley Spencer, Barbara Hepworth and Francis Bacon. Look out for decorative artwork by local artist James Cromar Watt and designer Bill Gibb. Many of the great 19th-century French painters feature strongly, with pieces by Monet, Renoir, Degas and Toulouse-Lautrec.

(11) 🖌 🖥 📷

Gordon Highlanders Museum

📍St Luke's, Viewfield Rd
⏰10am–4:30pm Tue–Sat
🌐gordonhighlanders.com

This excellent museum, west of the city centre, documents the illustrious history of one of Scotland's most famous regiments, founded in 1794 and described by Winston Churchill as "the finest regiment that ever was". The collection comprises medals, weapons and uniforms; there's also a replica World War I trench and a beautifully arranged memorial garden.

(12) 🖥 📷

Maritime Museum

📍Shiprow ⏰10am–5pm Mon–Sat (noon–3pm Sun)
🌐aagm.co.uk

Overlooking the harbour is Provost Ross's house, which dates back to 1593. It now houses the Maritime Museum, which traces the history of Aberdeen's seafaring tradition from medieval times to the city's offshore oil boom during the 1970s right up to the present day.

(13)

Aberdeen Beach

It might come as something of a surprise to learn that Aberdeen possesses one of Britain's finest city beaches. Located an easy 2 km (1 mile) walk east of Union Street, this 3 km (2 mile) long unbroken sweep of sand is backed by a tidy esplanade, which makes for an exhilarating stroll at any time of the year.

DRINK

Tippling House
Best known for its innovative cocktail menu, this atmospheric cellar bar also serves excellent Scottish ales and a fine selection of whiskies. Small plates are available too.

📍4 Belmont St
🌐thetipplinghouse.com

Prince of Wales
A warm welcome is guaranteed in this venerable alehouse, popular for its Sunday evening folk sessions.

📍7 St Nicholas Lane
🌐belhavenpubs.co.uk

Dundee's inspirational V&A Museum of Design by architect Kengo Kuma ↑

2

DUNDEE

🅐 D5 🅐 Tayside ✈🚢🚌 ℹ️ 16 City Sq 🆆 dundee.com

A major shipbuilding centre in the 18th and 19th centuries, Dundee has undergone quite the transformation in recent years, not least with the regeneration of the riverside area, at the heart of which is the sparkling new V&A Design Museum.

① 🍽️ 🖥️ 🛍️
V&A Museum of Design

🅐 1 Riverside Esplanade 🕙 10am-5pm daily 🆆 vam.ac.uk/dundee

The most recent gem in Dundee's crown is the V&A Museum of Design, which opened in 2018. Sitting at the heart of the revitalized waterfront, this monumental modern building, designed by Kengo Kuma, is an outpost of London's prestigious V&A and showcases the best of Scottish and international design. Representing Scotland in the Scottish Design Galleries are the likes of Charles Rennie Mackintosh, Eduardo Paolozzi and Basil Spence. Alongside these permanent collections is a continually revolving series of world-class temporary exhibitions.

② ⚡ 🍽️ 🖥️
Discovery Point

🅐 Discovery Point 🕙 10am-6pm Mon-Sat (from 11am Sun); tours by appt only 🆆 rrsdiscovery.co.uk

Adjacent to the V&A, Discovery Point is an innovative visitor attraction centred on the royal research ship *Discovery*, which was built here in 1901 for the first of Captain Scott's voyages to the Antarctic. Berthed in dry dock, the vessel has been superbly restored, and it's now possible to wander the decks, cabins, corridors and wardrooms. Meanwhile, an adjacent visitor centre does a fine job relaying the history of the expedition, courtesy of cleverly conceived audio-visual displays and computer-generated interactive experiences.

③ 🖥️ 🛍️
McManus Art Gallery and Museum

🅐 Albert Institute, Albert Sq 🕙 10am-5pm daily 🆆 mcmanus.co.uk

These galleries are home to the city's main art and history collections. The ones to aim for are the Victoria Gallery, showcasing the likes of Henry Raeburn, and the 20th Century Gallery, featuring a fine selection of works by the much revered Scottish Colourists. Landscapes and Lives celebrates the city's natural heritage, while traditional shipbuilding and whaling industries are covered in Dundee and the World.

↑ Admiring paintings on display at the McManus Art Gallery and Museum

⑤ 🛹 🏛
HMS Unicorn

🏠 **Victoria Docks** ⏰ **Apr-Oct: 10am-5pm daily; Nov-Mar: 10am-4pm Tue-Sun** 🌐 **frigateunicorn.org**

Moored in Victoria Docks, across from Discovery Point, is HMS *Unicorn*. Built in 1824, this simple-looking wooden frigate is the oldest British warship still afloat – and one of only six surviving pre-1850 warships in the world.

⑥ 🛹 Ⓜ
Mills Observatory

🏠 **Balgay Hill** ⏰ **Times vary, check website** 🌐 **leisureandculture dundee.com**

Prominently sited atop Balgay Hill, a small volcanic outcrop some two miles west of the city centre, Mills Observatory was the UK's first public-built observatory, opened in 1935. A number of exhibits chart the history of the solar system, while there are plenty of telescopes to peer through

④ 🛹 🖥 🏛
Verdant Works

🏠 **West Henderson's Wynd** ⏰ **Apr-Oct: 10am-6pm Mon-Sat, 11am-6pm Sun; Nov-Mar: 10:30am-4:30pm Wed-Sun** 🌐 **verdantworks. co.uk**

Built in 1833, Verdant Works is not only a rare example of a courtyard-style mill, but it's the last working mill of its type anywhere in Scotland.

and, between October and March, planetarium shows. The observatory also hosts many free stargazing events throughout the year.

⑦ 🏛
Broughty Castle Museum

🏠 **Castle Approach** ⏰ **10am-4pm Mon-Sat, 12:30-4pm Sun** 🌐 **leisure andculturedundee.com**

Dominating the pretty fishing village of Broughty Ferry a few miles east of the city centre stands Broughty Castle. Pressed up hard against the seashore, it's an impressive looking structure, originally constructed in 1496 in order to defend the nation against potential invasion by the English navy, before being largely rebuilt in the 19th century. Its four floors now keep displays pertaining to local history. Best of all though are the impressive views out to the Tay Estuary.

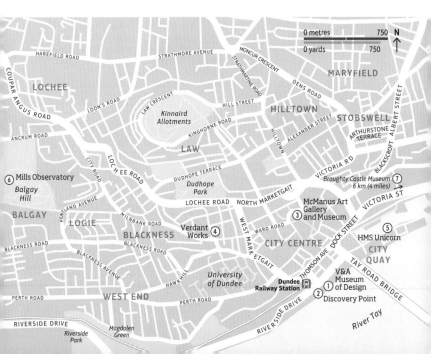

3

ST ANDREWS

E5 Fife Leuchars Station Rd 70 Market St (01334) 472021

Scotland's oldest university town and one-time ecclesiastical capital, St Andrews is now a shrine to golfers from all over the world. Its main streets and cobbled alleys are a delight to wander around.

①

St Andrews Cathedral

The Pends Daily (Apr-Sep: 9:30am-5:30pm; Oct-Mar: 10am-4pm historic environment.scot

Founded around 1160, St Andrew's was once the largest cathedral in Scotland. After its destruction during the reformation the cathedral was plundered, many of its stones used to build the town.

②

St Andrews University

st-andrews.ac.uk

Scotland's oldest university, and the UK's third oldest after Oxford and Cambridge, St Andrews was founded in 1413 by Bishop Henry Wardlaw. The university's buildings are scattered around town, but the two main sites are United College on North Street and St Mary's College on South Street, the latter dating from 1538 and home to the Faculty of Divinity and the King James Library. The Collections Centre keeps a wealth of artifacts; visits must be booked in advance.

③

St Andrews Castle

The Scores Daily (Apr-Sep: 9:30am-5:30pm; Oct-Mar: 10am-4pm) historic environment.scot

Built for the town's bishops and archbishops around 1200, St Andrews Castle was almost destroyed during the reformation; one remaining structure of note is the 14th-century Fore Tower. A modest visitor centre offers an interesting insight into the castle's history and there's a small collection of pictish stones to view.

④

British Golf Museum

Bruce Embankment 9:30am-5pm Mon-Sat, 10am-5pm Sun british golfmuseum.co.uk

Telling the story of how the city's Royal and Ancient Golf Club became the ruling arbiter of the game, this museum is a delight for seasoned golfers and novices. Exhibits include the world's oldest set of clubs (from the 17th century) and Seve Ballesteros' golf shoes, alongside trophies and pictures of golfing greats such as Tom Watson and Tiger Woods. You can even try your hand at putting on the museum's indoor green.

⑤

St Andrews Museum

Kilnburn Park 10:30am-4pm Mon-Sat (Oct-Mar: Wed-Sat) onfife.com

Often neglected in favour of the town's more obvious sights. this museum is well worth a visit. Its eclectic collection covers the history of the town in entertaining fashion.

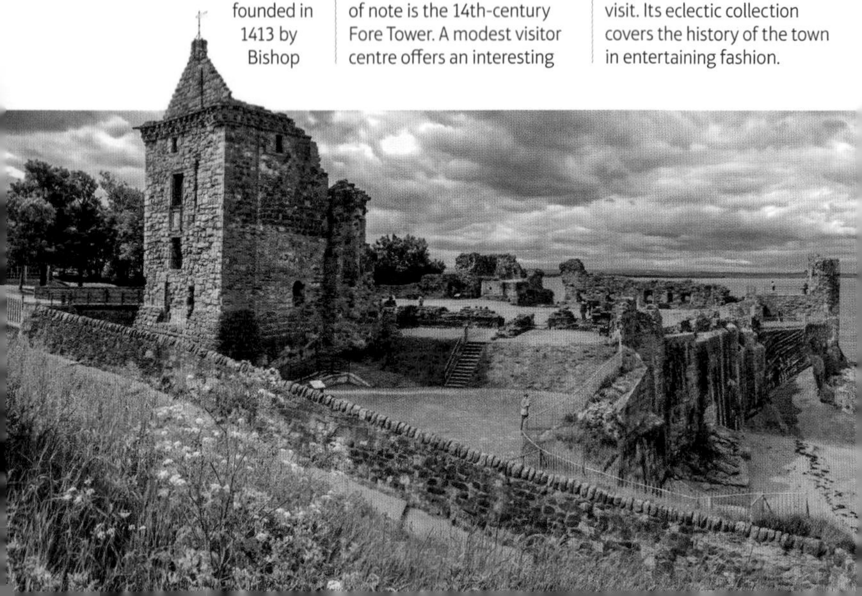

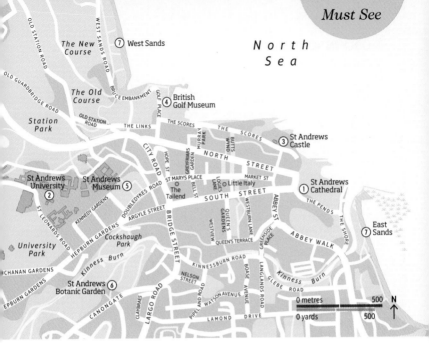

North
Sea

⑥ 🏷️ 🖼️ 🛍️

St Andrews Botanic Garden

📍 Canongate ⏰ Daily (Apr-Sep 10am-6pm; Oct-Mar: 10am-4pm) 🌐 standrews botanic.org

St Andrews Botanic Garden is a welcome respite from the busy town centre. Originally based at St Mary's College, the gardens were moved to the present site in the 1960s.

↓ Dramatic ruins of St Andrews Castle on its rocky promontory

Although covering a fairly modest 18 acres, there's much to enjoy here, including a rhododendron woodland, a 100-m- (330-ft-) long herbaceous border, and two glasshouses sheltering a marvellous collection of exotic plantlife. Between April and October visitors can explore an immersive butterfly house.

⑦ West Sands and East Sands

St Andrews is blessed with two fantastic sandy beaches. On the south side of the old harbour, East Sands is the smaller of the two, and is particularly popular with watersports enthusiasts, though there are some rock pools at the southern end of the beach for kids to muck around in. To the north of town lies West Sands, a vast sweep of sand that is best known for featuring in the opening sequence of the Oscar-winning film *Chariots of Fire* (1981). Packed with

sunlovers in summer, it's also a great spot for kite flying at any time of the year owing to the ferocious winds that frequently blow along this stretch of coast.

EAT

Little Italy
An absolute gem of an Italian restaurant with authentic decor and top notch food.

📍 2 Logies Lane 🌐 littleitaly.cc

£ £ £

The Tailend
Seafood restaurant renowned for its Arbroath Smokies among other dishes.

📍 130 Market St 🌐 thetailend.co.uk

£ £ £

GOLF IN SCOTLAND

The game of golf is synonymous with Scotland and has been played here for hundreds of years. As such, few countries can rival Scotland for the number, quality and variety of courses - over 550 at the last count, with new ones opening every year. Similarly, few golfing destinations can lay claim to such magnificent, unspoilt scenery. Golf is played by people of all ages and capabilities in Scotland - it really is a game for everyone to enjoy. Whether your game is suited to one of the legendary championship courses or to a less daunting challenge, you will be warmly welcomed here.

Did You Know?

Deemed a distraction from military training, golf was was banned from 1457 to 1502.

EARLY HISTORY

Variations on the game of golf as we know it today were being played across Europe as long ago as the 14th century, and possibly even in Roman times. However, it is in Scotland that the passion for golf was born, and by the middle of the 16th century the game had become a popular pastime among the highest levels of society - James VI himself was a keen player, as was his mother, Mary, Queen of Scots.

In 1744, the Gentlemen Golfers of Leith drew up the first Articles & Laws in Playing at Golf. These original rules formed the framework for the modern game of golf.

↑ A 19th-century illustration of golfers playing at St Andrews

TOP 3 FAMOUS COURSES

St Andrews Links
▲ E5 ⏴ St Andrews
Ⓦ standrews.com
Among its seven courses is the Old Course, the oldest and most iconic golf course in the world.

Royal Burgess
▲ D6 ⏴ Edinburgh
Ⓦ royalburgess.co.uk
Instituted in 1735, this is the oldest golfing society in the world.

Gleneagles
▲ D5 ⏴ Auchterarder
Ⓦ gleneagles.com
This luxurious resort is home to four courses. It's the only venue in Europe to have hosted both the Ryder Cup and the Solheim Cup.

→ One of the four courses at Gleneagles, one of Scotland's top golf resorts

TOOLS OF THE TRADE

The Scottish influence on golf was not to end there. Many of the professionals playing at the time were also skilled carpenters, instrumental in developing the clubs and balls used in the game. In the days before machinery, the wooden clubs were made entirely by hand. The earliest irons were also fashioned by hand, and the aluminium-headed clubs that followed differed very little from clubs today. Before the rubber-core ball in use today, there was the "guttie" ball, which was invented in 1848 to replace the expensive "feathery", thus making the game more affordable.

LONG-STANDING TRADITIONS

Many of Scotland's courses are steeped in history and tradition. Records show that golf has been played at St Andrews *(p170)* since 1457. The St Andrews Links Trust now operates seven superb courses on this hallowed stretch of seaside, the most venerable of which is the Old Course. Every golfer dreams of playing here and this legendary course is accessible to visitors at short notice via a democratic ballot system. Simply contact the Trust the day before you want to play to be included in the daily draw (successful applicants are posted on the club's website).

GOLFING EVENTS

Keen golfers may choose to combine a visit to Scotland with one of its many tournaments. Besides the famous Open Championship, held at least every other year, there's the Aberdeen Standard Investments Scottish Open (late summer), the Alfred Dunhill Links Championship (Sep), the Ladies' Scottish Open and, sometimes, the Women's British Open. Popular amateur events include the St Andrews Links Trophy (Jun) and the Scottish Amateur Championship (Jul–Aug). "Golf Weeks" (when non-members can play at a club) are held at St Andrews (Apr), Pitlochry (Jun), Royal Deeside and Machrihanish (both in May).

4

SCONE PALACE

D5 **Scone, Perthshire** **From Perth** **Apr & Oct: 10am–4pm daily; May–Sep: 9:30am–5pm daily** **scone-palace.co.uk**

The historic home of the Stone of Destiny, this ornate slice of Gothic grandeur was once the crowning place of Scottish kings and queens. Its opulent interior and annual events, such as the Perth Highland Games and medieval combat re-enactments, are quite the spectacle.

Pronounced "scoon", this magnificent palace in the heart of Perthshire dates back to the 12th century. The site was once a Pictish gathering place, and since then has been a Christian church, an Augustinian priory and the seat and the crowning place of Scottish monarchs. The last coronation in Scotland took place here in 1651, when King Charles II was crowned atop Moot Hill. Today the palace is one of the UK's finest examples of the late Georgian Gothic style, having been rebuilt in the early 19th century for William Murray, first Earl of Mansfield. It is now a breathtaking treasury of fabulous *objets d'art*. Portraits of the Murray family gaze down from the walls of the Long Gallery, while beautifully inlaid furnishings, marble busts, ornate sculptures from mythology and elaborately crafted 18th- and 19th-century timepieces are displayed in every room.

Scone's huge wooded gardens are home to red squirrels, roe deer and the rare Hawfinch, as well as peacocks who patrol the palace grounds. Stroll along the serene Laburnum Walkway, or climb to the top of Moot Hill, where famed Scottish kings, such as Macbeth and Robert the Bruce, were crowned.

THE STONE OF DESTINY

Scottish monarchs were crowned on the rough-hewn Stone of Destiny from the dawn of the Scots kingdom until 1296, when King Edward I took it with him to Westminster Abbey. In 1996 it was returned to Scotland, and it is now held at Edinburgh Castle (*p76*). A replica sits atop Moot Hill, marking the site of the original.

① In the palace grounds, 2,000 trees and 800 m (2620 ft) of paths make up the famous Murray Star Maze, a labyrinth leading to a central statue of the water nymph Arethusa.

② A piping ceremony at the unveiling of Scone Palace's restored 16th-century historic archway.

③ The ornate interior of the Long Gallery, adorned with paintings of the Murray family.

←
Red sandstone exterior and castellated roof of Scone Palace

LOCH LOMOND AND THE TROSSACHS NATIONAL PARK

🅰C5 🏠West Dunbartonshire, Argyll & Bute, Trossachs 🚉Balloch; Arrochar and Tarbet 🚌Callander; Balloch; Balmaha 🚶National Park Visitor Centre, Balmaha: (01389) 722 100 🌐lochlomond-trossachs.org

Combining the wild ruggedness of the Grampians with the pastoral tranquillity of the Borders, this beautiful region of craggy peaks, sparkling lochs and scenic waterfalls is the meeting place of the Lowlands and Highlands.

Loch Lomond

Of Scotland's many lochs, Loch Lomond is perhaps the most popular and best loved. Lying just 30 km (19 miles) northwest of Glasgow, its accessibility has helped its rise to prominence. Duncryne, a small hill some 5 km (3 miles) northeast of Balloch on the southern shore, gives an excellent view of the loch, while the western shore is the more developed, with villages such as Luss and Tarbet attracting many visitors.

Walkers pass by Loch Lomond's shores on the West Highland Way, Scotland's most popular long-distance footpath running from Glasgow to Fort William, and the 50 km (30 mile) Great Trossachs Path which runs between Callander and Inversnaid skirts its banks. Boat trips operate from Balloch Pier and can be rented from various points around the loch.

> **GREAT VIEW**
> **Ben Lomond**
>
> The 12-km (7.5-mile) hike to the summit of Ben Lomond, 990m (3,217 ft) above the lochside starting point at Rowardennan, calls for good boots and reasonable fitness. The path leads through oak and birch woods, then up to the summit for a breathtaking panoramic view.

↓ Walker overlooking Loch Katrine from the summit of Ben A'an, Trossachs

Loch Lomond as viewed from Beinn Dubh and *(inset)* Inversnaid Hotel Harbour ↑

The Trossachs

In 2002, 1,865 sq km (720 sq miles) of the Trossachs area was designated Scotland's first national park. Home to a variety of wildlife, including the golden eagle, peregrine falcon, red deer and the wildcat, the Trossachs have inspired many writers, including Sir Walter Scott *(p114)*. Loch Katrine, just north of Loch Lomond, was the setting of Sir Walter Scott's *Lady of the Lake* (1810). The Victorian steamer *Sir Walter Scott* cruises from Trossachs Pier. Callander is the most popular town from which to explore the Trossachs, while Queen Elizabeth Forest Park between Loch Lomond and Aberfoyle offers spectacular woodland walks through this vast tract of Scottish countryside.

Did You Know?

At 45 sq km (27.5 sq miles), Loch Lomond is the largest stretch of fresh water in Britain.

EXPLORING LOCH LOMOND AND THE TROSSACHS

① Balloch

Perched on the southwestern tip of Loch Lomond, Balloch is the loch's largest settlement. There's plenty to see here, including the **Loch Lomond Bird of Prey Centre**, which keeps a fantastic display of owls, kestrels and eagles. On the pier, the **Maid of the Loch** is an elegant 1950s paddle steamer. Balloch is also a starting point for loch trips with **Sweeney's Cruises**, who offer scenic excursions.

Loch Lomond Bird of Prey Centre

⊘ ⊕ 🕐May–Sep: 10am–5pm daily; Feb–Apr & Oct: 10am–4pm daily; Nov–Jan: 10am–4pm Sat & Sun 🔳llbopc.co.uk

Maid of the Loch

⊘ ⊕ 🕐May–Sep: 11am–4pm daily; Oct–Apr: 10am–4pm 🔳maidoftheloch.org

Sweeney's Cruises

🔳sweeneyscruiseco.com

② Luss

Originally built as a model village for workers employed by the Colquhouns, owners of the once lucrative slate quarry, Luss is by far the most popular spot on Loch Lomond. Set away from the main road on the western side of the loch, it's popular for its flower-covered cottages, sandy beach, and clutch of excellent rest-aurants. The village pier, meanwhile, serves as a busy hub for lake cruises. More recently Luss was the setting for the cult Scottish television series, *Take the High Road* (1980).

③ Balmaha and Inchcailloch

Tiny Balmaha is a stopping off point for folk walking the West Highland Way (p33). The National Park Visitor Centre is located here and has a small exhibition on the park's flora and fauna, while there are some good eating and drinking options in the village. More noteworthy is the island of Inchcailloch, which means "Island of the Old Woman," so-named after the Christian missionary St Kentigerna, who is said to have landed here in 717 AD. Now owned by Scottish Natural Heritage, Inchcailloch, which is accessible via ferry from the Balhama boatyard, has some lovely walks, as well as a pretty beach on the south-western side of the island.

④ Loch Katrine

At the heart of the Trossachs, the 12-km- (8-mile-) long Loch Katrine was the inspiration for

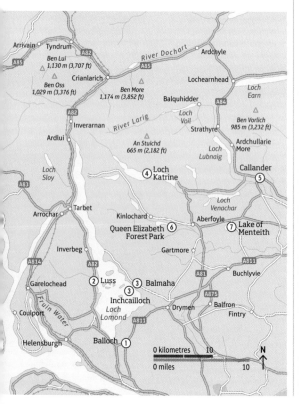

↑ Cyclists passing *The Lady of the Lake* cruise boat stationed on Loch Katrine

Sir Walter Scott's famous 19th-century poem *The Lady on the Lake*. So it is appropriate that the main activity here is a cruise on the *Sir Walter Scott*, a paddle steamer that has been plying the waters since 1899. An alternative, way to explore the lake is to hire a bike from Katrine Wheelz (*www.katrine wheelz.co.uk*), take the steamer up to Stronachlachar, then cycle back along the north shore. Walkers can climb the lofty Ben Venue from here – it's a challenging ascent but one which affords great views.

⑤
Callander
A busy little town on the eastern side of the Trossachs, Callander stands on one of the key routes into the Highlands – hence its popularity. The main thoroughfare is lined with shops and cafés.

It was in Callander that the Roman army was once stationed, and the fort remains are still visible. There are also some lovely walks close by, not least to the beautiful Bracklinn Falls, a three-mile long circuit that begins north of the town.

⑥
Queen Elizabeth Forest Park
Extending from the eastern shores of Loch Lomond to the mountains of Strathyre, the Queen Elizabeth Forest Park is an enticing mix of mountain, moorland, woodland and water – and the perfect spot to head to if it's peace and tranquility you're after. The park's Lodge Visitor Centre has live CCTV cameras where you can view ospreys, red deer and other residents. A network of cycle tracks and waymarked paths allow for extensive exploration through the forest, but if you're car-bound, there's the enjoyable Achray Forest Drive, which begins a couple of miles along from the visitor centre. If you fancy something a little more energetic, the Go Ape adventure course is a series of high rope bridges, swings and high-wire slides buried deep within the forest.

⑦
Lake of Menteith
Widely regarded as the only body of water in Scotland that is referred to as a lake (as opposed to a loch), the Lake of Menteith is the country's premier fly-fishing centre, attracting some of the world's finest anglers between May and August. From a cultural perspective, the lake is home to Inchmahome Priory, sited on the island of the same name. Founded in 1238, the priory remains an enticing prospect, with its roofless nave and superbly preserved effigies; it was here, in 1547, that a five-year old Mary Queen of Scots took refuge following the Scots' defeat at Pinkie Cluegh. Ferries shuttle passengers across to the island from the Port of Menteith on the lake's northern shore.

ROB ROY (1671–1734)
Robert MacGregor, known as Rob Roy (Red Robert) due to the colour of his hair, grew up as a herdsman near Loch Arklet. After a series of harsh winters, he took to raiding richer Lowland properties to feed his clan, and was declared an outlaw by the Duke of Montrose who burned his house to the ground. After this, Rob Roy's Jacobite sympathies became inflamed by his desire to avenge the crime. Plundering the duke's lands and repeatedly escaping from prison earned him a reputation similar to that of England's Robin Hood. He was pardoned in 1725 and spent his last years freely in Balquhidder, where he is buried.

6 🏛️ 🅜 🍴 🥤 🛍️

STIRLING CASTLE

🅐 D5 🏰 Castle Esplanade, Stirling 🚆🚌 🕐 Apr-Sep: 9:30am-6pm daily; Oct-Mar: 9:30am-5pm daily 🌐 stirlingcastle.scot

Rising high on a rocky crag, this magnificent castle, which dominated Scottish history for centuries, now remains one of the finest examples of Renaissance architecture in Scotland.

Overlooking the plains where some of Scotland's most decisive battles took place, Stirling Castle was one of the nation's greatest strongholds. Legend says that King Arthur wrested the original castle from the Saxons; however, the first written evidence of a castle is from 1100. The present building dates from the 15th and 16th centuries. From 1881 to 1964 it was used as a depot for recruits into the Argyll and Sutherland Highlanders.

Today you can explore the palace vaults, try your hand at some medieval crafts and rub shoulders with costumed characters as they bring the castle's fascinating history to life.

↑ Highland cattle grazing on pastures overlooked by Stirling Castle

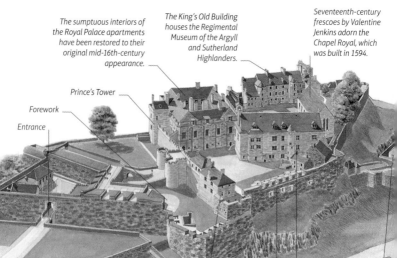

The sumptuous interiors of the Royal Palace apartments have been restored to their original mid-16th-century appearance.

The King's Old Building houses the Regimental Museum of the Argyll and Sutherland Highlanders.

Seventeenth-century frescoes by Valentine Jenkins adorn the Chapel Royal, which was built in 1594.

Prince's Tower

Forework

Entrance

Nether Bailey

The Grand Battery was built in 1708 to strengthen the castle's defences.

The Great Hall, built in 1500, has a roof similar to that of Edinburgh Castle (p76).

In the esplanade stands a statue of Robert the Bruce sheathing his sword.

The Elphinstone Tower was originally home to the constable of the castle.

Illustration of Stirling Castle detailing the buildings within its fortified walls ↑

STIRLING BATTLES

Standing at the highest navigable point of the Forth and holding the pass to the Highlands, Stirling occupied a key position in Scotland's many struggles for independence. Seven battlefields can be seen from the Stirling Castle; the 67-m (220-ft) Wallace Monument at Abbey Craig recalls William Wallace's defeat of the English army at Stirling Bridge in 1297, foreshadowing Robert the Bruce's victory in 1314.

1745

The year of the last military assault on Stirling Castle, led by the Jacobite army.

EXPERIENCE MORE

7
Stirling

🅰D5 🅰Stirlingshire 🚆🚌
🛈Old Town Jail, St John St;
🌐yourstirling.com

Between the Ochil Hills and the Campsie Fells, the city of Stirling grew up around its castle, historically one of Scotland's most important fortresses. Below the castle the Old Town is still protected by the original walls, built in the 16th century to keep Mary, Queen of Scots safe from Henry VIII. The medieval Church of the Holy Rude, on Castle Wynd, where the infant James VI was crowned in 1567, has one of Scotland's few surviving hammerbeam oak roofs. In front of the church, the ornate façade of Mar's Wark is all that remains of a grand palace, destroyed by the Jacobites in 1746.

Just 3 km (2 miles) south of Stirling, the **Battle of Bannockburn Experience** stands by the field where Robert the Bruce defeated the English in 1314 (*p62*), after which he dismantled the small castle that once stood there to prevent it from falling into English hands. A statue of Robert the Bruce on horseback commemorates the man who became an icon of Scottish independence.

Battle of Bannockburn Experience

♿😊🏛NTS 🅰Glasgow Rd
🕐Apr-Sep: 9:30am-5:30pm daily; Oct-Mar: 10am-5pm daily 🌐nts.org.uk

← The Bruce Monument at the site of his decisive victory

8

Stonehaven

🅰E4 🏠Aberdeenshire
🚆🚌Stonehaven

Situated on a long crescent of sandy beach, this small town is known for its annual Hogmanay Fireball Festival and its heated seawater **open-air swimming pool**. It is also infamous as the birthplace of the deep-fried Mars Bar. The **Stonehaven Tolbooth Museum** is housed in a 16th-century building on the quayside and once served as the town's courthouse and jail. It now displays a large collection of oddball, punishment-related artifacts such as the stocks and the crank, a distinctly horrible torture device.

Stonehaven Tolbooth Museum

🏠Old Pier, Stonehaven Harbour 🕐1:30–4:30pm Wed-Mon 🆆stonehaven tolbooth.co.uk

Open-air swimming pool

🏊 🏠Queen Elizabeth Park 🕐Times vary, check website; 🆆stonehavenopenairpool. co.uk

---

9 🏊

Dunnottar Castle

🅰E4 🚌X7, 107 from Stonehaven 🕐Apr-Sep: 9am-5:30pm daily; Oct-May: times vary, check website; may also close in bad weather 🆆dunnottar castle.co.uk

Perched on its sea-girt crag just 3 km (2 miles) south of Stonehaven, Dunnottar is the northeast's most spectacular castle. It featured in *Victor Frankenstein*, the 2015 sci-fi film adaptation of Mary Shelley's 1818 novel, starring Daniel Radcliffe, and also featured as Elsinore in Franco Zeffirelli's *Hamlet*. The castle sits on a superb natural stronghold, with steep cliffs on three sides and a narrow

Did You Know?

Dunnottar's Gaelic name is *Dùn Fhoithear*, meaning "fort on the shelving slope".

neck of rock connecting it to the land. The Scottish crown jewels were famously hidden from Oliver Cromwell's invading army here in the 17th century. Originally constructed for the Earl of Marischal in the 12th century, the surviving parts, mostly in ruins, date from the 15th and 16th centuries, and the 14th-century tower house is still in relatively good shape, though roofless. The castle is accessible by car, or via a steep well-marked clifftop path from Stonehaven.

10

Pennan

🅰E3 🏠Aberdeenshire
🚌From Aberdeen
Tiny Pennan is a picturesque fishing hamlet sandwiched between towering sandstone

> **Forvie National Nature Reserve is one of Scotland's most dramatic coastal stretches, and one of the largest areas of sand dunes in the UK.**

→ Crumbling ruins of Dunnottar Castle, poised on its clifftop precipice

cliffs and the choppy waters of the North Sea. This single row of pretty, whitewashed stone houses achieved fame as a location for the 1983 film *Local Hero* in which it doubled as the fictional village of Ferness. Look out for the iconic red phone box on the seafront; originally installed just for the movie, it is now a local landmark.

 11

Forvie National Nature Reserve

⚑ E4 ⌂ Forvie, Collieston, Ellon 🚌 61 or 63 from Aberdeen ⏱ Visitor Centre: Apr-Oct: daily 🌐 nature.scot

A bleak and beautiful expanse of windswept coast near Balmedie, a somnolent suburb of Aberdeen, Forvie National Nature Reserve is one of Scotland's most dramatic coastal stretches, and one of the largest areas of sand dunes in the UK. This unique environment, where stark, empty sand dunes meet the mudflats of the Ythan Estuary, is home to some spectacular wildlife including eider ducks, wading

oystercatchers and seals. Just 2.5 km (4 miles) south of Forvie, the opening of Trump International Golf Links in 2012 sparked controversy within the local community, as the previously protected Menie Estate was bulldozed to make way for the development. Donald Trump's grandiose promises of a $1.25 billion investment creating 6,000 jobs persuaded the Scottish government to ignore environmental considerations and approve the scheme. The local economy has not benefited as promised. The resort comprises one course

↑ Opulent Duff House, home to a priceless collection of artworks

(open only seven months of the year) and a 16-room hotel that employs fewer than 100 people.

 12

Duff House

⚑ E3 ⌂ Banff 🚆 Banff 🚌 35, 300 ⏱ Apr-Sep: 9:30am-5:30pm daily; Oct-Mar: 10am-4pm Fri-Sun 🌐 historic-environment.scot

This grand mansion is well off the tourist trail, but its spectacular collection of artworks and masterpieces by Scottish and European masters is a revelation. El Greco's *St Jerome in Penitence* is a highlight, and there are also works by Allan Ramsay, Sir Henry Raeburn and Dutch, German and Italian Renaissance painters. Surrounded by immaculate gardens, the house was designed by architect William Adam for William Duff, Earl of Fife, in 1735, but the two allegedly fell out over a structural flaw in the building, leading to a long-drawn-out court case, and Duff never actually moved into the finished house.

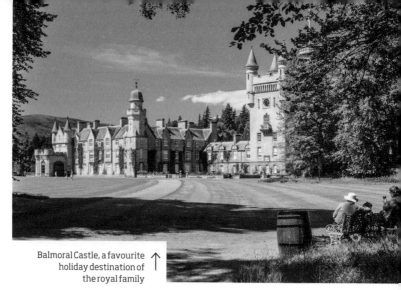

Balmoral Castle, a favourite holiday destination of the royal family ↑

13 🗺️ 🏛️ 💻 🛍️

Balmoral Castle and Royal Deeside

🗺️D3 🏠Balmoral Estate, Ballater 🚌201, 203 from Aberdeen ⏰Apr–Jul: 10am–5pm daily; Oct–Dec: selected dates, check website 🌐balmoral castle.com

Balmoral Castle is a kitsch Victorian vision that is the high point of any visit to leafy Royal Deeside. Queen Victoria bought the estate for 30,000 guineas in 1852, after its owner

VICTORIA AND ALBERT'S BALMORAL

It was the riverside setting that Queen Victoria fell for in 1848 when she first visited Balmoral, and it was her husband, Prince Albert, who worked with Aberdeen-born architect William Smith to create the white granite palace that replaced the old castle. It stands here still, a medley of fantastical turrets typical of the Baronial style.

choked to death on a fishbone. Her Prince Consort, Albert, had a hand in the design and it reflects his Teutonic tastes. These days, the royal family traditionally spend every August at Balmoral, hence the estate is off-limits to visitors during this time.

The grand ballroom is the only part of the castle generally open to the public, though visitors will find some compensation in the form of superb works of art, including those by Landseer and Carl Hagg; changing exhibitions are sometimes held here too. While access to the castle itself is limited, there's plenty else to see and do on the estate. First and foremost there are the grounds and manicured gardens, incorporating formal gardens with Victorian glasshouses, a water garden, and a walled kitchen garden, all of which you can explore with the help of an audio-guide. More exciting are the Land Rover safari tours, which entail a drive through the scenic grounds before heading

→

Dappled evening light illuminating Braemar Mountain in Aberdeenshire

off into the nearby Caledonian Pine forest (where there's a very good chance of spotting a capercaillie) and then up into the Lochnagar mountains.

***

14

Ballater

🗺️D4 🌐visitballater.com

Just 8 miles (12 km) east of Balmoral, the pretty little Victorian town of Ballater nestles contentedly within the heart of Royal Deeside. Despite its strong associations with the royal family – many

of the local shops once had royal warrants bestowed upon them – the town is just as well known for its spring water, which was discovered here in the early 19th century and widely thought to offer a cure for scrofula, a form of tuberculosis. While there's not a whole lot to see and do in Ballater itself, the recently restored **Old Royal Station** building – the line through here closed in 1966, then the building was destroyed by fire in 2015 – has an excellent visitor centre, also incorporating a library, café and restaurant. Ballater also makes a good base from which to strike out into the nearby mountains, especially Lock Muick, 9 miles (14 km) southwest of town.

Old Royal Station
📷 🖼 ⊘ 🏛 🅰 Station Sq
🕐 10am-5pm daily
(restaurant: 10am-4pm and 6pm-9pm Wed-Sun)

🅱 Braemar

🅰 D4 🌐 braemarscotland. co.uk

The small village of Braemar is famous, above all, for its Highland Games, the Braemar Gathering (p205), which is by some distance the most well known (and well attended) of all Scotland's Games. If you can't make it to the gathering itself, you can visit the new

Highland Games Centre, housed in a grand, lime-green coloured pavilion near the entrance to the arena. Courtesy of objects, costumes, banners and photographs, the museum colourfully documents the history and traditions of this most cherished event.

Highland Games Centre
🖼 😊 🅰 Princess Royal & Duke of Fife Memorial Park, Broombank Terrace 🕐 Apr-Oct: 10am-5pm daily
🌐 highlandgamescentre.org

🅲 Alford

🅰 D4 🌐 braemarscotland. co.uk

Although a rather nondescript town itself, Alford is worth a visit by virtue of the excellent **Grampian Transport Museum**, which charts the fascinating history of transport in northeast Scotland. On display is a marvellous collection of road vehicles, from tramcars and steam waggons to fire engines and dune buggies, though the exhibition does change from year to year.

If you plan on sticking around a while longer, there's also Craigievar Castle, some

> **Did You Know?**
>
> Ballater has hosted many royal residents and guests, including the Tzar of Russia in 1896.

10 km (6 miles) south of Alford. A distinctive shade of pastel pink, this charming castle is said to have been the inspiration behind Walt Disney's Cinderella Castle. Entertaining guided tours of this idiosyncratic 17th-century residence take in a dozen or so rooms run through with Jacobean woodwork and plaster ceilings. The castle grounds and woodland trails are a peaceful place to explore – look out for pine martens and red squirrels.

Grampian Transport Museum
🖼 😊 🅰 Montgarrie Rd
🕐 Apr-Oct: 10am-5pm daily
🌐 gtm.org.uk

Craigievar Castle
🖼 🖼 😊 🅝 🅰 Station Sq
🕐 Times vary; check website (castle grounds: dawn to dusk)
🌐 nts.org.uk

↑ Dingies setting sail from Findhorn's quiet harbour, on the Moray coast

⑰ Findhorn

ⒶD3 **Ⓜ**Moray 🚌
ℹFindhorn Foundation, Findhorn Ecovillage; www.ecovillagefindhorn.com

For an invigorating blast of fresh sea air, the coastal village of Findhorn, south of the Moray Firth and just a few miles from RAF Kinloss, makes for the perfect retreat. The town is known above all for the pioneering Findhorn Foundation, but many more people come here for its fine beach, a wide, dune-backed expanse that actually stretches for several miles up to and around Burghead Bay. The village itself is set around a pretty harbour lined with timeworn fishermen's cottages, while a small heritage centre relays the community's not inconsiderable fishing and shipping history.

FINDHORN FOUNDATION

Conceived in 1962 by Eileen and Peter Caddy and Dorothy MacClean, the Findhorn Foundation was set up on a caravan site to foster a simpler and more self-sustaining way of living. Still going strong, and with a community of around 500 people, the Foundation revolves around two main sites: the Park, a bustling eco-village nestled among the dunes, and Cluny Hill, a former hotel that's now used for experiential workshops and retreats.

---

⑱ Elgin

ⒶD3 **Ⓜ**Moray 🚆🚌
ℹElgin Library, Cooper Park; (01343) 562608

With its cobbled marketplace and crooked lanes, Elgin retains much of its medieval layout. The 13th-century cathedral ruins are all that remain of one of Scotland's architectural triumphs. Once known as the Lantern of the North, it was damaged in 1390 by the Wolf of Badenoch (son of Robert II) in revenge for his excommunication by the Bishop of Moray. Further damage came in 1576 when the Regent Moray had the lead roofing stripped. Among the remains is a Pictish cross-slab in the nave and a basin where one of the town benefactors, Andrew Anderson, was kept as a baby by his homeless mother. The **Elgin Museum** has anthropological and geological displays, and the **Moray Motor Museum** has vehicles dating back to 1904.

Elgin Museum

⑤ **Ⓐ**1 High St **Ⓞ**Apr-Oct: 10am-5pm Mon-Fri, 11am-4pm Sat **🌐**elginmuseum.org.uk

Moray Motor Museum

⑭🅿 **Ⓐ**Bridge St **Ⓞ**Easter-Oct: 11am-5pm daily **🌐**moraymotormuseum.org

---

⑲ Castle Fraser Garden and Estate

ⒶD3 **Ⓜ**Inverurie, Aberdeenshire **Ⓞ**Times vary, check website **🌐**nts.org.uk

Castle Fraser, within beautifully kept landscaped

→ Cardhu Distillery in Speyside, founded in 1811 in this remote spot

grounds, is an architectural riot of towers, turrets and crow-step gables. Most of these were added in the late 18th century, but the original castle, which is more than 400 years old, is one of the oldest and largest "z-plan" tower houses in Scotland. Inside, grand medieval halls and Regency salons house Fraser family portraits and exquisite Regency furniture.

20
Doune Castle

🅰️ D5 🔵 Doune 🚆 Doune, 🚌 From Stirling 🕐 Apr-Sep: 9:30am–5:30pm daily; Oct-Mar: 10am–4pm daily 🌐 historicenvironment. scot

Built as the residence of Robert, Duke of Albany, in the late 1300s, Doune Castle was a Stuart stronghold until it fell into ruin in the 18th century. Now fully restored, it offers a unique view into the life of the medieval royal household.

The Gatehouse leads to the central courtyard, then into the Great Hall. With its open-timber roof, minstrels' gallery and central fireplace, the Hall adjoins the Lord's Hall and Private Room, and retains its original privy and well-hatch. A number of private stairs and narrow passages illustrate the ingenious means

by which the royal family protected itself. The film *Monty Python and the Holy Grail* was shot here, and it has also featured in *Game of Thrones* and *Outlander*.

21
The Malt Whisky Trail®

🅰️ D3 🔵 Speyside, Moray 🌐 maltwhiskytrail.com

Due to its climate and geology, Speyside is home to half of Scotland's whisky distilleries. The signposted trail includes eight distilleries though one (Dallas Dhu) no longer makes whisky, and a cooperage, where barrels to store whisky are made.

There is no secret to whisky distilling (*p50*): barley is steeped in water and allowed to grow, a process called "malting"; the grains are then dried with peat smoke, milled, mixed with water and allowed to ferment in a double process of distillation. The final result is a raw, rough whisky that is then stored in old oak sherry casks for three to 16 years, during which time it mellows. Worldwide, an average of 30 bottles of Scotch whisky are sold every second.

The visitor centres at each of The Malt Whisky Trail® distilleries provide similar, and equally good, guided tours and informative audio-visual displays. Their entry charges can usually be redeemed against the purchase of a bottle of their whisky.

TOP 5 SPEYSIDE DISTILLERIES

Cardhu
🔵 Knockando, Aberlour 🌐 malts.com
Founded in 1811, Cardhu is the first distillery to be pioneered by a woman.

Macallan
🔵 Easter Elchies Estate, Aberlour 🌐 themacallan.com
The state-of-the-art Macallan visitor experience is the perfect place to sample the "Rolls Royce of single malts".

Glenlivet
🔵 Castleton Of Blairfindy 🌐 theglenlivet.com
Enjoy multi-sensory tours and tastings in this remote setting.

Glenfiddich
🔵 Dufftown 🌐 glenfiddich.com
Traditional craftman-ship and innovation come together at this family-run distillery.

Speyside Cooperage
🅰️ D3 🔵 Craigellachie 🌐 speysidecooperage.co.uk
Here visitors can learn about the making of the wooden casks that are used to store and age the whisky.

22 🏛

Loch Leven Castle and Heritage Trail

🅰 D5 🅰 Kinross Pier
🚌 From Kinross
🕐 Times vary, check website 🌐 pkct.org/loch-leven-heritage-trail

Sitting proudly atop a tiny island in the middle of Loch Leven, this eerie tower-house castle, often shrouded in mist, is one of Scotland's oldest, dating back to the 14th century. Mary, Queen of Scots was held captive here between 1567 and 1568, when she suffered a miscarriage and was subsequently forced to abdicate the throne to her infant son James VI. She escaped and was exiled to England, never to return. Other notable visitors include Robert the Bruce and Robert II, who was King of Scots from 1371 to his death in 1390. Boats depart regularly from the mainland pier; the crossing takes around 10 minutes. Tickets must be bought from the ticket office. The Loch Leven Heritage Trail is a 21-km (13-mile) gravel path that circles the loch – perfect for a scenic cycle or walk. Cycle hire is available at Kinross Pier.

> It was while on holiday in the countryside around Dunkeld that the children's author Beatrix Potter found inspiration for her Peter Rabbit stories.

23

Perth

🅰 D5 🅰 Perthshire 🚆🚌
🛈 45 High St 🌐 perthcity.co.uk

The capital of medieval Scotland, Perth's rich heritage is reflected in many of its buildings. In the Church of St John, founded in 1126, John Knox delivered fiery sermons that led to the destruction of many local monasteries. On North Port, the Victorianized Fair Maid's House (c. 1600) is one of the city's oldest, and the fictional home of the heroine of Sir Walter Scott's *The Fair Maid of Perth* (1828).

In **Balhousie Castle**, the Black Watch Museum commemorates the first ever Highland regiment, while the **Museum and Art Gallery** has local industry displays and Scottish art exhibitions.

Three km (2 miles) north of Perth, Gothic Scone Palace (p174) stands on the site of an abbey destroyed by John Knox's followers in 1559.

Between the 9th and 13th centuries, Scone guarded the sacred Stone of Destiny, now in Edinburgh Castle (p76).

Balhousie Castle

 🅰 RHQ Black Watch, Hay St 🕐 9:30am–4:30pm daily (Nov-Mar: 10am-4pm) 🌐 theblackwatch.co.uk

Museum and Art Gallery

🅰 78 George St 📞 (01738) 632488 🕐 10am–5pm Tue-Sat (Apr-Oct: also Sun)

24

Glamis Castle

🅰 D5 🅰 Glamis, outside Forfar, Tayside 🚆 Dundee then bus 🕐 Apr-Oct: 10am-5pm 🌐 glamis-castle.co.uk

Sporting the pinnacled outline of a Loire chateau, the imposing medieval tower house of Glamis Castle began as a royal hunting lodge in the 11th century, but later underwent a thorough reconstruction in the 17th

↑ Imposing exterior of Glamis Castle and one of the opulent bedrooms *(inset)*

century. It was the childhood home of the late Queen Elizabeth the Queen Mother, and her former bedroom can be viewed, including a youthful portrait by Henri de Laszlo (1878–1956). Her daughter, the late Princess Margaret, was born here.

Many rooms are open to the public, including Duncan's Hall, the oldest room in the castle and Shakespeare's setting for the king's murder in *Macbeth*. The castle's opulent rooms present china, paintings, tapestries and furniture spanning 500 years. In the extensive grounds stands a pair of wrought-iron gates made for the Queen Mother on her 80th birthday in 1980. In summer the spectacular gardens are in full bloom, with a fine array of rhododendrons and azaleas.

←

Loch Leven, at the heart of a national nature reserve

㉕
Dunkeld

◨ D5 ◨ Tayside
◨ Dunkeld & Birnam
◨ From Perth & Kinross

By the River Tay, crossed here by an elegant Thomas Telford bridge, this ancient and charming village was all but destroyed in the Battle of Dunkeld in 1689. The Little Houses lining Cathedral Street were the first to be rebuilt, and remain fine examples of an imaginative restoration.

The partly ruined 14th-century cathedral enjoys an idyllic setting on shady lawns beside the Tay, against a backdrop of steep and wooded hills. The choir is used as the parish church, and its north wall contains a leper's squint (a little hole through which lepers could see the altar during mass).

It was while on holiday in the countryside around Dunkeld that the children's author Beatrix Potter found inspiration for her Peter Rabbit stories.

STAY

Perth Parklands Hotel
In beautiful verdant grounds, this boutique townhouse offers chic, quality accommodation and friendly service. Its two rave-reviewed restaurants serve fabulous food and an exquisite afternoon tea.

◨ D5 ◨ 2 St Leonard's Bank, Perth
ⓦ theparklands hotel.com

ⓔⓔⓔ

Gleneagles Hotel
The "Riviera in the Highlands" comprises a five-star hotel, three golf courses, a spa, and country pursuits that include fishing and horse riding, and the only two-starred Michelin restaurant in Scotland.

◨ D5 ◨ Auchterarder
ⓦ gleneagles.com

ⓔⓔⓔ

↑ Pretty Culross, preserved by the National Trust for Scotland

26

Dunfermline

🅰D5 🄵Fife 🚌🚐

Scotland's capital until 1603, Dunfermline is dominated by the ruins of the 12th-century abbey and palace, which recall its royal past. The town first came to prominence in the 11th century as the seat of King Malcolm III, who founded a priory on the present site of **Dunfermline Abbey and Palace**. With its Norman nave and 19th-century choir, the abbey church contains the tombs of 22 Scottish kings and queens, including that of the renowned Robert the Bruce. The ruins of the palace soar over the gardens of Pittencrieff Park. Dunfermline's most famous son, the philanthropist Andrew Carnegie (1835–1919), had been forbidden entrance to the park as a boy. After making his fortune, he bought the entire Pittencrieff estate and gave it to the people of Dunfermline. Carnegie emigrated to Pennsylvania in his teens and, through iron and steel, became one of the wealthiest men in the world. He donated some $350 million for the benefit of mankind. The **Carnegie Birthplace Museum** tells his fascinating story.

Dunfermline Abbey and Palace
🄷 🄰St Margaret St 🄲Apr–Sep: daily (Oct–Mar: Sat–Wed) 🅆dunfermline abbey.com

Carnegie Birthplace Museum
🄰Moodie St 🄲Mar–Nov: daily (Sun pm only) 🅆carnegiebirthplace.com

27

Culross

🅰D5 🄵Fife 🚌🚐From Dunfermline & Perth 🅆nts.org.uk

An important religious centre in the 6th century, Culross is reputed to have been the birthplace of St Mungo in 514. Now a beautifully preserved 16th- and 17th-century village, Culross prospered in the 16th century due to the growth of its coal and salt industries, most notably under the genius of Sir George Bruce. Descended from the family of Robert the Bruce, Sir George took charge of the colliery in 1575 and created a drainage system called the "Egyptian Wheel" which cleared a mine 1.5 km (1 mile) long, running underneath the River Forth. The National Trust for Scotland began restoring the

town in 1932 and provides a guided tour from the visitor centre in the former prison.

Built in 1577, Bruce's palace has the crow-stepped gables, decorated windows and red pantiles typical of the period. Inside, its original painted ceilings are among the finest in Scotland. Crossing the square past Oldest House (1577), head for the Town House to the west. Behind it, a cobbled street known as the Back Causeway leads to the turreted Study, built in 1610 as a house for the Bishop of Dunblane. The main room, with a Norwegian ceiling, is open to visitors. If you continue north to the ruined abbey, fine church and Abbey House, don't miss the Dutch-gabled House with the Evil Eyes.

Palace, Town House and Study
🔲🄷(NTS) 🄲Apr–Sep: 10am–5pm daily; Oct: 10am–4pm daily

———

28

Falkirk Wheel

🅰D5 🄰Lime Rd, Tamfourhill, Falkirk 🚆Falkirk 🄲10am–5:30pm daily for boat trips 🅆scottishcanals.co.uk

This impressive, elegant boat lift is the first ever to revolve and the centrepiece of Scotland's ambitious canal regeneration scheme. Once important for commercial transport, the Union and the Forth and Clyde canals were blocked by numerous roads during the 1960s. Now the Falkirk Wheel gently swings boats between the two waterways for an uninterrupted link between Glasgow and Edinburgh. This huge, moving sculpture constantly rotates, lifting boats 35 m (115 ft), equivalent to 11 traditional locks, in just 15 minutes. Visitors can ride the wheel on boats that leave the visitor centre every 40 minutes.

Did You Know?

At 30 m (100 ft) high, *The Kelpies* are the largest equine sculptures in the world.

29 The Helix

🅐D5 🏠Falkirk 🕙9:30am–5pm daily 🌐thehelix.co.uk

Two amazing, glittering equine heads tower above the Forth and Clyde and Union canals. The Kelpies, 30-m- (98-ft-) tall metal sculptures created by sculptor Andy Scott, are the keynote landmark of The Helix, an expansive new canalside park with miles of walking and cycling trails. The visitor centre explains the history and renewal of the canals.

30 Antonine Wall

🅐D5 🏠Falkirk 🚆Falkirk 🕙Mon–Sat 🛈Falkirk Wheel, Lime Road; (01324) 620244 🌐antoninewall.org

The Romans invaded Scotland for a second time around AD 140, during the reign of Emperor Antonius, and built a 60-km (37-mile) earth rampart that stretched across Central Scotland from the Firth of Clyde to the Firth of Forth, further defended by ditches and forts at strategic points. One of the best-preserved sections of the wall can be seen at Rough Castle, west of Falkirk.

DRINK

Red Lion Inn
Hearty pub grub served in a quintessentially quaint setting.

🅐D5 🏠Low Causeway, Culross 🌐redlionculross.co.uk

£££

The Wine Library
Family-owned wine bar serving all manner of independent and unusual wines.

🅐D5 🏠1 Princes St, Falkirk 🌐thewinelibraryscotland.co.uk

£££

↑ The Falikirk Wheel connecting the Union, Forth and Clyde Canals

Sun setting over Andy Scott's *Kelpies,* Falkirk

EAT & DRINK

Mason Belles Kitchen

Part of the Old Churches House Hotel, this smart brasserie serves an accomplished menu featuring saddle fillet and curried monkfish tail - with lovely views of the cathedral too.

△D5 ⌂Cathedral Sq, Dunblane ⓦmasonbelleskitchen.co.uk

£ £ £

Tappit Hen

A real drinker's pub, the Tappit is an easy-going place with a selection of real ales and live music every night.

△D5 ⌂Kirk St, Dunblane ⓦbelhavenpubs.co.uk

£ £ £

Anstruther Fish Bar

This multi-award winning "chippy" is said to be the best in Britain (probably). A bold claim indeed, but it is pretty darn good.

△E5 ⌂42-44 Shore St, Anstruther ⓦanstrutherfishbar.co.uk

£ £ £

Wee Bear Cafe

This cosy, cottage-like café on the shores of the Loch of Lintrathen, west of Kirriemuir, serves breakfast, lunch and baked goodies.

△D4 ⌂Bridgend of Lintrathen ⓦlodgeatlochside.co.uk

£ £ £

---

31 🚶 (NTS)

Falkland Palace

△D5 ⌂Falkland, Fife ☎Ladybank, then bus ⓣTimes vary, check website ⓦnts.org.uk

This Renaissance palace was originally designed as a hunting lodge for the Stuart kings. Begun by James IV in 1500, most of the work was carried out by his son, James V, in the 1530s. The palace fell into ruin during the years of the Commonwealth, occupied briefly by the infamous Rob Roy, Scotland's Robin Hood, in 1715. After buying the estates in 1887, the third Marquess of Bute became the Palace Keeper and restored the building. The richly panelled interiors are filled with superb furniture and colourful and contemporary portraits of the Stuart monarchs. The royal tennis court, built in 1539 for King James V, is the oldest in Britain.

No less impressive are the palace gardens, fashioned in the 1940s by the pre-eminent garden designer of the time, Percy Cane. They are home to extensive formal gardens, a physic garden with Renaissance-era herbal plants, and an ancient orchard with wildflower meadow.

32

East Neuk

△E5 ⌂Fife ☎Leuchars 🚌Glenrothes & Leuchars 🅸St Andrews; (01334) 472021 ⓦwelcometofife.com

A string of pretty fishing villages peppers the shoreline of the East Neuk of Fife from Earlsferry to Fife Ness. Much of Scotland's medieval trade with Europe passed through here, reflected in the towns' Flemish-inspired architecture. The herring industry has since declined, but the sea still dominates village life.

The harbour is the heart of charming St Monans, while Pittenweem is the base for the East Neuk fishing fleet. A church stands among the cobbled lanes and colourful cottages of Crail; the stone by its gate is said to have been hurled from the Isle of May by the Devil himself. Today the town is known for its beautiful pottery and ceramics.

Anstruther is home to the **Scottish Fisheries Museum**, with boats, cottage interiors, and displays. From here you can visit the nature reserve on the Isle of May.

A statue of Alexander Selkirk in Lower Largo recalls his seafaring adventures that

Having garnered much of its recent fame thanks to local superstar tennis player Andy Murray, Dunblane has much to commend it.

inspired Daniel Defoe's novel *Robinson Crusoe* (1719). After disagreeing with his captain, Selkirk was put ashore on a deserted island for four years.

Scottish Fisheries Museum

🎨 🖼 🍴 🛍 🏛 St Ayles, Harbour Head, Anstruther
🕐 10am–4:30pm daily
🌐 scotfishmuseum.org

33
Dunblane

🗺 D5 🌐 dunblane.info

Having garnered much of its recent fame thanks to local superstar tennis player Andy Murray, Dunblane has much to commend it. Dominating the small town is its magnificent 13th-century cathedral, sporting both Romanesque and Gothic elements. The interior is blessed with some exquisite detail, including stained-glass windows, beautifully carved pews and a raft of memorials. Across the way, inside 17th-century

Dean's House, is the engaging little Dunblane Museum, which exhibits one of Murray's signed racquets alongside his cap and jacket from the 2012 London Olympics. Of course, Murray's gold-medal winning achievement is commemorated by a gold-painted letterbox on the High Street.

34
Kirriemuir

🗺 D4

Known as the Gateway to the Glens, the sandstone town of Kirriemuir was the birthplace of Peter Pan author, J M Barrie. A tiny whitewashed cottage now serves as **J M Barrie's Birthplace** museum. It once housed the family's ten children, but today the few

small rooms here are filled with all kinds of Barrie memorabilia, including first editions and personal effects. There's more in the **Gateway to the Glens Museum** on the main square, which also pays tribute to Kirrie's second most famous son, Bon Scott, the one-time lead singer of AC/DC. The town is also home to a **Camera Obscura**, one of only three in Scotland. This one was donated by Barrie himself.

J.M. Barrie's Birthplace

🎨 🛍 🏛 NTS 🏛 9 Brechin Rd
🕐 Apr–mid-Oct: 11am–4pm
Fri–Mon 🌐 nts.org.uk

Gateway to the Glens Museum

🏛 32 High St 🕐 10am–5pm Tue–Sat

Camera Obscura

🎨 🏛 Kirrie Hill
🕐 Apr–mid-Oct: 11am–4pm
Sat–Mon 🌐 kirriemuir cameraobscura.com

Exterior of Falkland Palace and *(inset)* the ornate 14th-century Royal Chapel

35

Pitlochry

🅰D5 🅰Perthshire
🚉🚌 🅸22 Atholl Rd
🆆pitlochry.org

Surrounded by beautiful pine-forested hills, Pitlochry became famous after Queen Victoria called it one of the finest resorts in Europe. In early summer, wild salmon leap up the ladder at the Power Station Dam to spawn upriver. Above the ladder are fine views of Loch Faskally, popular with anglers. Walking trails from here link with the pretty gorge at Killiecrankie. **Blair Atholl Distillery** offers guided tours, while the **Festival Theatre** in Port-na-Craig has shows all year.

Some 13 km (8 miles) from Pitlochry are the Falls of Bruar. It was a visit to these picturesque falls in 1787 that inspired Robert Burns to pen "The Humble Petition of Bruar Water", and it's certainly true that this has been a hugely popular beauty spot ever since. A path, constructed by the Duke of Atholl back in the 18th century, wends its way from the car park at the House of Bruar to the falls themselves, around a mile and a half distant, from where there are spectacular views of its tumbling waters. It's a fairly steep and, when wet, slippery walk in places, so be prepared.

Blair Atholl Distillery

🚫🚫🏠 🅰Perth Rd
🕙10am–5pm daily
🆆malts.com

Festival Theatre

🚫🚫🚫 🅰Port-na-Craig
🕙Mid-May–Oct: daily for plays 🆆pitlochryfestivaltheatre.com

THE FISH LADDER

Following the construction of Pitlochry Dam across the River Tummel in 1951, it became necessary to create a means by which the salmon could bypass the dam on their way upstream. Hence the ingenious Fish Ladder was born, a 310-m- (980-ft-) long tunnel next to the Pitlochry Power Station, consisting of 34 pools, three of which are resting pools. An observation chamber at the base of the dam helps to explain it all, while a couple of viewing windows allow you to observe the fish close up.

36

Tay Forest Park

🅰D5 🅰Perthshire
🅸Queen's View Visitor Centre; (01796) 474188
🆆forestryandland.gov.scot

Encompassing an area of roughly 195 sq km (75 sq miles) across Highland Perthshire, Tay Forest Park is actually a network of seven woodland sites, each with their own designated trails. The best place to start is the Queen's View Visitor Centre at the east end of Loch Tummel, from where you can strike out towards Allean, site of a ruined Pictish ring fort, or Faskally on the shores of Loch Dunmore with its beautiful specimen trees. Head to

Drummond Hill, on Loch Tay itself, and you're quite likely to spot Capercaillie. More generally, the park lies at the heart of Scotland's so-called Big Tree Country – spend enough time here and you'll soon see why.

---

③⑦

Aberfeldy

🅰D5 🄰Perthshire

First made famous by Robert Burns in his poem "The Birks of Aberfeldy", and Scotland's first fairtrade town, bustling Aberfeldy merits an extended visit thanks to several attractions. Most popular is **Dewar's World of Whisky**, where you can join a tour of the distillery and visit the heritage museum before trying a few samples. West of town, the 16th-century **Castle Menzies**, former seat of the Menzies clan, is under going a lengthy programme of restoration but can still be

Did You Know?

Pitlochry is the furthest Scottish town from the sea.

visited. A mile or so up the road at **Highland Safaris**, you can learn about, and feed, red deer, but much more fun are the extended Land Rover safari trips up into the spectacular nearby mountains and around Loch Tay.

About 13 km (8 miles) southwest of Aberfeldy is the fascinating **Scottish Crannog Centre**, a reconstructed Iron Age Crannog (ancient loch dwelling). Soak up the atmosphere of the timber roundhouse and watch demonstrations of ancient crafts and cooking on a guided tour.

Dewar's World of Whisky
⊛🅧🄳🄰 🄲Apr-Oct: 10am-6pm Mon-Sat, noon-4pm Sun; Nov-Mar: 10am-4pm Mon-Sat 🕸dewars.com

Castle Menzies
🅧 🄲Apr-Oct: 10:30am-5pm Mon-Sat, 2-4pm Sun 🕸castlemenzies.org

Highland Safaris
⊛🅧🄳🄰 🄲Mar-Oct: 9am-5pm daily; Nov-Feb: 9am-5pm Tue-Sun 🕸highlandsafaris.net

Scottish Crannog Centre
⊛🅧 🄰Kenmore 🄲10am-5:30pm daily (advance booking required) 🕸crannog.co.uk

---

③⑧ 🅧 (NTS)

Meigle Sculptured Stone Museum

🅰D5 🄰Meigle 🚌Bus from Dundee 🄲Apr-Sep: 9:30am-5:30pm daily 🕸historicenvironment.scot

The tiny village of Meigle is home to one of western Europe's most important collections of early Christian

←

The main street, lined with restaurants, in the Victorian spa town of Pitlochry

↑ A Pictish cross-slab showing horsemen and centaurs, Meigle Museum

and pictish stones. The Picts were a loose confederation of tribes that came together to oppose the Romans. Reposed within the Meigle Sculptured Stone Museum are 26 carved stones dating from the 8th to 10th centuries, which were recovered from a nearby churchyard. Mostly grave markers or cross slabs, the carvings variously depict birds, animals or horsemen, though their exact meaning remains something of a mystery. The most impressive is Meigle 2, a 2.5-m- (8-ft-) high stone bearing reliefs of men on horseback, mythical animals and Daniel in the lions den.

> 🄰 GREAT VIEW
> ### Schiehallion Summit
>
> From a path starting at Braes of Foss, midway between Aberfeldy and Loch Rannoch, the broad ridge of Schiehallion is an undemanding hike compared to most munros, yet the summit views are among the best in the Highlands.

A DRIVING TOUR
ROYAL DEESIDE SCENIC TOUR

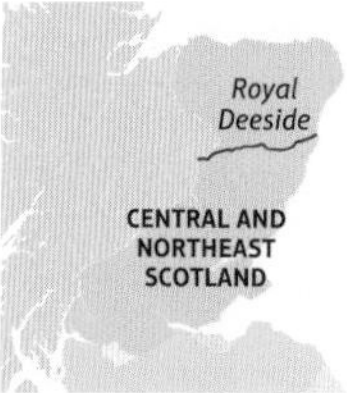

Distance 111 km (69 miles) **Stopping-off points** Crathes Castle café (open May–Sep: 10:30am–4pm). The castle grounds are home to a GoApe treetop adventure course.

Since Queen Victoria's purchase of the Balmoral Estate in 1852, Deeside has been best known as the summer home of the British Royal Family, though it has been associated with royalty since the time of Robert the Bruce in the 1300s. This route follows the Dee, one of the world's most prolific salmon rivers, through some magnificent Grampian scenery.

Locator Map
For more detail see p160

Royal Deeside

CENTRAL AND NORTHEAST SCOTLAND

*An information centre on the A97 provides an excellent place from which to explore the **Muir of Dinnet Nature Reserve**, a beautiful mixed woodland area, formed by the retreating glaciers of the last Ice Age.*

Balmoral Castle (p184) *was bought by Queen Victoria for 30,000 guineas in 1852, after its owner choked to death on a fishbone. The castle was rebuilt in the Scottish Baronial style at Prince Albert's request.*

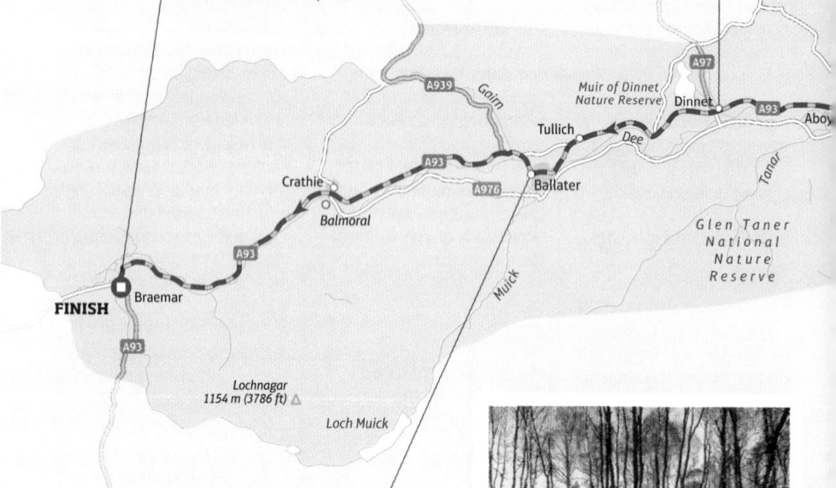

A939

Goirn

Muir of Dinnet Nature Reserve Dinnet A93 Aboy

A97

Tullich *Dee*

Crathie A93

A976 Ballater

Balmoral *Tanar*

A93

Muick *Glen Taner National Nature Reserve*

FINISH Braemar

A93

Lochnagar 1154 m (3786 ft) △

Loch Muick

*The old railway town of **Ballater** has royal warrants on many of its shop fronts. It grew as a 19th-century spa town, its waters reputedly providing a cure for tuberculosis.*

↑ Tranquil waters at the Muir of Dinnet Nature Reserve

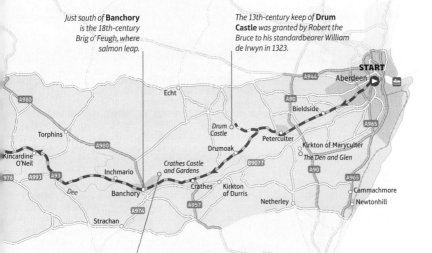

Autumn leaves add a splash of colour to the forest surrounding the Brig O'Feugh, just south of Banchory ←

*Just south of **Banchory** is the 18th-century Brig o' Feugh, where salmon leap.*

*The 13th-century keep of **Drum Castle** was granted by Robert the Bruce to his standardbearer William de Irwyn in 1323.*

START
Aberdeen ▶

A944

Echt

A90

Bieldside

A965

Drum Castle

Peterculter

Torphins

A980

Kirkton of Maryculter

The Den and Glen

Kincardine O'Neil

Drumoak

B9077

A90

976

A993 A93

Inchmario

Crathes Castle and Gardens

Dee

Banchory

Crathes

Kirkton of Durris

A957

A965

Cammachmore

Netherley

Newtonhill

Strachan

A974

Crathes Castle is the family home of the Burnetts, who were made Royal Foresters of Drum by Robert the Bruce. Along with the title, he gave Alexander Burnett the ivory Horn of Leys, which is still on display here.

0 kilometres   6
0 miles   6

N ↑

↑ Crathes Castle and Gardens, owned by the National Trust for Scotland

THE HIGHLANDS AND ISLANDS

Most of the stock images of Scottishness – clans and tartans, whisky and porridge, bagpipes and heather – originate in the Highlands, and enrich the popular picture of Scotland as a whole. But for many centuries the Gaelic-speaking, cattle-raising Highlanders had little in common with their southern neighbours. Clues to the non-Celtic ancestors of the Highlanders lie scattered across the Highlands and islands in the form of stone circles, brochs and cairns spanning over 5,000 years. By the end of the 6th century, the Gaelic-speaking Celts had arrived from Ireland.

For over 1,000 years, Celtic Highland society thrived under a clan system built on family ties to create loyal groups dependent on a feudal chief. However, the clans were systematically broken up by England after 1746, following the defeat of the Jacobite attempt on the British crown at the Battle of Culloden led by Bonnie Prince Charlie.

A more romantic vision of the Highlands began to emerge in the early 19th century, thanks largely to Sir Walter Scott's novels and poetry depicting the majesty and grandeur of a country previously dismissed as merely poverty-stricken and barbaric. Another great popularizer was Queen Victoria, whose passion for Balmoral Castle helped establish the trend for acquiring Highland sporting estates. But behind the sentimentality lay harsh economic realities that drove generations of Highland farmers and their families away from their homes. Some went willingly in search of a new life in America, Canada and Australia, others were forcibly removed by wealthy landowners to make way for livestock.

CAPE WRATH AND THE NORTH COAST **47**
Faraid Head
Durness
Heilam
Kinlochbervie
HANDA ISLAND **49**
Scourie
Achfary
Drumbeg
Kylesku
Tongue
Ben Hope 927 m (3,041 ft)
Altnaharra
Lochinver
Ben More Assynt 998 m (3,274 ft)
Shinness
Reiff
Elphin
Lairg
Drumrunie
Strathcanaird
FALLS OF SHIN **46**
Port of Ness
Lewis
Barvas
North Tolsta
Shawbost
Carloway
Stornoway
Portnaguran
Timsgarry
Arivruaich
Flannan Isles
Hushinish
Lemreway
Harris
Ardhasaig
OUTER HEBRIDES **8**
Scarastavore
St Kilda 60 km (38 miles)
Tigharry
North Uist
Lochmaddy
Clachan-a-Luib
Creagorry
Benbecula
Stilligarry
South Uist
Daliburgh
Lochboisdale
Kilbride
Eriskay
Barra

INVEREWE GARDEN **44**
ULLAPOOL **45**
Beinn Dearg 1,084 m (3,556 ft)
GAIRLOCH **39**
Red Point
WESTER ROSS **43**
Ben Wyvis 1,045 m (3,428 ft)
STRATHPEFFER **35**
Kilmaluag
Talladale
Achnasheen
Muir of Ord
Staffin
Kinlochewe
Uig
Lusta
Shieldaig
Sgurr Na Lapaich 1,150 m (3,773 ft)
Kensalleyre
Balnacra
SKYE **5**
Portree
Applecross
Lochcarron
APPLECROSS PENINSULA **41**
Stromeferry
Drumnadrochit
Bracadale
Plockton
Carn Eige 1,182 m (3,878 ft)
Peinchorran
Broadford
LOCH NESS **4**
Sea of the Hebrides
Drumfearn
Glenelg
Elgol
Kinloch Hourn
THE GREAT GLEN **4**
Teangue
Armadale
Inverie
GLEN SHIEL **42**
Invergarry
CANNA
MALLAIG **15**
RUM **16**
KNOYDART PENINSULA **40**
GLENFINNAN **29**
Clunes
Moy
MUCK
EIGG
Lochailort
Kinlocheil
FORT WILLIAM **28**
BEN NEVIS **1**
ARDNAMURCHAN PENINSULA **23**
Ardtoe
Strontian
GLENCOE **26**
COLL **22**
Sorisdale
Glenbeg
Tobermory
Portnacroish
TIREE **22**
Caolas
Calgary
Dervaig
Bridge of Orchy
Scarinish
MULL **17**
Benderloch
Tyndrum
IONA **18**
Croggan
OBAN **21**
Fionnphort
Bunessan
Kilchrenan
Dalmally
Clachan
LOCH AWE **19**
INVERARAY CASTLE **9**
AUCHINDRAIN TOWNSHIP **10**
Lochgoilhead
CRARAE GARDENS **11**
Strachur
Kiloran
Ardentinny
Garvard
Tayvallich
Buchlyv
Tighnabruaich
Colintraive
Balloc
JURA **13**
Sound of Jura
Glasgow Airport
Sanaigmore
Tarbert
Rothesay
Glasgo
Port Askaig
Kilberry
Kennacraig
Barrhead
Bridgend
ISLAY **12**
Kilmory
BUTE **25**
Bowmore
Claonaig
GIGHA **14**
Port Ellen
Ardbeg
Tayinloan
Pirnmill
Muasdale
Kilchenzie
ARRAN **24**
KINTYRE **20**
SOUTHERN SCOTLAND
p108

The Minch

The Minch

Atlantic Ocean

THE HIGHLANDS AND ISLANDS

Northern Isles

THE HIGHLANDS AND ISLANDS

Must Sees

1. Ben Nevis
2. Cairngorms National Park
3. Inverness
4. Loch Ness and the Great Glen
5. Skye
6. Orkney Islands
7. Shetland Islands
8. Outer Hebrides

Experience More

9. Inveraray Castle
10. Auchindrain Township
11. Crarae Gardens
12. Islay
13. Jura
14. Gigha
15. Mallaig
16. Rum, Eigg, Muck and Canna
17. Mull
18. Iona
19. Loch Awe
20. Kintyre
21. Oban
22. Coll and Tiree
23. Ardnamurchan Peninsula
24. Arran
25. Bute
26. Glencoe
27. Rannoch Moor
28. Fort William
29. Glenfinnan
30. Blair Atholl
31. Black Isle
32. Moray Firth
33. Fort George
34. Culloden
35. Strathpeffer
36. Cawdor Castle
37. Dornoch
38. Helmsdale
39. Gairloch
40. Knoydart Peninsula
41. Applecross Peninsula
42. Glen Shiel
43. Wester Ross
44. Inverewe Garden
45. Ullapool
46. Falls of Shin
47. Cape Wrath and the North Coast
48. Dunnet Head
49. Handa Island

Fast and Furious Highland Sport

Camanachd (shinty), the fast and fearsome sport of the Highlands, plays out much like a ferocious clan battle. Players raise their sticks to hit the ball in the air and physical contact is allowed. Men's and Women's finals for the Camanachd and Valerie Fraser cups take place in September. Check www. shinty.com for local fixtures.

$\rightarrow$

Players engaged in the traditional Highland sport of Camanachd, or shinty

HIGHLAND
TRADITIONS AND CULTURE

After the Battle of Culloden in 1746, the British government set out to destroy Highland culture. Some say this only strengthened Highlanders' resolve to celebrate their heritage, which continues to this day in the form of clan gatherings, spectacular sporting tournaments, and Highland Games.

Traditional Highland Games

Kilted muscle-men (and women) are a high point of any Highland Games, where athletes toss mighty cabers, hurl massive hammers and throw mammoth weights. Over 80 events take place in villages, castle grounds and Highland estates across the country every weekend from May to September.

$\leftarrow$

Competitor in a Highland Games hammer-tossing competition

Royal Edinburgh Military Tattoo

After the defeat of the Jacobites, clans who fought for Bonnie Prince Charlie (p64) were recruited to fight for King George. The Black Watch is the oldest of these kilted regiments, which in 2006 were merged to create the Royal Regiment of Scotland. They can be seen (and heard) in their full tartan glory at the Edinburgh Military Tattoo, which is held at Edinburgh Castle during the month of August.

←

Soldiers from the 5th Battalion of the Royal Regiment of Scotland

BEHIND THE KILT

In the 16th century, the kilt was a full-length garment, with the upper half worn as a cloak. An elaborate code lays down who can wear what tartan. Most clans have at least two tartans – a bold pattern for formal dress and a second more muted version for everyday wear. Up to 20 new tartans are created every year and kilts in stripes or polka dots, accessorized with fake-fur sporrans in rainbow colours, are a fun alternative to the traditional plaid.

INSIDER TIP
The Royal National Mòd

Listen to traditional pipe and clarsach (harp) music and melancholy Gaelic song and verse at the Royal National Mòd, which is held in a different location in the Scottish Highlands every year.

Braemar Gathering, Ballater

Held annually in Ballater, the Braemar Gathering hosts one of the most prestigious and renowned Highland clan gatherings in the country. Thousands attend to enjoy the spectacle. Watch Highland dancers compete for style points as hundreds of pipers and drummers march in unison, and sample all manner of traditional Scottish food and drink.

→

Kilted dancers perform a traditional Highland Fling at a Highland Gathering

CLANS AND TARTANS

As far back as the 12th century Highland society was organized into various clans. The word is derived from the Gaelic term *clann* meaning offspring. This clan system divided communities into tribal groups led by autocratic chiefs, known as clan chiefs or chieftains. All members of the clan bore the name of their chief, but not all were related by blood. Nonetheless loyalty to the clan chief was of utmost importance. Though they had noble codes of hospitality, the clansmen also had to be fierce warriors to protect their land and herds. Each clan had its own territory, motto and distinct tartan – traditions that are continued to this day.

HIDDEN GEM
Lochcarron

Tartan lovers should take a tour of the mill and learn all about tartan production at the Lochcarron Visitor Centre in Selkirk *(loch carron.co.uk)*. The on-site shop stocks clothes and accessories in over 700 different tartan designs, and there's a great café here too.

A BAN ON TARTAN

After the Battle of Culloden *(p64)*, all the clan lands were forfeited to the British Crown, and the wearing of tartan – seen as a rejection of British rule – was banned for nearly 100 years. The Black Watch, raised in 1729 to keep peace in the Highlands, was one of the Highland regiments in which the wearing of tartan survived. After 1746, civilians could be punished by exile for up to seven years for wearing tartan.

HIGHLAND CLANS TODAY

Once the daily dress of the clansmen, the kilt continues to be a symbol of national pride. The one-piece *feileadh-mòr* has been replaced by the *feileadh-beag*, or "small plaid", made from approximately 7 m (23 ft) of material with a double apron fastened at the front with a silver pin. Though they exist now only in name, the clans are still a strong source of pride for Scots, and many still live in areas traditionally belonging to their clans. The wearing of one's clan tartan is customary at formal events such as weddings and ceilidhs.

↑ Lithograph of a member of the Clan Buchanan wearing his clan tartan

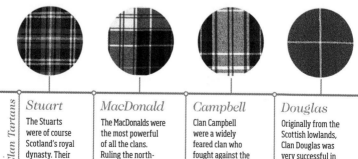

Clan Tartans

Stuart	MacDonald	Campbell	Douglas
The Stuarts were of course Scotland's royal dynasty. Their clan motto was "no one harms me with impunity".	The MacDonalds were the most powerful of all the clans. Ruling the north-west islands, they held the title of Lords of the Isles.	Clan Campbell were a widely feared clan who fought against the Jacobites in the Battle of Culloden in 1746.	Originally from the Scottish lowlands, Clan Douglas was very successful in Scotland and beyond, with territories in France and Sweden.

↑ Tartan production on a loom at Lochcarron, the world's leading manufacturer of tartan

TRACING GENEALOGY

From the time of the infamous Highland Clearances of the 18th century onwards, Scots have emigrated to Australia, Canada, New Zealand, South Africa, the US and elsewhere in search of an easier life. There are now millions of foreign nationals who can trace their heritage back to Scotland, and uncovering family history is a popular reason for visiting the country. Professional genealogists can be commissioned, but those interested in conducting investigations themselves should try the General Register House *(nrscotland.gov.uk)* which has records of births, deaths and marriages dating from the 1500s, or the Scottish Genealogy Society *(scotsgenealogy.com)*, both of which are in Edinburgh.

PLANT BADGES

Each clan has a plant associated with its territory. It was worn on the bonnet, especially on the day of battle.

Scots pine was worn by the MacGregors of Argyll.

Rowan berries were worn by the Clan Malcolm.

Ivy was worn by the Clan Gordon of Aberdeenshire.

Spear thistle, now the national symbol of Scotland, was the badge of the Stuarts.

Cotton grass was worn by the Clan Henderson.

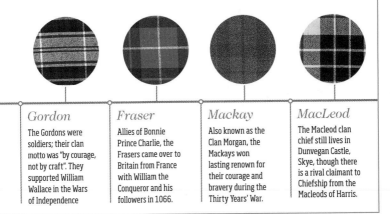

Gordon
The Gordons were soldiers; their clan motto was "by courage, not by craft". They supported William Wallace in the Wars of Independence

Fraser
Allies of Bonnie Prince Charlie, the Frasers came over to Britain from France with William the Conqueror and his followers in 1066.

Mackay
Also known as the Clan Morgan, the Mackays won lasting renown for their courage and bravery during the Thirty Years' War.

MacLeod
The Macleod clan chief still lives in Dunvegan Castle, Skye, though there is a rival claimant to Chiefship from the Macleods of Harris.

Snow-capped Ben Nevis reflecting on the calm surface of Loch Linnhe ↑

❶

BEN NEVIS

🅐C4 🅐Lochaber 🚆Fort William 🚌Glen Nevis 🄸Glen Nevis Visitor Centre, Fort William; open summer: 8:30am-6pm daily; spring and autumn: 9am-5pm daily; winter: 9am-2:30pm daily

In a land where spectacular mountains and mist-shrouded peaks abound, Ben Nevis reigns king. Standing at a whopping 1,345 m (4,413 ft), Britain's highest peak offers walking routes to suit all abilities, and the breathtaking views from the summit reward hikers handsomely for their efforts.

With its summit in cloud for about nine days out of ten, and capable of developing blizzard conditions at any time of the year, Ben Nevis is a mishmash of metamorphic and volcanic rocks. The sheer northeastern face poses a technical challenge to experienced rock climbers, while thousands of visitors each year make their way to the peak via the western trail known as the Old Bridle Path. This can be joined from the visitor centre, Achintee House, or 400 m (440 yds) beyond the campsite.

←

Dappled sunlight on the verdant slopes of Glen Nevis, near Fort William

→
Hikers walking through
Glen Nevis towards the
summit of Ben Nevis

On rare fine days, visitors who make their way to the summit will be rewarded with breathtaking views. On a cloudy day, a walk through Glen Nevis may be more rewarding than making an ascent, which will reveal little more at the summit than a ruined observatory and memorials testifying to the tragic deaths of walkers and climbers. For a more leisurely pace, head to the Nevis Range Gondola in Torlundy just north of Ben Nevis, which climbs 650 m (2,130 ft) to the mountain ski centre and restaurant on the north face of Aonach Mor.

Climbing Ben Nevis

In Gaelic *Beínn Níbheís* means "the terrible mountain", but don't be put off. Almost anyone can add Ben Nevis to their list of exploits. In 2019, three-year-old Jaxon Krzysik became the youngest person to reach the summit, and the oldest was reportedly 82.

The main footpath is relatively gentle, but the nine-hour walk to the summit and back is no easy stroll. Weather quickly changes from fine to foul (check www.bennevisweather.co. uk). Walking boots and warm, weatherproof outerwear are essential. Bring plenty of food and water, a compass and a map as mobile reception is patchy.

> In Gaelic *Beínn Níbheís* means "the terrible mountain", but don't be put off. Almost anyone can add Ben Nevis to their list of exploits.

THE BEN NEVIS RACE

Held on the first Saturday in September, the Ben Nevis Race brings a whole new energy to Glen Nevis, as experienced hill runners and adrenaline junkies prepare to conquer this formidable mountain. The first event was run by local barber William Swan in 1865. The current record for men was set in 1984 by Kenny Stuart in a time of 1hr 25mins 34 seconds, while the fastest woman is Victoria Wilkinson, who in 2018 set a record of 1hr 43mins 1 second.

CAIRNGORMS NATIONAL PARK

🗺️D4 **🏠The Highlands** **🚌🚆Aviemore** **ℹ️7 The Parade, Grampian Rd, Aviemore; (01479) 810930** **🌐visitcairngorms.com**

There is no better place in Scotland to get away from it all than this rolling, near-Arctic massif of moors and lochs dotted with mountain peaks. This vast wilderness, home to reindeer, red deer, golden eagles and mountain hare, is within easy reach of Scotland's major cities. The Cairngorm plateau is dominated by Ben Macdhui which, at 1,309 m (4,296 ft), is Britain's second-highest mountain and can be ascended from both Speyside and Deeside. However, the brooding peak of Lochnagar, with its magnificent northern corrie, is perhaps the most coveted munro of the lot. It was immortalized in verse by Lord Byron, who lauded its wild crags and the "steep frowning glories of dark Lochnagar".

① Aviemore

🚌🚆 **🌐visitaviemore.com**

The lively little town of Aviemore is the gateway to the Cairngorms, thronged with visitors throughout the year. During summer, it's packed with hikers, climbers and mountain bikers heading for the surrounding hills, then during winter it's taken over by skiiers out to enjoy the nearby slopes. As a result, there's a plentiful supply of hotels, restaurants and cafés, and outdoors shops along the main street stretching away from the train station. The extensive grounds of the nearby **Rothiemurchus Estate** afford the possibility to participate in various outdoor activities, from cycling and walking to kayaking and fishing.

Rothiemurcus Centre

🚲🏇🚣☕ **🏠Rothiemurcus** **🕐Times vary, see website** **🌐rothiemurcus.net**

② Glenmore Forest Park

🏠Glenmore, Aviemore **🌐forestryandland.gov. scot**

One of Scotland's six forest parks, Glenmore lies at the foot of the Cairngorms and sits within the National Park's boundary. It is renowned for its magnificent Caledonian pinewoods that fringe beautiful Loch Morlich, which itself is situated in the very heart of the park. A walk around the loch should take about two hours; it comes as something of a surprise to discover a sandy little beach here. Otherwise, the park offers dozens of forest paths and biking trails, and in winter, cross-country skiing becomes the main activity. Several trails fan out from the Glenmore Forest Park Visitor Centre, the

← Serene waters at Loch Morlich and snowcapped peaks of the Cairngorms

for being something of a mecca for both summer and winter climbers. Just five miles south of the River Dee on the Balmoral estate, the magnificent mountain looms high above one of Scotland's most beautiful corries. There are a couple of routes to the summit, the most popular of which begins at the Balmoral Visitor Centre *(p184)*, passing picturesque Meikle Pap on the way. Be warned – if you are hillwalking in the area when there is snow underfoot, an ice axe and crampons are essential, as is experience of this type of terrain.

④ ⓜ 🛍 🖥

Cairngorm Ski Area

🏠 Ski Area, Cairngorm 🚌 🌐 cairngormmountain. co.uk

A short drive southeast of Aviemore, also reachable by a regular bus service, the Cairngorm ski area is

best of which is the trek up to Meall a'Bhuachallie, meaning "Hill of the Shepherd", from which there are great views of the Cairngorm Plateau.

③

Lochnagar

One of the Cairngorms' highest and most popular mountains, Lochnagar (1155m/3789 ft) is renowned

the country's largest snowsports resort, popular with both beginners and experts alike. But even if you're not here to ski, the area offers some terrific walks around the high mountain plateau; if you don't fancy going it alone, between May and October there are guided walks every Thursday up to the summit which begin at the Ranger's Base next to the Coire Cas car park. The base also houses an exhibition on the Cairngorms, shedding light on its history, flora and fauna and other aspects of the mountain.

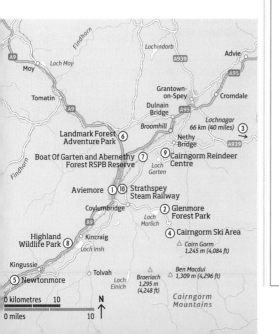

↑ Historical buildings at the open-air Highland Folk Museum, Newtonmore

⑤ 🐾

Newtonmore

🏠 Wildcat Centre; Main St
🌐 wildcatcentre.org

The little town of Newtonmore is known for its all-conquering shinty team, with its biggest rivals, Kingussie, just a few miles down the road. It has also become popular – among families in particular – for its Wildcat Experience, whereby visitors can track down over 130 colourfully painted wildcat models which are dotted around town and on the scenic trails beyond; a trackpack can be obtained from the **Wildcat Centre**. On the edge of town lies the **Highland Folk Museum**, a large open-air museum containing a fine assemblage of historical buildings, many of which have been moved from their original location; among them is an Inverness school dating from 1925, a blackhouse from Lewis, and a rural post office and store

Did You Know?

The Cairngorms is home to Scotland's two highest villages: Tomintoul and Dalwhinnie.

complete with sweet shop – actors in period costume help bring the whole experience to life. Allow a good couple of hours to enjoy the museum.

Wildcat Centre
🎯 🏠 Main St
🌐 wildcatcentre.org

Highland Folk Museum
🍴🅿️ 🏠 Kingussie Rd
🕐 Daily (Apr–Aug: 10:30am–5:30pm; Sep & Oct: 11am–4:30pm) 🌐 highlandlife.com

---

⑥ 🎿 💻 🏛

Landmark Forest Adventure Park

🏠 Carrbridge 🕐 10am–6pm daily 🌐 landmarkpark.co.uk

Great fun for both kids and adults, the Landmark Forest Adventure Park in Carrbridge comprises all manner of family friendly indoor and outdoor activities, from treetop trails and climbing walls to a Lost Labyrinth maze and a handful of theme park style rides. There are more sedate attractions too, such as a tropical hot house with multiple species of butterfly, and Bamboozeleum, an indoor gallery of magic and illusions. The most recent addition is Dinosaur Kingdom, a collection of 20 life-size models complete with moving parts and scary sound effects.

TOP 4 WALKS IN THE CAIRNGORMS

Loch Brandy
An easy half-day walk from Clova village to a mirror-calm loch.

Glen Doll
A two- to three-hour stroll on a well-surfaced path from Glen Doll to Corrie Fee, a dramatic natural amphitheatre.

Lairig Ghru
This age-old mountain trail runs from Speywaide to Deeside and climbs to 835 m (2,740 ft). A tough but rewarding full-day hike with amazing views.

Jock's Road
This iconic long-distance trail traverses three Munro summits. Allow a full day to complete the walk.

---

⑦

Boat of Garten

🚂 🌐 boatofgarten.com

Boat of Garten is a quaint little village lying on the fringes of the National Park adjacent to the River Spey. It's also, rather romantically, known as the Osprey village, on account of the large number of ospreys that nest here. The best place to get a close up view of these magnificent birds is at the nearby **Abernethy Forest RSPB Reserve**, a couple of miles east of the village on the shores of Loch Garten. Here, an observation centre has telescopes and live CCTV footage of the nest. The area is also home to a wealth of other birds and wildlife species.

Abernethy Forest RSPB Reserve
🎯 🕐 Reserve: daily; visitor centre: Apr–Aug 10am–5:30pm daily 🌐 rspb.org.uk

> **The brooding peak of Lochnagar, with its magnificent northern corrie, is perhaps the most coveted munro of the lot.**

⑧

Highland Wildlife Park

📍 Kincraig, Kingussie
🕐 Daily (Jul-Aug: 10am-6pm; Apr-Jun, Sep & Oct: 10am-5pm; Nov-Mar: 10am-4pm) 🌐 highland wildlifepark.org.uk

Part of the Royal Zoological Society of Scotland, the Highland Wildlife Park is a cut above your average zoo, with spacious enclosures and a collection of animals rarely seen elsewhere in the UK. The park's most famous residents are four polar bears, one of which (Hamish) was the first polar bear to be born in the UK in 25 years in 2018. Other species present are snow leopards, including two cubs born here in 2019, arctic foxes, red pandas and the native wildcat. The park has a strong focus on conservation and education. There's also a drive through safari, where elk, bison and the critically endangered Przewalski's horses roam free, while an area of enclosed woods is home to wolves and Bukhara deer. If you don't have your own car, guides are on hand to drive you around.

⑨

Cairngorm Reindeer Centre

📍 Glenmore 🕐 10am-5pm daily 🌐 cairngorm reindeer.co.uk

The ever popular Cairngorm Reindeer Centre is home to Britain's only herd of wild reindeer, the first of which were reintroduced to the Cairngorms in 1952; there are currently around 150 of these iconic animals here. To get the most out of a visit, venture out on one of the excellent guided hill trips, which entails a combined hike and drive up to the mountain where you can walk among, and feed, the herd. If time is limited, you can content yourself with a quick visit to see the deer in the paddock by the visitor centre.

⑩

Strathspey Steam Railway

📍 Aviemore to Boat of Garten 🚆 🕐 Departure times vary, see website for timetable 🌐 strathspey railway.co.uk

Aviemore is the departure point for the marvellous Strathspey Steam Railway. Originally part of the Inverness and Perth Junction Railway, the line opened in 1863, only to then be axed in the 1960s. Following a long, painstaking restoration project, the service was finally restored between Aviemore and Boat of Garten in 1978, then extended to Broomhill, which is where the train puffs its way to today. It's a delightful 90-minute round trip with some gorgeous scenery to savour along the way – make sure to nab a window seat and sit on the right-hand side leaving from Aviemore. For a little extra you can travel first class, and there's also the possibility to enjoy a delicious afternoon tea on board the train.

↑ Locomotive 848 puffing its way along the Strathspey Steam Railway to Broomhill

SCOTLAND'S MOUNTAINS

Scotland's hills vary from the heathery domes of the Southern Uplands to the craggy eminences in the far west. Narrow ridges such as Glencoe's Aonach Eagach and the Cuillins of Skye are a particular challenge. Most hills can be climbed in a day, but some may require an overnight camp, or a stay in a simple hut known as a "bothy". Winter mountaineering needs extra skills but it also offers the most breathtaking scenery.

INSIDER TIP
Weather Watch

Weather changes in an instant, particularly in the highlands. Always check ahead (www.metoffice.gov.uk) before heading for the hills.

ROCK AND ICE CLIMBING

Rock and ice climbing in Scotland has a distinguished history stretching back over a century. The main climbing areas, such as Glencoe, the Cairngorms and Skye, have proved tough training grounds for many climbers who have gained world-renown. All year the northern faces of Ben Nevis offer a multitude of climbs at all levels. New areas, including the far northwest and the islands, have been developed more recently, as have disciplines such as sea-stack climbing. Scotland's wild winter weather produces ice climbs that are among the most serious and demanding in the world. The only "closed season" on Scotland's mountains is the period from July until late October, when restrictions apply in certain rural areas during the stag-shooting season.

↑ Rock climber scaling an advanced route in Skye's Cuillin mountains

MUNROS, CORBETTS, GRAHAMS AND MORE

Scotland's mountains are categorized according to their height. Hills rising just above 914 m (3,000 ft) are called "Munros" after Sir Hugh Munro, first president of the Scottish Mountaineering Club (SMC). In 1891 Munro published the first list of mountains fulfilling this criterion. The list has been maintained by the SMC ever since, and the hills' principal summits are now officially classed as Munros, while lesser summits are called "Tops". The list now totals 282 hills and dedicated Munroists known as "Munro baggers" strive to tick them all off in their lifetime.

In the 1920s, J Rooke Corbett published a list of the 222 summits that measured 760-915 m (2,500-3,000 ft), and they became known as "Corbetts". A third list exists of summits of 610-760 m (2,000-2,500 ft) called "Grahams". The most recent additions are "Donalds" - lowland hills 600 m (2000 ft) or over with prominence of 30 m (100 ft) or more - and "Marylins" - any hill with a drop of 150 m (492 ft) on all sides.

SKIING AND SNOWBOARDING

There are five main ski centres in Scotland: Glencoe, Nevis Range, The Lecht, Cairngorm and Glenshee. The Lecht tends to have the gentlest runs; Glencoe has the steepest.

↑ Glenshee Ski Centre offers skiing and snowboarding facilities

Nevis Range, Glenshee and Cairngorm offer good facilities and runs for all abilities as well as nursery slopes for those starting out. Ski centres are usually open from December to April, depending on the amount of snow cover. Most hotels and guesthouses in ski areas offer weekend and midweek packages, and there are ski schools in all the areas. Crosscountry or Nordic skiing is also becoming increasingly popular. As long as there is good snow cover, there are many suitable areas from the Southern Uplands to the hills of the north and west, as well as hundreds of miles of forest trails all over the country.

↑ Hikers walking the trail through Glen Nevis to the lofty summit of Ben Nevis

SAFETY IN THE MOUNTAINS

The mountains of Scotland demand respect at any time of the year, and this means being properly prepared. You should always take with you full waterproofs, warm clothes and food and drink. Take a map and compass and know how to use them. Good boots are essential. Winter mountaineering demands knowledge of ice-axe and crampon techniques and is not recommended for inexperienced climbers. Scotland has a well organized network of voluntary mountain rescue teams. Calls for rescue should be made to the police on 999. Glenmore Lodge in Aviemore *(p212)* offers courses in skiing, hill craft and mountaineering.

③

INVERNESS

🅐D3 🏛**Inverness-shire** 🚌🚆 **ℹ36 High St**
🌐**visitinvernesslochness.com**

In the Highlands, all roads lead to Inverness, the region's "capital". Despite being the largest city in the north, the atmosphere is more townlike, with a compact and easily accessible centre, where cultural and natural heritage await, including the bountiful River Ness.

① 🎨

Inverness Castle

🏛**Wynd St** 🕐**Apr-Oct:
daily; Nov-Mar: Fri-Mon**
🌐**highlifehighland.com**

Perched upon high ground above the city, the red sandstone castle that you see today is a late-19th-century structure, which belies the fact that a fortress has stood here since the 11th century. Robert the Bruce destroyed

> 🔍 HIDDEN GEM
> **Victorian Market**
>
> This beautiful indoor arcade is a blast from Inverness' Victorian past. Shops sell all manner of cute and curious trinkets, while quaint tearooms offer up sweet treats.

the first one during the Wars of independence, before a succession of sieges gradually saw to the rest of it. Although most of the heavily castellated castle is no longer open to the public – it now functions as the Inverness sheriff court – one of the towers has opened up as a viewing point offering unrivalled views of the city, and it's also possible to wander around the grounds.

② 🖥

Inverness Museum and Art Gallery

🏛**Castle Wynd** 🕐**Apr-Oct:
Tue-Sat; Nov-Mar: Thu-Sat**
🌐**highlifehighland.com**

Below the castle, the newly refurbished town museum and gallery offers a comprehensive trawl through the history of the Highlands, with a particular emphasis on

the Vikings and Jacobites, although there is also an excellent assemblage of Pictish stones here, dating from as early as the Iron Age. One of the museum's more peculiar attractions is a stuffed puma, named "Felicity", who was captured in Inverness in 1980 before being placed in a local zoo. The art gallery, meanwhile, is almost exclusively devoted to temporary exhibitions.

③ 🎨 🛍

Scottish Kiltmaker Visitor Centre

🏛**4-9 Huntly St** 🕐**9am-
6pm daily** 🌐**highland
houseoffraser.com**

This imaginative centre offers an intriguing insight into the history, culture and tradition of the kilt, with audio-visual, costume and tartan displays. After viewing the exhibition, head through to the work-shop to watch the highly skilled kiltmakers at work, from those who cut the cloth to those who pleat and stitch.

You'll probably want to visit the shop too. Here, you can peruse all manner of tartan goodies – indeed, you'll do well not to leave without purchasing some item of knitwear, even if you aren't brave enough to don a kilt just yet.

Clearances. The first stretch opened in 1822. Popular with paddle steamers in the 1930s, today it is used for both commerce and leisure, with a regular stream of cruise boats competing for space with oceangoing yachts, fishing boats and the occasional naval vessel along this most picturesque of waterways. For the best view of the bustle of the canal, make for Tomnahurich Swing Bridge.

↑ Inverness city centre, located on the banks of the River Ness

④ Ness Islands

A group of small, elongated islands in the middle of the Ness River, the Ness Islands have been a popular strolling spot for locals and visitors alike since the first suspension bridges were built in the late 19th century. Aside from walking among the mature Scots pines, beech and fir, the main attraction here is a miniature railway, which runs at weekends between Easter and October.

④ Caledonian Canal

Connecting Scotland's west coast at Inverness with the east coast at Corpach, near Fort William, the 97-km- (60-mile-) long Caledonian Canal was designed by the Scottish civil engineer Thomas Telford in the early 19th century, in order to help create employment at the time of the Highland

All year round, however, you'll have the opportunity to spy some of the islands' surprisingly abundant wildlife. Look out for deer hiding among the trees, otters frolicking in the water and the occasional bat wheeling in the sky at dusk.

EAT

Cafe 1
Stylish bistro offering innovative dishes, such as tempura monkfish with black pudding and pea puree.

⌂ 75 Castle St
Ⓦ cafe1.net

£ £ £

Mustard Seed
Located in a converted church, Mustard Seed serves exciting modern Scottish food.

⌂ 16 Fraser St
Ⓦ mustardseed restaurant.co.uk

£ £ £

DRINK

Hootananny's
Enjoy live music here, including ceilidh sessions on Saturday afternoons.

⌂ 67 Church St
Ⓦ hootanannys inverness.co.uk.

The Malt Bar
As the name suggests, this is the place to head for whisky.

⌂ 34 Church St
Ⓦ themaltroom.co.uk

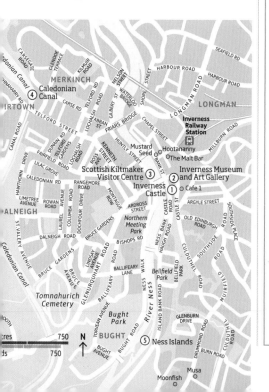

Did You Know?

Visitor interest in Nessie reportedly contributes £40 million a year to Scotland's economy.

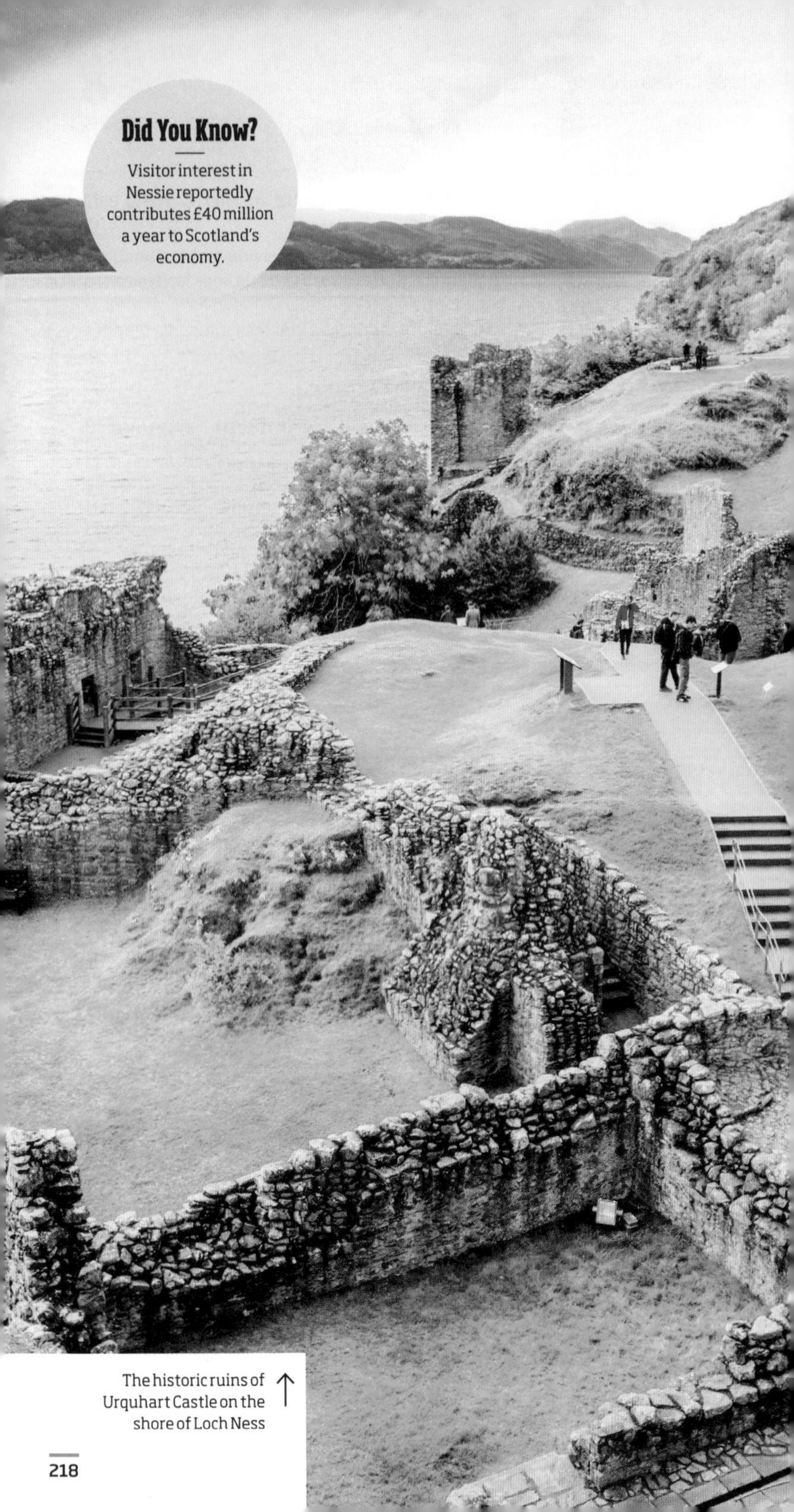

The historic ruins of Urquhart Castle on the shore of Loch Ness ↑

❹

LOCH NESS AND THE GREAT GLEN

🅐C4 🅷The Highlands ✈️Inverness 🚌🚂Inverness, Fort William
ℹ️36 High St, Inverness; (01463) 252401 🆆visitinvernesslochness.com

Centuries ago, the Great Glen was born of a geological rift that split Scotland from coast to coast. Glaciers deepened the trench and the result today is a long valley of steep-sided mountains and deep, dark, lochs. Castles and forts abound, reminding us of the area's strategic importance and evoking a sense of nostalgia and intrigue. Most intriguing of all, however, is the legendary monster that inhabits the watery depths of Loch Ness – or so the story goes.

Loch Ness

Almost 230 m (750 ft) deep and 37 km (23 miles) long, Loch Ness is Scotland's largest body of water. Flanked by mountains, castle and abbey ruins, and several charming villages, Loch Ness is worthy of its fame. Jacobite lake cruises start from the north road along its bank.

Urquhart Castle

Magnificently situated on the edge of Loch Ness, Urquhart Castle was once one of Scotland's largest castles. Although now all that remains of it are ruins, a fine tower house still stands, and the views from the top are well worth the climb. The visitor centre is state-of-the-art and displays an array of medieval artifacts.

→

Falls of Foyers thundering down the hillside to Loch Ness

THE LOCH NESS MONSTER

First sighted by St Columba in the 6th century, "Nessie" has attracted attention since photographs - later revealed to be faked - were taken in the 1930s. Though serious investigation is often undermined by hoaxers, sonar techniques continue to yield enigmatic results: plesiosaurs, giant eels and too much whisky are the most popular explanations. The Loch Ness Centre presents the photographic evidence and a wide variety of scientific explanations.

THE GEOLOGY OF SCOTLAND

Scotland is a geologist's playground, with rocks displaying three billion years of geological time. Starting with the hard granitic gneiss in the Western Isles, which was formed before life developed on earth, the rocks tell a story of lava flows, eras of mountain-building, numerous ice ages and even a time when the land was separated from England by the ancient Iapetus Ocean. Four major fault and thrust lines, running across Scotland from northeast to southwest, define the main geological zones.

A walking group exploring the dramatic landscapes of Torridon ↑

TYPICAL FEATURES

This cross-section is an idealized representation (not to scale) of some of the distinctive geology of the Highlands and islands of northwest Scotland. The tortuously indented coastline of this part of the country is a result of extremely high precipitation in the area during the last Ice Age which heavily eroded the layers of ancient rock, leaving a beautiful and contrasting landscape of boulder-strewn glens and deep sea lochs and coastal inlets.

Freshwater loch

Rock layers in a stepped effect

The action of sea tides and waves continually erodes the existing coastline.

Plateau-topped hills on the island are the exposed remains of a basalt lava flow.

Did You Know?

22,000 years ago, a large ice sheet covered Scotland entirely, and went as far south as the Midlands.

Lewisian gneiss is one of earth's oldest substances, created in the lower crust three billion years ago and later thrust up and exposed. Hard, infertile and grey, it forms low plateaus filled with thousands of small lochs in the Western Isles.

Quartzite peaks soar above a base of sandstone. The quartzite can often be mistaken for snow from a distance.

The Highland Boundary Fault runs from Stonehaven, on the east coast, to Arran on the west.

Serpentine

Old lava flow

Deep sea loch

CHANGING EARTH

About 500 million years ago Scotland was part of a landmass that included North America, while England was part of Gondwana. After 75 million years of continental breakup and drift, the two countries "collided", not far from the modern political boundary.

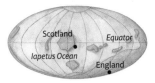

Scotland

Equator

Iapetus Ocean

England

○ Ancient Landmass

The last Ice Age, which ended around 10,000 years ago, was the most recent chapter in Scotland's geological history when, as was the case in Scandinavia, it became glaciated.

Scandinavia

Scotland

○ Glaciation in the last ice age

··· Present-day national boundaries

Formations

U-shaped Valleys
△ The movements of glaciers broke off spurs, rounding out the existing river valleys.

Gabbro
△ The dark rock of Skye's Cuillins was created by subterranean magma in the Tertiary period.

Devonian Sandstone
△ In places, the sea has eroded the horizontally layered rock into cliffs and sea stacks.

Basalt Columns
△ Lava that cooled slowly fractured in a hexagonal pattern like those found on the Isle of Staffa.

↑ Lone walker exploring other-worldly rock formations at The Storr

⑤

SKYE

🅰B3,B4 🅰Inner Hebrides 🚆Kyle of Lochalsh 🚌Portree
🚢From Mallaig or Glenelg 🌐isleofskye.com

The largest of the Inner Hebrides, Skye boasts some of Britain's most dramatic scenery. From rugged volcanic plateaus to ice-sculpted peaks, the island is divided by numerous sea lochs. Limestone grasslands dominate in the south, where hills are scattered with ruined crofts abandoned during the Clearances.

①

Portree

🛈 Bayfield House, Portree; (01478) 612992

With its harbour lined with colourful houses, Portree (meaning "port of the king") is Skye's mini-metropolis. The town received its name after a visit made by James V in 1540 in a bid to bring lasting peace to local warring clans. With stunning views of the surrounding mountains, and its fair share of cosy pubs, restaurants and B&Bs, Portree is an excellent base from which to explore this beautiful and rugged island.

Although the town itself is devoid of conventional sights, there are one or two areas which reward a brief trip. Somerled Square is the town's nucleus and the location of Portree's bus station. The 19th-century harbour, which is a short walk away from the square, is the most obvious attraction; its colourful harbourfront houses make for a pretty picture. From the wharf, you can sit with a coffee in hand and watch local fishermen land the day's catch. Close by is The Lump, a scenic headland once notorious for hosting public hangings. These days it's rather more sedate, offering elevated views across Loch Portree.

↑ Boats moored in the still waters of Portree harbour at sunset

> On the Trotternish Peninsula, overlooking the Sound of Raasay, the erosion of a basalt plateau has resulted in a series of other-worldly rock formations known as The Storr

② The Storr

On the Trotternish Peninsula, and looking out towards the Sound of Raasay, the erosion of a basalt plateau has resulted in a series of other-worldly rock formations known as The Storr. The highest, and most iconic, of these curious structures is the Old Man of Storr, a mono-lith rising to 49 m (160 ft). The rock itself was first climbed in 1955 by Don Whillans, and there have been several more successful attempts since; the Old Man has also featured in several films, including *The Wicker Man* (1973) and *Snow White and the Huntsman* (2012).

You can hike the 2.6-mile (3.8-km) Storr Ascent, accessed from the main road from Portree to Staffin, and head to the north side for spectacular views of these rocky pinnacles. Be warned – this is one of the most popular hikes in all of Scotland, so be prepared for crowds all year round.

③ The Quiraing

North of the Storr, and easily accessed from the Uig to Staffin road, the strangely named Quiraing is a spec-tacular landscape of bizarre rock formations – towering pinnacles, high cliffs, spikes and towers – all the result of a massive landslip centuries ago. The Quiraing – whose name comes from the Norse word Kvi Rand, meaning "Round Fold" – is notable for three distinctive landmarks: a pyramidal peak called the "Prison", the 40-m- (131-ft-) high "Needle" and the "Table", a smooth, grassy plateau, which requires a further 15-minute climb upwards.

Starting at the car park by the cemetery, the Quiraing walk is a wonderful, not-too-strenuous 7-km (4-mile) loop, although there is some rough and rocky terrain in places.

④ The Skye Museum of Island Life

🏠 Kilmuir ⏰ Easter-Sep: 9:30am–5pm Mon-Sat
🌐 skyemuseum.co.uk

Discover what island life was like 100 years ago at this award-winning museum, which takes visitors back in time to an old Highland village comprising a small community of well-preserved thatched cottages and crofts.

The largest and perhaps most impressive of these buildings is the Old Croft House, which functioned as a family home until as recently as 1957. It even has some of its original furnishings. Behind the complex is the grave of Flora MacDonald, famous Jacobite heroine and erstwhile companion of Bonnie Prince Charlie (p64), whose head-stone is engraved with an epitaph by Dr Johnson. There are fine views from here across to the Western Isles.

EAT

Three Chimneys
A sublime cottage restaurant in a remote setting. Expect fantastic dishes, such as langoustines with a smoked mussel ketchup.

🏠 Colbost, Dunvegan
🌐 threechimneys.co.uk

£££

Scorrybreac
Calum Munro, the head chef at this intimate restaurant, utilizes the island's produce to exciting effect.

🏠 7 Bosville Terrace, Portree 🌐 scorry breac.com 🚫 Mon & Sun

£££

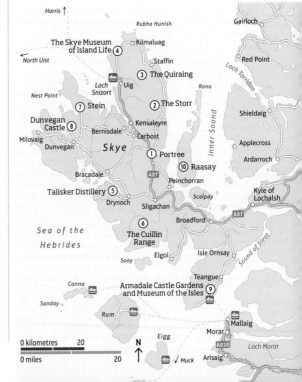

⑤ 🥃 Ⓜ

Talisker Distillery

📍 Carbost 🕐 Mar–Oct:
9:30am–5pm Mon–Sat (from
10am Sun); Nov–Feb: 10am–
4:30pm daily 🌐 malts.com

Overlooking the Black Cuillins
from the pretty banks of Loch
Harport at Carbost, Talisker is
the oldest working distillery
on the island. It is famed for
its sweet, full-bodied Highland
malts which are often
described as "the lava of the
Cuillins". Founded in 1830 by
Hugh and Kenneth Macaskill,
the distillery houses five stills:
three spirit stills and two wash
stills. The 45-minute tours
take in these stills, as well as
worm tubs and the warehouse,
but the main draw is getting to
sample a "wee dram" at the

Talisker Distillery,
situated in a
beautiful location,
and (inset) the
bottles of whisky
produced here

end. True whisky connoisseurs
should splash out on a two-
hour Masterclass Tour, where
they will learn the intricacies
of the process in fine detail.

___

⑥

The Cuillin Range

Britain's finest mountain range
is within walking distance of
Sligachan, and in summer
boats sail from Elgol to the
desolate inner sanctuary of
Loch Coruisk. As he fled across
the surrounding moorland,
Bonnie Prince Charlie reportedly said: "even the Devil shall
not follow me here!"

A particular highlight of
the area, at the foot of Skye's
"Black Cuillins" on the River
Brittle, are the Fairy Pools.
Here, white water cascades
into deep stone cauldrons
filled with clear pale-turquoise
water. The pools are also a
favourite with wild swimmers
daring enough to plunge into
their chilly waters. It's around
an hour to follow the riverside

trail that leads to the most
spectacular upper pools, with
breathtaking views of the
Cuillins along the way.

___

⑦

Stein

Overlooking Loch Bay, Stein
is easily the prettiest village
on the Waternish Peninsula,
even if it is little more than a
row of whitewashed 18th-
century cottages. It was
originally planned as a fishing
village by the British Fisheries
Society, designed by Thomas
Telford in 1790 – though this
never came to be. Stein's
signature sight is the medieval
shell of the Trumpan Church,
whose peaceful location

→

Dunvegan Castle, the
medieval fortress-home of
Clan MacLeod

🔺 GREAT VIEW
Neist Point

The most westerly
headland on Skye
features stunning cliff
scenery, a lighthouse
and a cracking view of
the Outer Hebrides. It is
one of the most photo-
graphed points on the
island – though this title
is hotly contested.

belies the fact that this was the site of one of the island's bloodiest battles – the 1578 slaughter of the MacDonalds at the hands of the MacLeods.

8
Dunvegan Castle

🏠 Dunvegan 🕐 Apr–mid-Oct: 10am–5:30pm daily 🌐 dunvegancastle.com

For over eight centuries, Dunvegan Castle has been the seat of the chiefs of the Clan MacLeod – indeed, the current chief, Hugh Magnus MacLeod, lives here with his family today. Dramatically sited atop a rocky outcrop on the east side of Loch Dunvegan, the castle's architecture is a unique mix of building styles due to the numerous renovations that took place over the years.

Many of the rooms display historical artifacts, but the single most important exhibit is the so-called Fairy Flag, a now somewhat dishevelled silk standard that was allegedly brought back to Skye by King Harald Hardrada following the Battle of Stamford in 1066. The formal gardens make for pleasant wandering while seal-spotting adventures and fishing trips on the loch depart from the castle.

9
Armadale Castle Gardens and Museum of the Isles

🏠 Armadale, Sleat 🕐 Apr–Oct: daily; Mar & Nov: Mon–Fri 🌐 armadalecastle.com

Once the seat of Clan Donald, who reigned over the area as Lords of the Isles, this ruined castle and its impressive grounds make for a fascinating day out.

The main reason to visit the castle, however, is for the Museum of the Isles, where visitors can discover the story of Scotland's most powerful clan. Its six galleries also cover Highland history, displaying some superb exhibits on the Jacobites, including a snuff mull and firing glasses belonging to Bonnie Prince Charlie. Other noteworthy exhibits include Highland bagpipes, beautifully studded shields and pistols, and a pair of cannonballs fired at the castle from HMS *Dartmouth*.

10
Raasay

Lying off Skye's western coast, Raasay – meaning "Isle of the Roe Deer" – measures just 16 km (10 miles) long. Other than the **Isle of Raasay Distillery**, there are few major tourist sights, which is

TOP 4 SCENIC HIKES

Storr Ascent
Skye's most popular walk takes in the iconic Old Man of Storr *(p222)*.

Point of Sleat
An easy 10-km (6-mile) walk to the peninsula's southernmost point, taking in a sandy beach along the way.

The Quiraing
This circuit starts at a roadside car park 4 km (2.5 miles) from Staffin, and rewards hikers with incredible views *(p233)*.

Camasunary
A terrific 11-km (7-mile) hike to a bay via the Cuillin mountains.

its chief appeal. Visitors come for the solitude and to hike its rugged hills, the best of which is the 1,456-ft (443-m) Dun Caan. There is also a lovely walk up to the atmospheric ruins of Brochel Castle. The island is rich in flora and fauna too, with golden eagles and Raasay voles among the many species to keep an eye out for.

Isle of Raasay Distillery
🏠 Borodale House, Iverarish 🌐 raasaydistillery.com

6

ORKNEY ISLANDS

🄰 D1, E1 🄰 Orkney ✈ Kirkwall 🚢 From Scrabster or Gill's Bay (Caithness),
Aberdeen, Lerwick (Shetland), and John O'Groats (May–Sept only)
ℹ West Castle Street, Kirkwall; (01856) 872856 🆆 orkney.com

Beyond the Pentland Firth, less than 10 km (6 miles) off the Scottish mainland,
the Orkney archipelago consists of some 70 islands and rocky skerries boasting the
densest concentration of archaeological sites in Britain. Today, only about 16 of
these islands are permanently inhabited. Orkney's way of life is predominantly
agricultural – it's said that, whereas the Shetlanders are fishermen with crofts, the
Orcadians are farmers with boats.

The Mainland is the archipelago's main island, home to Orkney's two largest towns, Kirkwall and Stromness. Almost 5,000 years ago, rings of colossal stone walls enclosed a complex of temples at Ness of Brodgar, the most recently rediscovered of Orkney's Neolithic relics. In 1999, sites including the chambered tomb at Maeshowe and the Standing Stones of Stenness and the Ring of Brodgar were granted UNESCO World Heritage status, and archaeologists continue to unearth exciting finds that tell of a sophisticated ancient culture that flourished here long ago.

Hoy, Orkney's second-largest island, takes its name from the Norse word for "high island", which refers to its spectacular cliff-lined terrain. Hoy is very different from the rest of the archipelago, and its northern hills make excellent walking and bird-watching country.

Orkney's outlying islands are sparsely populated and mostly the preserve of seals and seabirds. Rousay is known as the "Egypt of the North" for its many archaeological sites, and Egilsay was the scene of St Magnus's grisly murder in 1115. The 12th-century round-towered church dedicated to his memory is a rare example of Irish-Viking design. Sanday is the largest of the Northern Isles, its fertile farmland fringed by sandy beaches, while North Ronaldsay, the northern most of the Orkney Islands, is noted for its hardy, seaweed-eating sheep and rare migrant birds.

↑ Ancient stone monoliths form the Ring of Brodgar Neolithic henge, Orkney

① Kirkwall

Orkney's capital is lined with period houses. Opposite **St Magnus Cathedral**, an 870-year-old masterpiece of red and yellow stone, lie the ruins of the **Bishop's Palace**, dating from the 16th century. The **Orkney Museum** tells the history of the islands, while the **Highland Park Distillery** dispenses a fine dram at the end of its guided tours.

St Magnus Cathedral

⊛ ⊛ ⬛ Broad St ⬛ Mon–Sat
🔲 stmagnus.org

Bishop's Palace

⊛ ⬛ Watergate
🔲 Apr–Oct: daily 🔲 historic environment.scot

Orkney Museum

⬛ Broad St ⬛ Mon–Sat
🔲 orkney.gov.uk

Highland Park Distillery

⊛ ⊛ ⊛ ⬛ Holme Rd
🔲 Times vary, check website
🔲 highlandparkwhisky.com

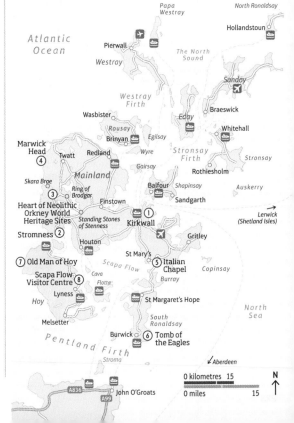

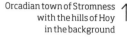

Orcadian town of Stromness with the hills of Hoy in the background ↑

② Stromness

Many of the waterfront buildings in Stromness date from the 18th and 19th centuries. Among them, the **Pier Arts Centre** contains a fine collection of 20th-century works. **The Stromness Museum** traces Orkney's history as a trading port.

Pier Arts Centre

 ⚑ 28–36 Victoria St
🕐 10:30am–5pm Tue–Sat
Ⓦ pierartscentre.com

Stromness Museum

⚑ 52 Alfred St 🕐 Daily (Nov–Mar: Mon–Sat) Ⓦ stromness museum.org.uk

---

💬 INSIDER TIP
Day Trips to Remote Islands

There are flights from Kirkwall to a dozen outlying islands several times a week, as well as daily ferries. Inter-island transport is weather-dependent.

---

③ Heart of Neolithic Orkney World Heritage Sites

⚑ Various locations on Central & West Mainland
🕐 Daily Ⓦ historic environment.scot

Almost 5,000 years ago, rings of colossal stone walls more than 100 metres long enclosed the complex of temples at Ness of Brodgar, the most recently discovered of Orkney's Neolithic relics. Said to date from around 2750 BC, Maeshowe is a chambered tomb aligned with the winter solstice. Vikings plundered it around 1150, leaving a fascinating legacy of runic graffiti on the walls. Nearby are the huge Standing Stones of Stenness and the Ring of Brodgar, a megalithic henge of 36 stones. The Neolithic village of Skara Brae was discovered when a storm stripped dunes from the site in 1850 to reveal relics of everyday Stone Age life. In 1999 these ancient sites were granted UNESCO World Heritage status.

④ Marwick Head

The cliffs of Marwick Head, overlooking Birsay Bay, are one of several RSPB reserves on West Mainland, home to thousands of nesting seabirds in early summer. A memorial Commemorates Lord Kitchener and the crew of HMS *Hampshire*, which was sunk off this headland by a German mine in 1916.

---

⑤ Italian Chapel

⚑ Lambholm, Hoy
🕐 Daily (Mass: 1st Sun of month, Apr–Sep)

East of Kirkwall, the road runs through quiet agricultural land over a series of causeways linking the southernmost islands to Mainland. The Churchill Barriers were built by Italian prisoners of war in the 1940s to protect the British fleet stationed in Scapa Flow. In their spare time, these POWs constructed the Italian Chapel, containing beautiful frescoes.

---

⑥ 🎿 🖥 🛍

Tomb of the Eagles

📍 South Ronaldsay
🕐 Mar-Oct: daily
🌐 tomboftheeagles.co.uk

On South Ronaldsay, the 5,000-year-old Tomb of the Eagles, or Isbister Chambered Cairn, was discovered by a local farmer. Some 340 burial sites were later unearthed, along with stone tools and the talons of many sea eagles. The mile-long walk from the visitor centre to the tomb through a Bronze Age excavation site teems with birdlife and wild flowers.

⑦

Old Man of Hoy

The Old Man of Hoy, a 137-m (450-ft) vertical stack off the western coast, is the island's best-known landmark, a popular challenge to keen rock climbers. Near Rackwick, the 5,000-year-old Dwarfie Stane is a unique chambered cairn cut from a single block of stone.

---

⑧

Scapa Flow Visitor Centre

📍 Lyness, Hoy 🕐 For renovation until 2021
🌐 orkney.gov.uk

On the eastern side of Hoy, the Scapa Flow Visitor Centre contains a fascinating exhibition on this deep-water

STAY

Merkister Hotel
Only 15 minutes from Stromness and close to the Neolithic Orkney World Heritage Sites, this family-run hotel offers cosy rooms, exquisite home cooking set against fabulous sunset views.

🗺 D1 📍 Harray
🌐 merkister.com

£ £ £

The Creel
Multi-award-winning seafront B&B and restaurant in a timeless stone village. Quaint rooms and imaginative cooking - try the wolf-fish broth.

🗺 E1 📍 St Margaret's Hope 🌐 thecreel.co.uk

£ £ £

naval haven. Temporarily rehoused in Hoy Hotel, the exhibition recounts the events of 16 June 1919, when the captured German fleet was scuttled on the orders of its commanding officer to prevent handover: 74 ships were sunk. Many have been salvaged; others provide one of the world's great wreck-diving sites. Tours from Houton Pier, using a remote-controlled vehicle fitted with an underwater camera, give a glimpse of this sub-aquatic graveyard. Guided tours of the former Royal Naval Base depart at 11am every Tuesday and Thursday from the Ferry Waiting Room.

←

Orkney's iconic sea stack, the Old Man of Hoy is a popular rock climbing spot

Did You Know?

The last inhabitants
of the Island of Mousa,
the Smith family, left
the island in 1853.

St Ninian's Isle, separated
from Mainland by a thin
isthmus of white sand ↑

7
SHETLAND ISLANDS

🅰 F1, F2 🅰 Shetland 🚌✈ From Aberdeen and Stromness, Orkney
ℹ Lerwick; www.shetland.org

With the North Sea to the east, and the Atlantic Ocean ravishing its western shores,
this windswept archipelago is where Scotland meets Scandinavia, and the sense
of transition here tangible. Shetland's rugged coastline, oceanic climate and
fascinating geology will delight all who venture to this most northerly enclave.

More than 100 rugged, cliff-hemmed islands
form Scotland's most northerly domain.
Nowhere in Shetland is further than 5 km
(3 miles) from the sea, and fishing and salmon
farming are mainstays of the economy,
boosted in recent decades by North Sea oil.
Severe storms are common in winter, but in
summer, the sun may shine for as long as 19
hours, and a twilight known as the "simmer
dim" persists throughout the night.

Mainland is home to Shetland's main town,
Lerwick, and the quiet port of Scalloway. North
of Lerwick, Shetland rises to its highest point
at Ronas Hill (454 m/1,475 ft) amid tracts of
bleak, empty moorland. The west coast has
spectacular natural scenery, notably the red
granite cliffs and blow-holes at Esha Ness,
from where you can see the wave-gnawed
stacks of The Drongs and a huge rock arch
called Dore Holm.

The northern isles of Yell, Fetlar and Unst
have regular, though weather-dependent,
boat connections to Mainland. Beyond the
lighthouse of Muckle Flugga is Out Stack,
Britain's most northerly point.

West of Mainland, Foula has dramatic sea
cliffs, while Fair Isle, midway between Orkney
and Shetland, is owned by the National Trust
for Scotland. There are regular internal flights
to Fair Isle, Foula and Papa Stour, as well as
inter-island ferries. Most routes depart from
Tingwall, on Central Mainland.

0 kilometres 15
0 miles 15
N

Burrafirth
Hermaness National Nature Reserve ⑥ Haroldswick
Cullivoe *Unst*
Gutcher Belmont
Isbister *Fetlar*
A970 Houbie
Yell
Ollaberry
Burravoe
Stenness Mossbank *Out Skerries*
Scatsta
Brae Vidlin
Muckle Roe Whalsay
Papa Stour Voe
Aith *Bergen*
Garth *Mainland* Weisdale
Walls Laxfirth
Foula **Tingwall**
Ham Skeld *Vaila* Lerwick ①
② Noss
Scalloway ③ ② Bressay
West Burra *East Burra*
South Havra *Mousa*
St Ninian's Isle Sandwick
Dunrossness ④ Mousa Broch
Sumburgh
Jarlshof Prehistoric and Norse Settlement ⑤ Sumburgh
Sumburgh Head *Fair Isle, Aberdeen ↓*

FAIR ISLE KNITWEAR

Fair Isle sweaters have been knitted by hand from hand-spun wool by the island's womenfolk for more than 200 years. Each garment takes up to 100 hours to create and is a unique work of art, using traditional patterns in muted shades of grey, blue, brown and yellow, reflecting the tones of the Shetland Isles' flora, fauna and natural landscapes. Skills are passed on from mothers to daughters, and learning them takes up to four years. Prices are high and would-be buyers may have to wait several years for their garment to be completed.

①

Lerwick

Shetland's chief town is a pretty place of grey stone buildings and narrow, flag-stoned lanes. First established by Dutch fishermen in the 1600s, it grew to become wealthy from the whaling trade. The increase in North Sea oil traffic has made the harbour area very busy. At the heart of the town is Commercial Street, its northern end guarded by Fort Charlotte, which affords fine views from its battlements. At the **Shetland Museum and Archive**, on Hay's Dock, you can admire a fine collection of historic boats, archaeological finds and Shetland textiles tracing the islands' unique and fascinating history.

On Lerwick's outskirts lie the Clickminin Broch, a prehistoric fort dating from around 700 BC, and the 18th-century **Böd of Gremista**, birthplace of Arthur Anderson, co-founder of the P&O shipping company, which now houses a textile museum.

Shetland Museum and Archive

Ⓐ Ⓑ ◐ Daily ⓦ shetland museumandarchives.org.uk

Böd of Gremista

Ⓐ ◐ May–Sep: Tue–Sat ⓦ shetlandtextilemuseum. com

② Bressay and Noss

🚢 From Lerwick

Sheltering Lerwick from the winter gales is Bressay, an island with fine walks and views. The Bressay ferry departs from Lerwick every hour, weather-dependent, and boats run from Lerwick to Noss, off Bressay's east coast. **Noss National Nature Reserve** is home to thousands of breeding seabirds, including gannets and great skuas (or bonxies), while both islands are outstandingly beautiful and abundant in

↑ Shetland Pony grazing on gentle grasslands of West Burra, Scalloway Islands

bird and mammal life. **The Bressay Heritage Centre** holds seasonal exhibitions on the island's culture, history and natural heritage, and is open from May to September.

Noss National Nature Reserve
⊛ 🕐May–Aug: Tue, Wed, Fri–Sun 🌐nature.scot

Bressay Heritage Centre
⊛ 🕐May–Sep: 1am–4pm Wed, Fri & Sun 🌐shetlandheritage association.com

③ Scalloway

West of Lerwick is the quiet fishing port of Scalloway, Shetland's second town and the islands' former capital. Scalloway Castle is a fortified tower dating from 1600, while the **Scalloway Museum** contains an exhibition on the "Shetland Bus", a wartime resistance operation that used fishing boats to bring refugees from German-occupied Norway. North of Scalloway, near Weisdale, the fertile region of Tingwall is a well-known angling centre. Connected by bridges to Central Mainland's west coast are the islands of Burra and

Trondra, with lovely beaches and coastal walks. Fishing and crofting are the main industries and both islands are known for their rich arts and crafts culture.

Scalloway Museum
⌂ Castle St ⏰ Times vary, check website 🌐 scalloway museum.org

___

④

Mousa Broch

⌂ Mousa ⏰ Apr-Sep: Mon-Fri & Sun 🌐 mousa.co.uk

The ornate Mousa Broch, on an easterly islet reached by a ferry (running Apr-Sep) from Sandwick, is the best example of this type of ancient fortified tower in Britain. These drystone roundhouses, which are unique to Scotland, consist of two concentric walls, between which is a narrow passage containing a stone stairway to the top. Thought to have been constructed in around 300 BC, Mousa is the tallest of all the remaining brochs in Scotland. Its 13-m- (42-ft-) tall towering walls are clearly visible from the main road, and make ideal nestboxes for a colony of storm petrels.

SHETLAND'S BIRDLIFE

Millions of migrant and local birds can be admired on these islands. Over 20 species of seabirds regularly breed here, and over 340 different species have been recorded passing through Fair Isle, one of the world's great staging posts. Inaccessible cliffs provide excellent security at vulnerable nesting times for huge colonies of gannets, guillemots, puffins, kittiwakes, fulmars and razorbills. Species found here but in very few other UK locations include great skuas and storm petrels.

⑤

Jarlshof Prehistoric and Norse Settlement

⌂ Sumburgh 🚌 Jarlshof ⏰ Apr-Sept: 9:30am-5:30pm daily 🌐 historic environment.scot

Jarlshof, in the far south, spans over 3,000 years of occupation from Neolithic to Viking times. Preserved under layers of sand and grit for thousands of years, this ancient site was discovered in the 1890s thanks to powerful storms that ravished the land to reveal ancient treasures hidden underneath the ground. Explore ancient Bronze Age dwellings, Iron Age wheelhouses and Viking longhouses and outbuildings, and evidence of the island's

←

Clifftop lighthouse at Sumburgh Head on the southern tip of Mainland

Norse occupation, all set against the dramatic backdrop of the beautiful West Voe of Sumburgh.

___

⑥

Hermaness National Nature Reserve

⌂ Muckle Flugga Shorestation 🚌 Unst 🚌 From Lerwick to Haroldswick ⏰ Daily (Visitor Centre: Apr-Sep only) 🌐 nature.scot

Of all Shetland's islands, Unst has the most varied scenery and the richest flora and fauna, plus an excellent visitor centre at the Hermaness National Nature Reserve, home to thousands of seabirds. Here visitors can learn about the local birdlife, and stroll along the clifftop paths and grassy moorland. Beyond the lighthouse of Muckle Flugga is Out Stack, Britain's most northerly point.

Cliffs and sea stacks near Mangersta, on the west coast of Lewis ↑

8

OUTER HEBRIDES

🅰 A3, B2 🅰 Western Isles, Outer Hebrides 🛫 Stornoway, Benbecula, Barra ⛴ from Uig (Skye), Oban, Mallaig, Kyle of Lochalsh & Ullapool ℹ 26 Cromwell St, Stornoway, Lewis 🅦 visitouterhebrides.co.uk

Western Scotland ends with this remote chain of islands, made of some of the oldest rock on earth. Barren landscapes are divided by countless waterways, while the western, windward coasts are edged by white sandy beaches.

Hundreds of windswept and beautiful islands lie scattered off Scotland's northwest coast. Some are tiny rocky skerries inhabited only by seabirds, while others are home to bustling farming and fishing communities. White sandy bays fringe these rugged coasts, bordered by sweet-smelling natural wild-flower meadows known as *machair* that pepper the land with splashes of yellow, white, blue and pink.

In the low-lying hinterlands, vast peat bogs provide many homes with fuel, and the rich tang of peat smoke is the signature scent of the isles. These are some of the longest-inhabited parts of Scotland, with ancient standing stones attesting to over 6,000 years of human settlement, though abandoned dwellings and monuments attest to the difficulties in commercializing traditional local skills. Home to Scotland's largest Gaelic-speaking community, many islanders use the ancient Celtic tongue as their first language.

↑ Sheep in wild-flower meadows on rugged and remote Harris

① Lewis

Lewis is the largest and most populous of the Western Isles. Its administrative centre is Stornoway, a bustling harbour town with colourful house fronts. It is also the site of Lews Castle, home to the **Museum nan Eilean**, which offers insight into the culture, language and traditions of the people of the Outer Hebrides.

The island's northwest coast is the location for some of the country's most important prehistoric remains: standing some 9 m (30 ft) high, Dun Carloway is a 2,000-year old dry-stone broch (fortified tower), though perhaps more impressive are the **Callanish Standing Stones**, some 50 neatly cut slabs arranged in an almost complete circle; the nearby **Callanish Visitor Centre** sheds light on the reason for their existence. No less evocative is the **Arnol Blackhouse**, a superbly preserved late 19th-century blackhouse; a pungent-smelling peat fire is lit each morning, making the experience all the more authentic. The west coast road winds up at the Port of Ness, a comely fishing village with a gorgeous beach sited at the northern tip of Lewis.

Museum nan Eilean

♿ 📷 🏪 🅿 Lews Castle grounds, Stornoway Apr–Sep: 10am–5pm Mon–Wed, Fri & Sat; Oct–Mar: 1–4pm

🌐 lews-castle.co.uk

Callanish Standing Stones and Visitor Centre

♿ ⓘ 📷 🏪 🅿 Loag Road, Callanish ⏰ Times vary, check website

🌐 callanishvisitorcentre. co.uk

Arnol Blackhouse

♿ 📷 🅿 Arnol, Bragar
📞 (01851) 710 395
⏰ Times vary, check website
🌐 historicenvironment.scot

> **White sandy bays fringe these rugged coasts, bordered by sweet-smelling natural wild-flower meadows known as *machair*.**

②

Harris

South of the rolling peat moors of Lewis, a range of mountains marks the border with Harris, which is entered via the head of Loch Seaforth. The ferry port of Tarbert stands on a slim isthmus, separating North and South Harris. Believe it or not, this sleepy town, with its quaint stone houses and winding streets, is the hub of the island. The opening of the **Isle of Harris Distillery** in 2015 was a boon for the community. As well as gin and whisky, visitors can sample a taste of real island hospitality.

The more mountainous North Harris is a paradise for hill walkers, offering views of the distant islands of St Kilda 80 km (50 miles) to the west – at 799 m (2621 ft), the Clisham is the highest peak anywhere in the Western Isles. The main road north from Tarbert passes Bunavoneadar, then beyond the privately-owned Abhainnsuidhe Castle before winding up at the crofting village of Hushinish. Here, a slipway serves the island of Scarp, once home to over 200 people but now uninhabited.

By way of contrast, the lower-lying southern Harris is characterized by a dramatic coastline pocked with small bays and pristine beaches, the most impressive of which is Luskentyre on the west coast, though the competition is fierce. Harris is, of course, best known for the production of tweed, a high-quality woollen cloth that has been crafted here for centuries and is still hand woven in many island homes; some weavers still use indigenous plants to create the dyes. The **Harris Tweed** shop sells this sought-after material by the reem.

> **CROFTING**
>
> Crofts are small parcels of agricultural land. They originated in the early 1800s when landlords decided to lease out poor-quality land on the coast in an effort to clear the people from more fertile areas. Crofters became dependent on wages from either fishing or collecting kelp, which was used to make commercial alkali. When these sources of income diminished, they endured extreme hardship through famine, high rents and lack of security. In 1886 an Act was passed to allow crofting families the right to inherit (but not own) the land. Today there are 17,000 registered crofts, almost all in the Highlands and islands. Most crofters raise sheep, but recent trends include tree planting and providing habitats for rare birds.

TOP 5 HEBRIDEAN BEACHES

Tràigh Mhòr, Barra
This stretch of white sand doubles as the island's runway when the tide is out.

Berneray, North Uist
A spectacular bay where white sands are lapped by turquoise waters.

Hushinish, Harris
Pristine, white shell sand beach looking out over Hushinish Bay.

Luskentyre, Harris
This remote beach boasts silvery-white sands, epic mountain views and rolling dunes.

Uig Sands, Lewis
An enormous stretch of sand is surrounded by machair meadows.

The remote community of Stockinish, a fishing harbour in East Harris ↑

Harris Tweed

🏠 Caberfeidh, Tarbert 🕐 9am-5:30pm Mon-Sat 🌐 harristweedisleofharris.co.uk

Isle of Harris Distillery

🕐🍽🛍 🏠 Tarbert 🕐 10am-4pm Mon-Fri; 10am-12:30pm Sat 🌐 harrisdistillery.com

---

③

The Uists and Benbecula

After the dramatic scenery of Harris, the lower-lying, largely waterlogged southern isles may seem an anticlimax, though they nurture secrets well worth discovering. Long, white, sandy beaches fringe the Atlantic coast, edged with one of Scotland's lesser-known natural treasures: the lime-rich soil that nurtures the islands' unique flora. During the summer months, the soil is covered with wild flower meadows known as machair, the unique fragrance of which can be detected far out to sea.

From Lochmaddy, North Uist's main village, the A867 crosses 5 km (3 miles) of causeway to Benbecula, the isle from which the brave Flora MacDonald smuggled Bonnie Prince Charlie to Skye (p222). Benbecula is a flat island covered by a mosaic of small lochs. Like its neighbours, it is known for its excellent trout fishing. Here, and to the north, the Protestant religion holds sway, while Catholicism prevails in the southern islands. Benbecula's chief source of employment is the Army Rocket Range, which has its headquarters in the main village of Bailivanich. Another causeway leads to South Uist, which has golden beaches that are renowned as a National Scenic Area. The east side of the island is mountainous, with the highest peak, Beinn Mhòr, reaching 620 m (2034 ft).

EAT

Harris and Lewis Smokehouse

Contemporary dining in a stunning setting; expect supreme local meat and fish dishes.

🏠 Sandwick Rd, Stornoway, Lewis 🌐 harrisandlewis.co.uk

£££

Harris Hotel

Long-established hotel whose menu typically features traditional dishes such as pigeon breast with haggis and sweet plum.

🏠 Scott Rd, Tarbert 🌐 harrishotel.com

£££

Berneray Bistro

Shop and bistro offering a daytime menu of breakfast rolls, grilled wraps and ciabattas. The evening menu is something extra special.

🏠 Berneray 🌐 berneray shopandbistro.co.uk

£££

Langass Lodge

Locally caught seafood and produce from Langass's own garden feature on the menu at this small restaurant.

🏠 Locheport, North Uist 🌐 langasslodge.co.uk

£££

Café Kisimul

This family-run café offers an eclectic menu including a selection of Indian dishes.

🏠 Castlebay, Barra 🌐 cafekisimul.co.uk

£££

→

Village bay and abandoned settlement of the Island of Hirta, St Kilda

④

Eriskay

One of the smallest and most enchanting of the Western Isles, Eriskay epitomizes the peace and beauty of the Outer Hebrides. The island is best known for the wrecking of the SS *Politician* in 1941, which inspired the book and 1949 film *Whisky Galore!* by writer Compton Mackenzie. A bottle from its cargo and other relics can be seen in the island's only bar, Am Politician.

It was at the beautiful beach of Coilleag A'Phrionnsa (Prince's beach) that Bonnie Prince Charlie first set foot on Scotland at the start of his 1745 campaign to lead the Jacobite rebellion. It is said that the pink flowers that bloom in Eriskay's machair grasses grew from seeds he dropped on his arrival.

It was only in early 2000 that the causeway connecting Eriskay to South Uist by road was finally completed – making the island more accessible to visitors.

⑤

Barra

The most dramatic way to arrive on the pretty southerly island of Barra is by small passenger plane. The vast white sands of the stunning Tràigh Mhòr Beach (more commonly known as Cockle Strand) in the north of the island doubles as the airstrip, with the timetable dictated by the tide. When planes aren't taking off or landing on this impressive beach, locals gather cockles.

The island itelf has a central core of hills and circular road, with beaches mostly strung along the western coast.

Did You Know?
Uist is one of the last Gaelic-speaking strongholds in Scotland.

Castlebay – aptly named after the brooding fortress of **Kisimul Castle** that dominates the bay from this picturesque little islet – is Barra's only settlement of any real size. Kisimul is the fifteenth seat of the Clan MacNeill; although it's mostly off limits pending restoration, it's great fun taking the boat across the water to the island. Another beauty spot, the view over Castlebay from the Madonna and Child statue atop Heaval Hill is particularly fine.

West of town, the charming little **Barra Heritage Centre** (Dualchas) offers worthwhile insight into the peoples and landscapes of the island, and you can grab a decent coffee and homemade cake from the café here too.

South of Castlebay, the road continues south across a causeway to Vatersay, an oddly shaped island divided into two peninsulas connected by a finger-like isthmus. It's here that you'll see the Annie Jane Monument,

St Kilda is the UK's westernmost island chain, comprising three islands and three spectacular sea stacks each with sheer, soaring cliffs.

Kisimul Castle
⊛ 🄲 (01871) 810313
🅆 historicenvironment.scot

Barra Heritage Centre
🄰 Castlebay 🄾 Times vary, check website 🅆 barra heritage.com

―――――――――――

⑥
St Kilda

These "Islands on the Edge of the World" were the most isolated habitation in the country until the ageing population requested to be evacuated in 1930. Now a UNESCO World Heritage Site, St Kilda is the UK's westernmost island chain, comprising three islands and three spectacular sea stacks, each with sheer, soaring cliffs rising as high as 425 m (1,400 ft). Such is the islands'

isolation that separate subspecies of mouse and wren have evolved here. But St Kilda's big attraction is its gannetry – one of the world's largest with 40,000 pairs – while it also has the UK's largest colony of puffins.

The only island on which visitors can land is Hirta, with tours run by **Kilda Cruises** and **Island Cruising**. Otherwise, volunteers can occasionally pay to join summer work parties through the **St Kilda World Heritage Site**, organized by the National Trust for Scotland. Also on Hirta is the island's only settlement, at Village Bay, where there's a small museum and ranger's office.

Island Cruising
⊛ ⊛ 🄰 1 Erista, Uig, Lewis 🄾 May–Sep
🅆 islandcruising.com

Kilda Cruises
⊛ ⊛ 🄰 Isle of Harris
🄾 May–Sep 🅆 kildacruises. co.uk

St Kilda World Heritage Site
🄽🅃🅂 🅆 nts.org.uk

―――――――――――

erected to commemorate more than 300 emigrants who tragically lost their lives when the eponymous ship ran ashore here in 1853. There are some stunning stretches of sandy beaches on Vatersay, the best of which lie on the island's southern reaches.

CYCLING THE HEBRIDEAN WAY

Inaugurated in 2017 and stretching along the entire length of the Outer Hebrides, the Hebridean Way is an exhilarating long-distance route, comprising a 250-km (156-mile) walking trail and a 297-km (185-mile) cycle trail. The cycle route begins in Vatersay. With the prevailing wind at your back, a series of causeways and ferry crossings punctuate the journey north through the lower-lying islands – Eriskay, waterlogged South Uist, Benbecula and the burnished hillsides of North Uist. Harris will astound with its breathtaking scenery, before the road extends all the way up to the Butt of Lewis in the north. The scenery here is as varied as it is dramatic; craggy mountains, shimmering lochs and stunning beaches are in no short supply. Pedalling at a leisurely pace, you should be able to complete the route in five or six days.

Windswept Nisabost Beach, Harris

EXPERIENCE MORE

9

Inveraray Castle

🅰C5 🅰Inveraray, Argyll & Bute 🚌Dalmally, then bus 🚌From Glasgow 🕐Apr-Oct: 10am–5:45pm daily (last admission 5pm) 🌐inveraray-castle.com

This multi-turreted mock Gothic palace is the family home of the powerful Clan Campbell, the Dukes of Argyll since 1701. Building started in 1746 by architects Roger Morris and William Adam on ruins of a 15th-century castle. The conical towers were added after a fire in 1877.

The magnificent interiors, designed by Robert Mylne in the 1770s, form a backdrop to such treasures as Regency furniture, a huge collection of Oriental and European porcelain and portraits by Ramsay, Gainsborough and Raeburn. The Armoury Hall contains early weaponry collected by the Campbells to fight the Jacobite rebels, and there's a fascinating exhibition on Scotland's most famous outlaw Rob Roy, complete with his belt, sporran and dirk (small dagger) handle.

10

Auchindrain Township

🅰C5 🅰Inveraray, Argyll & Bute 🚌Inveraray, then bus 🕐Apr-Oct: 10am–5pm daily 🌐auchindrain org.uk

The first open-air museum in Scotland, Auchindrain illuminates the working lives of the kind of farming community typical of the Highlands until the late 19th century. Constituting a township of some 20 thatched cottages, the site was communally farmed by its tenants until the last one retired in 1962. Visitors can wander through the houses, most of which combine living space, kitchen and a cattle shed all under one roof. They are furnished with box beds

Did You Know?

The final scenes of the 1963 James Bond film *From Russia With Love* were filmed around Argyll and Bute.

and rush lamps, and edged by herb gardens. Auchindrain is a fascinating memorial to a time before the Highland farmers made the transition from subsistence to commercial farming.

11

Crarae Gardens

🅰C5 🅰Crarae, Argyll & Bute 🚌Inveraray, then bus 🕐Apr-Sep: 9am–5pm daily; Oct-Mar: 9:30am–4pm Thu–Mon 🌐nts.org.uk

Considered to be the most beguiling of all the gardens of the West Highlands, the Crarae Gardens were created in 1912 by Lady Grace Campbell. She was the aunt of explorer Reginald Farrer, whose specimens from Tibet were the beginnings of a collection of exotic plants. The gardens now resemble a Himalayan ravine, nourished by the warmth of the Gulf Stream and the region's high rainfall. Unusual Himalayan rhododendrons flourish here, but the gardens are also home to exotic plants from Tasmania, New Zealand and the US.

12

Islay

🅰B6 🅰Argyll & Bute 🚢From Kennacraig 🛈Bowmore 🌐islay jura.com

With nine exceptional distilleries to choose from, whisky-lovers can't go wrong in Islay. The most southerly of Scotland's Western Isles, Islay is famous for its pungent, peaty and powerful Highland malts, such as **Lagavulin** and smoky **Laphroaig**. The charming village of **Bowmore** is home to the island's oldest

↑ Romantic Inveraray Castle, with its Gothic and Baroque features

Copper stills used to make single malt whisky at Laphroaig Distillery *(inset)*, on Islay

distillery, while the latest addition is **Ardnahoe Distillery**, opened in 2018 on a scenic spot on the island's east coast. On the shores of Loch Indaal, the effortlessly cool **Bruichladdich** distillery produces innovative malts as well as the famous Botanist gin. The usual tours and tastings are available here, but the Be the Botanist tour, which includes a tasting and cocktail making class, is a particular highlight.

The **Museum of Islay Life** in Port Charlotte covers the island's social and natural history. East of Port Ellen, the Kildalton Cross, a block of local green stone inscribed with Old Testament scenes, is one of the UK's most impressive 8th-century Celtic crosses. Also worth a visit is the medieval stronghold of the Lords of the Isles, Finlaggan, which is under excavation.

Some of Islay's superb beaches support a variety of birdlife, which can be seen at the Royal Society for the Protection of Birds (RSPB) reserve at Gruinart.

Lagavulin Distillery
⊛⊛🅟 🅐 Port Ellen
🅞 Times vary, check website
🆆 malts.com

Laphroaig Distillery
⊛⊛🅟 🅐 School St, Bowmore
🅞 Times vary, check website
🆆 laphroaig.com

Ardnahoe Distillery
⊛⊛🅣🅟🅓 🅐 Ardnahoe, Port Askaig 🅞 10am–5pm daily
🆆 ardnahoedistillery.com

💬 INSIDER TIP
Fèis Ìle

Time your visit to coincide with Fèis Ìle, a spirited festival held in the last week of May that celebrates Islay's culture, featuring toe-tapping music, highland flings, whisky tastings, local produce and more.

Bruichladdich Distillery
⊛⊛🅟 🅐 Port Charlotte
🅞 Times vary, check website
🆆 bruichladdich.com

Museum of Islay Life
⊛ 🅐 Port Charlotte
🅞 10:30am–4:30pm daily (Apr & Oct: Mon–Fri)
🆆 islaymuseum.org

Whisky-lovers can't go wrong in Islay. The most southerly of Scotland's Western Isles, Islay is famous for its pungent, peaty and powerful Highland malts.

⓭ Jura

🅐 B5, B6 🏛 Argyll & Bute
🚢 From Kennacraig to Islay, Islay to Jura

Just a five-minute ferry ride from Port Askaig on Islay (p243), the island of Jura couldn't be more different: barren, mountainous and remote, it's the perfect spot if it's complete solitude you're after. The island is said to take its name from the Norse word *dyr-oe*, meaning Deer Island, entirely appropriate as deer outnumber humans here by at least 30 to one – indeed, the west coast is almost entirely uninhabited, while the island's only road runs down the east coast. Jura's only village is Craighouse, which is home to what few facilities the island has, including a hotel, restaurant, shop and post office, and of course the famous **Jura Distillery**, where tours and tastings are offered.

The island offers superb hill walking, especially on the slopes of the three main peaks known as the Paps of Jura – the tallest of these is Beinn An Oir at 784 m (2,572 ft);

note that for visitors' own safety, hiking is restricted in certain areas during the deer-stalking season, between July and October.

Beyond the northern tip of the are the notorious whirlpools of Corryvreckan. The author George Orwell, who came to the island to write his final novel, *1984*, nearly lost his life here in 1946 when he fell into the water. Legend tells of Prince Breackan who drowned in his attempt to win the hand of a princess. He tried to keep his boat anchored in the whirlpool for three days, held by ropes made of hemp, wool and maidens' hair, until one rope, containing the hair of an unfaithful girl, finally broke.

Jura Distillery

◍◍◍ 🏠 Craighouse
🕐 10am-5pm Mon-Sat (Nov-Mar: 10am-4pm Mon-Fri) 🌐 jurawhisky.com

⓮ Gigha

🅐 X9 🏛 Argyll & Bute
🚢 Tayinloan, Kintyre Peninsua 🌐 gigha.org.uk

Three miles off the west coast of Kintyre, and accessible by regular ferry from Tayinloan, Gigha is an attractive proposition thanks to the numerous white, sandy beaches sprinkled around its coastline. Ferries dock in Ardminish, Gigha's only village, where you can hire a bike from the Gigha Boats Activity Centre and go explore the island; they also have paddleboards and rowing boats if you want to get out onto the water.

A particular place of note is **Achamore Gardens**, acquired by James Horlick (inventor of the much-loved hot drink) in 1944; the house itself is now privately owned and off limits, but there's much to enjoy within the sub-tropical gardens, which are famous for their large rhododendrons, a bamboo maze and beautiful walled garden.

> Jura is said to take its name from the Norse word *dyr-oe*, meaning Deer Island, entirely appropriate as deer outnumber humans here by at least 30 to one.

Achamore Gardens
⊛ 🏠 Achamore House
📞 (01583) 505390 🕐 Dawn to dusk daily

Gigha Boats Activity Centre
Ardminish Bay
📞 (07876) 506520
🕐 Apr-Oct: 9am-6pm Mon-Sat, 11am-6pm Sun

15
Mallaig

🅰B4 🏠 Lochaber
🚌🚃🚢 From Ardvasar, Skye
ℹ Fort William; (01397) 701801

There's a good chance that you'll end up in Mallaig, as it's the main port for ferries to Skye (p222) and the Small Isles (p246), as well as being the terminus for the wonderful West Highland Railway from Fort William (p253) – the line along which the famous Jacobite Steam Train runs.

The village was founded in the 1840s, when the owner of the North Morar Estate, Lord Lovat, moved his tenants to the western part of the peninsula and encouraged fishing as a way of life. By 1851 Mallaig was the largest settlement in the area. The 1901 railway extension linking Mallaig to the national mainline was a further boon to the local economy and way of life.

↑ Colourful fishing boats line the pier in the busy port town of Mallaig on the West Coast

Today Mallaig is a classic west coast port town, the ambience more commercial than leisurely, but it is set in an area of outstanding beauty. At its heart is the harbour, which still has an active fishing fleet and is also the departure point for boat trips and wildlife cruises operated by **Western Isle Cruises**. The **Mallaig Heritage Centre** is a fascinating local history museum covering the impact of fishing, railways and ferries on local life.

Mallaig Heritage Centre
⊛ 🕐 🏠 Station Rd
🕐 Apr-Oct: 11am-4pm Mon-Sat 🌐 mallaigheritage. org.uk

Western Isle Cruises
⊛ 🕐 🏠 The Pier Office
🕐 Reduced service Nov-Mar
🌐 westernislecruises.co.uk

EAT

Tea Garden Café
This quirky café is famed for its delicious pint of prawns, hauled straight from the harbour and served with a zingy squeeze of lemon.

🅰B4 🏠 Backpackers Lodge, Station Rd, Mallaig 🌐 mallaig backpackers.co.uk

£ £ £

Boathouse
This well regarded, nautically themed restaurant offers a glorious seafood menu featuring the likes of Gigha halibut with chorizo and saffron potato.

🅰B6 🏠 Ardminish Bay, Gigha 🕐 Oct-Mar 🌐 boat houseongigha. com

£ £ £

↑ Jura whisky distillery and hotel, where tours and tastings of this famous dram are offered

16

Rum, Eigg, Muck and Canna

🅰B4 🏠Small Isles 🚢From Mallaig or Arisaig 🛈Fort William; (01397) 701801

Each of the four Small Isles has its own individual character, but shares a sense of tranquillity. Canna is a narrow island surrounded by cliffs and has a scattering of unworked archaeological sites. Once owned by Gaelic scholar John Lorne Campbell, it now belongs to the National Trust for Scotland and has very few inhabitants.

Eigg is the most varied island. Dominated by the distinctive sugarloaf hill, the Sgurr of Eigg, it has a glorious beach with "singing sands" that make odd noises when moved by feet or by the wind. Here the islanders symbolize the spirit of community land ownership, having successfully led a campaign to buy their island from their landlord.

Muck takes its name from the Gaelic for "pig", which it is said to resemble in shape. The smallest of the islands, but no less charming, it is owned by a family who live and farm on the island.

Rum is the largest and most magnificent island, with scabrous peaks that are home to an unusual colony of Manx shearwater birds. The island's rough tracks make it best suited to the active visitor. Now owned by Scottish Natural Heritage and a centre for red deer research, it previously belonged to the wealthy Bullough family who built the lavish **Kinloch Castle**.

Kinloch Castle

🏠Rum 🌐kinlochcastle friends.org

17

Mull

🅰B5 🏠Argyll 🚢Oban, Lochaline and Kilchoan 🛈Craignure; (01680) 812377

The largest of the Inner Hebridean islands, Mull features rough moorlands, the rocky peak of Ben More and a splendid beach at Calgary. Most roads follow the coastline, affording wonderful sea views.

On a promontory east of Craignure lies the 13th-century **Duart Castle**, home of the chief of Clan Maclean.

At the northern end of Mull is the picturesque town of Tobermory, with its brightly coloured buildings and a kaleidoscope of houses along the seafront. Built as a fishing village in 1788, it is now a popular port for yachts. The harbourside **Mull Aquarium** is Europe's first catch and

↑ Brightly coloured buildings line the street on Tobermory Harbour

release aquarium. With its touch pools and cinema, it holds great appeal for kids. Next door is the **Tobermory Distillery**, where both whisky and gin are distilled.

Duart Castle

♿🚻🅿 🏠Off A849, near Craignure 🕐Apr: 11am-4pm Sun-Thu; May-Oct: 10:30am-5pm daily 🌐duartcastle.com

Mull Aquarium

🏠Taigh Solais, Tobermory 🕐Mar-Oct: 9:30am-5pm daily 🌐mullaquarium.co.uk

Tobermory Distillery

♿🚻🅿 🏠Ledaig, Tobermory 🕐11am-5pm daily; tours hourly 🌐tobermorydistillery.com

---

18

Iona

🅰B5 🚢Fionnphort, Mull 🌐welcometoiona.com

The small and beautiful island of Iona is one of the biggest attractions on Scotland's west coast. The passenger only

↑ European shag perched on a rock on the tiny island of Canna

ferry from Fionnphort on Mull takes just five minutes to cross to Baile Mór, which consists of little more than a few cottages, a shop, restaurant and hotel. From here it's a short walk to the atmospheric remains of a 14th-century Augustinian nunnery, and then a further five minutes to the **Iona Heritage Centre**, with displays on the island's history including part of the stern of the steamer Guy Mannering, which sank offshore in 1865. But of course it's Iona Abbey that most people make a beeline for. The restored abbey stands on the site where Irish missionary St Columba began his crusade in 563 and made Iona the home of Christianity in Europe. In the graveyard of the abbey,

48 Scottish kings are said to be buried and four historic high crosses can be seen, two of them along the medieval Street of the Dead. Since 1938, when the Iona Community was formed, this has again been a religious centre. During the summer months the abbey has a large influx of visitors.

If you are lucky with the weather, head to **Fingal's Cave** on the Isle of Staffa. A true natural wonder, the cave is surrounded by "organ pipes" of basalt, said to be the inspiration for Mendelssohn's *Hebrides Overture* (1833). Boat trips run there from Ulva and Fionnphort and to the seven **Treshnish Isles**. These uninhabited islands are a sanctuary for thousands of seabirds, including puffins, razorbills, kittiwakes and skuas. Lunga is the main stop for tour boats.

Iona Heritage Centre
🕐 Easter–Oct: 9am–5pm Mon–Sat 🌐 ionaheritage. co.uk

Fingal's Cave and Treshnish Isles
⊛ 🅰 Staffa, west of Mull 🗓 Easter–Oct 🕐 Timetable varies, check website 🌐 staffatours.com

📷 PICTURE PERFECT
Tobermory Harbour

For that iconic snap of Tobermory's colourful waterfront, head to the aquarium end of Main Street. A lookout point here offers an excellent shot of the harbour, twinkling with the reflections of brightly coloured buildings.

EAT

Café Fish
Super-fresh seafood straight off the boat and a surprising wine list are on offer here. There's also a delightful quayside terrace in summer.

🅰 B5 🅰 23 Main St, Mull 🕐 Mid-Mar–Oct 🌐 thecafefish.com

£ £ £

Tobermory Fish and Chip Van
This cracking chippie van serves mackerel and scallops alongside the traditional fish'n'chips.

🅰 B5 🅰 Fisherman's Pier, Mull 🌐 tobermory fishandchipvan.com

£ £ £

Argyll Hotel
Crofters and local fishermen keep this cosy restaurant well-stocked with lamb, game, beef and seafood.

🅰 B5 🅰 Iona 🌐 argyllhotel iona.co.uk

£ £ £

19

Loch Awe

C5 · Argyll · Dalmally
loch-awe.com

One of the longest freshwater lochs in Scotland, Loch Awe stretches 40 km (25 miles) across a glen in the south-western Highlands. A short drive east from the town of Lochawe are the remains of Kilchurn Castle, abandoned after being struck by lightning in the 18th century. Dwarfing the castle is Ben Cruachan. The huge summit of 1,126 m (3,694 ft) can be reached by the narrow Pass of Brander, where Robert the Bruce fought the Clan MacDougal in 1308. Near the village of Taynuilt is the preserved Lorn Furnace at Bonawe, which serves as a reminder of the iron-smelting industry that destroyed much of the area's woodland in the last centuries.

On the A816, to the south of the loch, is **Kilmartin Museum**, displaying artifacts from local prehistoric sites, as well as reconstructions of boats, utensils and jewellery, and providing a vivid glimpse into what life was like in prehistoric Scotland.

Kilmartin Museum

Kilmartin
Daily · kilmartin.org

Did You Know?

The first transatlantic telephone cable landed at Oban during the Cold War.

20

Kintyre

B6 · Argyll & Bute
Oban · Campbeltown
wildaboutargyll.co.uk

A long, narrow peninsula stretching far south of Glasgow, Kintyre has superb views across to the islands of Gigha, Islay and Jura. The 14-km (9-mile) Crinan Canal, which opened in 1801 and has a total of 15 locks, bustles with pleasure craft in the summer. The town of Tarbert (meaning "isthmus" in Gaelic) takes its name from the neck on which it stands, which is narrow enough to drag a boat across, between the waters of Loch Fyne and West Loch Tarbert. This feat was first achieved by the Viking King Magnus Barfud who, in 1198, was granted by treaty as much land as he was able to sail around.

Travel further south past Campbeltown and the B842 road ends at the headland known as the Mull of Kintyre, which was made famous when former Beatle Paul McCartney, who had a home in Kintyre, added lyrics and commercialized a traditional pipe tune of the same name. Westwards from Kintyre lies the isle of Rathlin. It is here that Robert the Bruce learned patience in his constant struggles against the English by observing a spider weaving an elaborate web in a cave.

21

Oban

C5 · Argyll
North Pier · oban.org.uk

Known as the "Gateway to the Isles", this bustling port on the Firth of Lorne commands fine views of the Argyll coast. Shops crowd the seafront around the "little bay" which gives Oban its name, and fresh fish is always for sale on the busy pier. Regular ferries leave for Mull, Coll, Tiree,

Barra, South Uist, Islay, Colonsay and Lismore, making Oban one of the most-visited places on the west coast. Built on a steep hill, the town is dominated by the immense McCaig's Tower, an eccentric Colosseum-like structure built in the 1800s. Other major landmarks are the pink granite cathedral and the 600-year-old ruined keep of Dunollie Castle, once the northern outpost of the Dalriadic Scots. Among Oban's other attractions are working centres for glass and pottery, and Oban Distillery, producers of fine malt whisky. On rainy days a good option is the old-fashioned **Oban War and Peace Museum** which offers an interesting insight into local culture.

At the end of July, yachts converge on the town for West Highland Week, while at the end of the month, Oban's Highland Games take place. Nearby Kilmore, Taynuilt and Tobermory, on Mull, also host summer Highland Games.

A few miles north of Oban, off the A85, is the 13th-century **Dunstaffnage Castle** where Flora MacDonald was briefly imprisoned for helping Bonnie Prince Charlie *(p64)* escape in 1746. South of Oban is the Isle of Seil, reached via the 18th-century "Bridge over the Atlantic". On the tiny island of Easdale, just off Seil, the **Easdale Folk Museum** houses displays on the region's fascinating slate-mining history. Further south, on the Isle of Luing (reached via the Cuan car ferry), the superb **Atlantic Islands Centre** traces the development of the Slate Islands which lie opposite – there's a terrific café here too. Back on the mainland, **Arduaine Garden**, is noted for its rare varieties of spring-blooming rhododendrons and azaleas.

← Kilchurn Castle, on a rocky peninsula on Loch Awe

↑ The beautiful white sands of Balevullin Beach on the windswept island of Tiree

Oban War and Peace Museum
Corran Esplanade Mar-Nov: daily obanmuseum.org.uk

Dunstaffnage Castle
Connel Apr-Sep: daily; Oct-Mar: Sat-Wed historicenvironment.scot

Easdale Folk Museum
Easdale Apr-mid-Oct: 11am-4pm daily easdale museum.org

Atlantic Islands Centre
Barcaldine, near Connel Times vary, see website isleofluing.org

Arduaine Garden
Arduaine Apr-Sep: 9:30am-5pm daily; Oct-Mar: 9:30am-4pm daily nts.org.uk

22

Coll and Tiree

B4, A5 Argyll From Oban From Glasgow to Tiree only Oban visitcoll.co.uk; isleoftiree.com

Despite frequent winter gale warnings, these islands, the most westerly in the Inner Hebrides, often record more hours of sunshine than the rest of Britain. They offer beautiful white-sand beaches and impressive surf. Tiree's soil is 60 per cent shell sand, so no trees can grow. As a result, it is perhaps the windiest place in Scotland. Wild flowers flourish here in spring.

Breacachadh Castle (not open to the public), the 15th-century home of Clan Maclean until 1750, overlooks a bay in south Coll. Tiree has two free museums, the Trenish Isles Exhibition, about the natural history of this group of islands, visible from Tiree, and the Skerryvore Lighthouse Museum in Hynish. The lighthouse stands 20 km (12 miles) offshore.

23
Ardnamurchan Peninsula

🅰B4 🅰Argyll 🚢Corran Ferry on A82 from Glencoe to Fort William, or Fishnish (Mull) to Kilchoan 🅦west highlandpeninsulas.com

The Ardnamurchan Peninsula and the adjacent areas of Moidart and Morvern are some of the west coast's best-kept secrets. They are characterized by a sinuous coastline, rocky mountains and beaches. Some of the best beaches are at the tip of the peninsula, which also happens to be the most westerly point of mainland Britain.

The **Ardnamurchan Lighthouse Visitor Centre** at Kilchoan explores the fascinating history of lighthouses and light-keeping. The 1846 lighthouse was designed by Alan Stevenson, uncle of author Robert Louis Stevenson, and is one of many built by the Stevenson family throughout Britain.

The award-winning **Ardnamurchan Natural History Visitor Centre** at Glenmore has encouraged wildlife to inhabit its "living building", and wild red deer can even graze on its turf roof. An enchanting wooded road runs from Salen to Strontian, or head north to Acharacle.

Ardnamurchan Lighthouse Visitor Centre

🅰Kilchoan 🅒Apr-Oct: 10am-5pm daily 🅦ardnamurchanlighthouse.com

Ardnamurchan Natural History Visitor Centre

🅰Glenmore 🅒Mar-Oct: 9am-5pm Sun-Fri 🅦ardnamurchannaturalhistorycentre.com

24
Arran

🅰C6 🅰North Ayrshire 🚢From Ardrossan to Brodick; from Claonaig (Mull of Kintyre) to Lochranza (Apr-Oct only) 🛈The Pier, Brodick; (01770) 303774 🅦visitarran.com

With dramatic mountain peaks, serene beaches, inland lochs and stunning scenery, Arran offers all the beauty of rural Scotland in one tiny package. Arran is thought to have been populated as long ago as the end of the last Ice Age. The island's Neolithic chambered burial tombs, such as the one at Torrylinn near Lagg in the south, are an indication of this. Bronze Age stone circles can also be seen around Machrie on the west coast. Vikings arrived from about AD 800 and exerted an influence for more than four centuries.

GREAT VIEW
Arran's Goatfell Mountains

The three-mile Glen Rosa to Brodick walk is one of the best on the island, and it offers some stunning views over the island's Goatfell mountains. Keep your eyes peeled for deer and golden eagles too.

> The Ardnamurchan Peninsula and the adjacent areas of Moidart and Morvern are some of the west coast's best-kept secrets.

After the Battle of Largs in 1263, when Alexander III defeated the Norsemen, Scotland bought Arran from the Vikings in 1266.

Robert the Bruce stayed on Arran on his return to Scotland in 1307. His followers had already been harassing the garrison at **Brodick Castle**, then occupied by supporters of the King of England. Legend states that it was from Arran that Bruce saw a signal fire on the Ayrshire coast that told him it was safe to return to the mainland and launch the campaign against the English. Parts of the castle still date from the 13th century, though it has had many later additions.

Today, visitors tend to come to Arran for outdoor pursuits. Golf is especially popular, with seven golf courses on the island, including 18-hole courses at Brodick, Whiting Bay and Lamlash.

Brodick is the island's only real town. The more mountainous parts offer some of the most spectacular hill walking in Central Scotland. The Goatfell ridge to the east of Glen Rosa and Beinn Tarsuinn to the west has a rugged beauty.

In the north of the island is the **Lochranza Distillery**, the island's first legal distillery, and one of few remaining independent distilleries in Scotland. Until the 19th century, Arran was known for its illicit malt whisky known as "Arran Water".

Brodick Castle
⑥ ⑧ ⑳ ⓝⓣⓢ 🏰 Brodick
🕐 Apr-Oct: 10am-5pm daily; gardens all year 🌐 nts.org.uk

Lochranza Distillery
⑥ ⓘ ⑳ ⑥ 🏰 Lochranza
🕐 10am-5pm daily (Oct-Mar: to 4pm) 🌐 arranwhisky.com

←

Serene Artdoe Beach on the northeast side of the Ardnamurchan Peninsula

↑ One of many opulent bedrooms inside Mount Stuart House on the isle of Bute

㉕
Bute

🅰️C6 🏰 Argyll & Bute
🚢 From Wemyss Bay to Rothesay or Colintraive to Rhubodach 🚢 From Dunoon ℹ️ Rothesay; (01700) 507043

Bute is almost an extension of the Cowal Peninsula, and the small ferry from Colintraive takes only five minutes to cross the Kyles of Bute to Rhubodach on the island. It's is a long drive from Glasgow, however, and most people travel via Wemyss Bay on the Firth of Clyde to the main town, Rothesay.

Just 25 km (16 miles) long by 8 km (5 miles) at its widest point, Bute has been occupied since at least the Bronze Age. The remains of the chapel at St Ninian's Point on the west coast date from around the 6th century, while **Rothesay Castle**, now ruined, is mostly a 12th-century structure. It saw struggles between islanders and Vikings in the 13th century, but over the last 120 years, it has played a more placid role as a holiday resort.

Bute's main attraction is **Mount Stuart House**, 5 km (3 miles) south of Rothesay. Built in 1877, the house's Gothic features reflect the Marquess's interests in mythology, religion and astronomy.

Rothesay Castle
⑧ 🏰 Castle Hill St, Rothesay
🕐 Apr-Sep: 9:30am-5:30pm daily; Oct-Mar: 10am-4pm Mon-Wed, Sat & Sun
🌐 historicenvironment.scot

Mount Stuart House
⑥ ⑧ ⑳ 🏰 Mount St
🕐 Apr-Oct: 11am-5pm daily
🌐 mountstuart.com

The vast wilderness of Rannoch Moor and Schiehallion in the distance ↑

26 Glencoe

🅰C4 🏠Lochaber 🚍Fort William 🚌Glencoe 🛈NTS Visitor Centre, Glencoe; Open Mar-Oct: 9:30am-5:30pm daily, Nov-Feb: 10am-4pm daily 🌐nts.org.uk

Renowned for its awesome scenery and savage history, Glencoe was compared by Dickens to "a burial ground of a race of giants". The precipitous slopes of Buachaille Etive Mòr and the knife-edged ridge of Aonach Eagach offer a formidable challenge even to experienced mountaineers. Against a backdrop of craggy peaks and the tumbling River Coe, the Glen offers superb hill walking. The Visitor Centre has details of routes, ranging from an easy walk near Signal Rock (from which the signal was given for the massacre of Glencoe) to a stiff 10-km (6-mile) haul up the Devil's Staircase. Guided walks are offered in summer by NTS Rangers. Take the chairlift at the **Glencoe Mountain** resort for dramatic views.

To the southwest, beautiful Glen Etive leads to the head of impressive Loch Etive, which emerges on the coast at the Connel Bridge north of Oban. At the Ballachulish Bridge a side road branches to Kinlochleven, at the head of a long attractive loch.

Glencoe Mountain

⊘ 🏠Kingshouse, Glencoe ⏰Daily 🌐glencoe mountain.co.uk

27 Rannoch Moor

🅰D5 🏠Perthshire

Curlews call and buzzards mew as they circle above this desolate expanse of wet and wild moorland, dotted with ponds, rivers and lochans. Rannoch Moor is one of the last remaining wildernesses in Europe, stretching far north and west from Rannoch Station, where exhilarating walking trails begin. In the shadow of Schiehallion, the moor is home to an abundance of wildlife, including herds of wild deer. The Black Wood of Rannoch quilt the mountain's lower slopes, and Alpine flora flourish on the bare rocky slopes of 1,214-m (3,983-ft) Ben Lawers.

MASSACRE OF GLENCOE

In 1692, the Glencoe MacDonalds chief was five days late with an oath of submission to William III, providing an excuse to root out a nest of Jacobite supporters. For ten days 130 soldiers, under Robert Campbell, were hospitably entertained by the MacDonalds before, in a terrible breach of trust, the soldiers turned on them and killed them. A political scandal ensued, but there were no official reprimands for three years.

West Highland Museum

🏛 🅰 Cameron Square
🕐 Daily (Sep-Jun: Mon-Sat)
🅦 westhighlandmuseum.
org.uk

Jacobite Steam Train

🚂 Fort William 🕐 Departs
10:15am & 2:40pm (Apr, May:
Mon-Fri; Jun-Sep: daily)
🅦 westcoastrailways.co.uk

29
Glenfinnan

🅰 C4 🅰 Highand 🅦 visit
fortwilliam.co.uk

One of Scotland's most iconic
sights is the Glenfinnan
viaduct, a 21-arched structure
completed in 1898 by Sir
Robert McAlpine. The viaduct
will be especially familiar to
fans of Harry Potter, as the
Hogwarts Express puffed
along it in several of the films.
In the village stands the
18-m- (60ft-) high **Glenfinnan
Monument**, erected by
Alexander MacDonald in 1815
to commemorate the moment
when Bonnie Prince Charlie
raised his battle standard
sixty years earlier; the lone
Highlander at the top was a
later addition. The **Visitor
Centre** opposite explains the
1745 uprising. Another point
of interest in the village is the
Glenfinnan Station Museum,
which relays the history of the
West Highland railway.

Glenfinnan Monument and Visitor Centre

♿ 🚻 🅝🅣🅢 🅰 Glenfinnan,
Lochaber 🕐 Times vary,
check website 🅦 nts.org.uk

Glenfinnan Station Museum

♿ 🚻 🏛 🅰 Station Road,
Glenfinnan 🕐 Apr-mid-Oct
daily 🅦 glenfinnanstation
museum.co.uk

28
Fort William

🅰 C4 🅰 Highand 🅦 visit
fortwilliam.co.uk

Fort William, one of the major
towns on the west coast, is
noted not for its looks but for
its convenient location at the
foot of Ben Nevis (p208). In
fact Fort William now has
something of a reputation as
the outdoor capital of Britain,
thanks to the plethora of
mountain and watersports
activities available nearby.
A number of outlets rent out
bikes, as well as kayaks for
use on Loch Linnhe, while
mountaineering guides lead
various expeditions.

For a rainy day activity, the
West Highland Museum is
worth a visit for its displays
on all aspects of Highland life.

**The Jacobite Steam
Train**, which doubles as the
Hogwarts Express, runs the
magical route from here to
Mallaig (p245).

→

The Jacobite Steam Train
chugging along the
Glenfinnan Viaduct

← Blair Castle's grand ballroom, built for the Atholl Highlanders

Blair Castle and Gardens

🖐️🕐👜 🅰️ Blair Atholl Estate 🕐 Apr-Oct: 9:30am-5:30pm daily (last admission for castle tours: 4:30pm) �🅦 blair-castle.co.uk

Atholl Country Life Museum

🖐️👜 🅰️ Old School, Blair Atholl 🕐 Apr-Oct: 10am-5pm daily �🅦 blairatholl.org.uk

---

㉛

Black Isle

🅰️D3 🄰 Ross & Cromarty 🚆🚌 Inverness ⓦ black-isle. info

Believed to have taken its name from either the gaelic word *dubh*, meaning black, or the mild climate which often leaves the frost-free fields a distinct black colour, the Black Isle is a broad peninsula largely made up of low rolling hills, extensive tracts of farmland and pretty fishing villages. The most appealing of these is Cromarty, which was an important 18th-century port. Many of its merchant houses still stand, but it is its associations with the author and geologist Hugh Miller (1802–56) that attracts most people.

㉚

Blair Atholl

🅰️D4 🄰 Lochaber 🚆🚌 ⓦ blair-castle.co.uk

The neat and orderly village of Blair Atholl is home to the spectacular **Blair Castle**, a rambling, turreted affair that has been altered so often in its 700-year history that it now provides a unique insight into the history and ever-changing tastes of aristocratic life in the Highlands. The elegant 18th-century wing displays the gloves and pipe of Bonnie Prince Charlie *(p64)*, who came to gather support for a Jacobite uprising. Family portraits span 300 years and include paintings by such masters as Johann Zoffany and Sir Peter Lely. Sir Edwin Landseer's *Death of a Hart in Glen Tilt* (1850) also features. In 1844 Queen Victoria conferred on its owners, the Dukes of Atholl, permission to maintain a private army, the existing Atholl Highlanders. On the hour, one of the Highlander pipers plays for a few minutes in front of the castle entrance.

The castle aside, there are a couple of other worthwhile sites in the village; down by the River Tilt, the 15th-century watermill cranks into action each summer, though more appealing is its delightful little tearoom. Close by, the **Atholl Country Life Museum,** with its three small galleries, reconstructed post office and a fascinating audio-visual display, offers a thorough trawl through Highland life and provides a unique insight into the Blair Atholl community from ancient times to present day. Among the numerous displays, its star exhibit is, bizzarely, a rather dishevelled-looking stuffed Highland cow.

HIGHLAND CLEARANCES

During the heyday of the clan system, tenants paid their land-holding chieftains rent in the form of military service. However, with the destruction of the clan system after the Battle of Culloden, landowners began to demand a financial rent, which their tenants were unable to afford, and the land was gradually bought up by Lowland and English farmers. In what became known as "the year of the sheep" (1792), thousands of tenants were evicted, sometimes forcibly, to make way for live stock. Many emigrated to Australia, America and Canada. The ruins of their crofts can still be seen today, especially in Sutherland and Wester Ross.

Did You Know?

The Moray Firth dolphins are the biggest bottlenose dolphins in the world.

The **Hugh Miller Museum** recalls his life in detail, with a marvellous collection of his fossils alongside many personal effects including his desk, mallet and walking stick. Next door is the cottage where he was born, now restored to represent what it was like during Miller's day. The nearby **Cromarty Courthouse** runs tours of the town.

A mile along from Fortrose is Rosemarkie, with a lovely sandy beach and the terrific **Groam House Museum**, which has 15 Pictish standing stones, a collection that's second only to those in the Meigle Museum *(p197)* just outside Blairgowrie.

Hugh Miller Museum

⊘ 🏛 NTS 🏠 Church St, Cromarty ⏰ Mid-Apr–Sep: 1–5pm daily; Oct: 1–5pm Sat-Mon 🌐 nts.org.uk

Cromarty Courthouse

⊘ 🏠 Church St, Cromarty ⏰ Apr–mid-Oct: noon–4pm Sun-Thu; mid-Oct–Apr: by appointment 🌐 cromarty-courthouse.org.uk

Groam House Museum

⊘ 🏠 High St, Rosemarkie ⏰ Apr–Oct: 11am–4:30pm Mon-Fri, 2–4:30pm Sat & Sun 🌐 groamhouse.

32
Moray Firth

🅰 D3 🏠 Moray 🚆 Elgin 🌐 morayspeyside.com

Renowned for its wildlife-spotting opportunities, most notably from the popular viewing spot at Chanonry Point, the Moray Firth is home to a wealth of marine life. Harbour seals, porpoises, white-beaked and bottlenose dolphins and several species of whale come here to feed. Sightings vary from year to year, but the whales are most commonly spotted between July and late September. Learn more about the Moray Firth's resident and visiting sealife at the **WDC Scottish Dolphin Centre** at Spey Bay. Dolphin spotting tours are available.

WDC Scottish Dolphin Centre

⊘ 😊 🏛 🏠 Spey Bay, Fochabers, Moray ⏰ Times vary, check website 🚫 mid-Dec–mid-Feb 🌐 dolphincentre.whales.org

Fort George

🅰 D3 🏠 Inverness 🚆🚌 From Inverness ⏰ Apr–Sep: 9:30am–5:30pm daily; Oct–Mar: 10am–4pm daily 🌐 historicenvironment.scot

One of the finest examples of European military architecture, Fort George holds a commanding position on the Moray Firth. Completed in 1769, it was built after the Jacobite risings to discourage further rebellion, and is still a military garrison.

The **Regimental Museum** of the Highlanders Regiment is in the Fort, and some barrack rooms show the conditions of common soldiers more than 200 years ago. The **Grand Magazine** contains an outstanding collection of arms and military equipment. Fort George's battlements also offer views of dolphins playing in the Moray Firth.

Dolphins playing in the Moray Firth, best seen off Chanonry Point ↑

34 (NTS)

Culloden

🗺 D3 📍 Inverness-shire
🚌🚂 From Inverness

The desolate battlefield of Culloden looks much as it did on 16 April 1746, when the last battle was fought on British soil. Here the Jacobite cause, under Bonnie Prince Charlie's leadership (p64), perished from the attack of nearly 9,000 troops, led by the Duke of Cumberland. Visitors can roam the battlefield, visit the clan graves and experience the audio-visual displays at the **NTS Visitor Centre**.

Roughly 1.5 km (1 mile) east of Culloden are the outstanding Neolithic burial sites at Clava Cairns.

NTS Visitor Centre
⊗ ⓘ 🍴 🏠 📍 On the B9006
🕙 Daily 🌐 nts.org.uk

35

Strathpeffer

🗺 C3 📍 Ross & Cromarty
🚂 Dingwall 🚌 Inverness
🌐 strathpeffer.org

Standing 8 km (5 miles) east of the Rogie Falls, the holiday centre of Strathpeffer still retains the refined charm that made it well known as a Victorian spa and health resort. The town's huge hotels and gracious layout recall the days when European royalty and lesser mortals flocked to the chalybeate- and sulphur-laden springs, believed to alleviate tuberculosis. It is still possible to sample the water at the unmanned **Water Tasting Pavilion** found in the town centre.

Water Tasting Pavilion
📍 The Square 🕙 Easter-Oct: daily

36

Cawdor Castle

🗺 D3 📍 On B9090 (off A96)
🚂 Nairn, then bus or taxi
🚌 From Inverness 🕙 Mid-Apr-early Oct: 10am-5:30pm daily (last entry 5pm) 🌐 cawdorcastle.com

With its turreted central tower, moat and drawbridge, Cawdor Castle is one of the Highlands' most romantic stately homes. Though the castle is famed for being the 11th-century home of Shakespeare's tragic character Macbeth, and the scene of his murder of King Duncan, it is historically unproven that either figure came here. An ancient holly tree that is preserved in the vaults is said to be the one under which, in 1372, Thane William's donkey stopped for a rest during its master's search for a place to build a fortress. According to legend, this was how the site for the castle was chosen. Now, after 600 years of continuous occupation (it is still the home of the Thanes of Cawdor) the house contains a number of rare tapestries and portraits by the 18th-century painters Joshua Reynolds (1723–92) and George Romney (1734–1802).

Elegant furniture in the Pink Bedroom and Woodcock Room includes fine work by the 18th-century designers Chippendale and Sheraton. In the Old Kitchen, the huge Victorian cooking range stands as a shrine to below-stairs drudgery.

STAY

Culgower House
Between Brora and Helmsdale, on the East Sutherland coast, this quaint family home is nestled in wooded hills. Rooms have sea views and breakfasts are a dream.

🗺 D3 📍 Loth, Helmsdale
🕙 Dec-Mar 🌐 culgower house.com

££££

Bannockburn Inn
Watch dolphins swim in the Moray Firth from this beautifully renovated 18th-century fisherman's cottage with stunning sea views.

🗺 D3 📍 Stafford St, Helmsdale 🌐 bannock burninn.co.uk

££££

↑ The Black Water tumbling over Rogie Falls, Ross-shire

Dunrobin Castle, seat of the Earls of Sutherland since the 13th century

The castle grounds provide beautiful nature trails, as well as a nine-hole golf course.

37
Dornoch

D3 **Sutherland**
Golspie, Tain
Inverness, Tain
Carnegie Court House, Castle Street **visit dornoch.com**

With its first-class golf course and extensive sandy beaches, Dornoch is a popular holiday resort, but it has retained a peaceful atmosphere. The medieval cathedral (now serving as the parish church) was all but destroyed in a clan dispute in 1570; it was eventually restored in the 1920s for its 700th anniversary. Recently, the American singer Madonna chose the cathedral for the christening of her son and for her own wedding in 2000.

A stone at the beach end of River Street marks the place where Janet Horne, the last woman to be tried for witchcraft in Scotland, was executed in June 1722.

Nineteen kilometres (12 miles) to the northeast is the stately, Victorianized pile of **Dunrobin Castle**, magnificently situated in a great park with gardens overlooking the sea. Since the 13th century this has been the seat of the Earls of Sutherland. Many of its rooms are open to visitors.

The peaceful town of Tain to the south became an administrative centre for the Highland Clearances, when the tolbooth was used as a jail. All is explained in the heritage centre, **Tain Through Time**.

Dunrobin Castle
Near Golspie
Apr-Oct: daily
dunrobincastle.co.uk

Tain Through Time
Tower St
Jun-Aug: Mon-Sat; Apr, May, Sep & Oct: Mon-Fri
tainmuseum.org.uk

→ Helmsdale's Emigrants Statue commemorating Scottish diaspora

38
Helmsdale

D2 **Sutherland**
From Inverness

Founded by Vikings, Helmsdale was settled in the 19th century by crofters turfed off their land by the Duke of Sutherland. A flotilla of fishing boats crewed by their descendants still bobs in a harbour surrounded by neat stone houses. The **Timespan Heritage Centre** tells the story of Helmsdale's fascinating history and of the gold rush that followed the discovery of small amounts of the precious metal in the Helmsdale River in 1868. The Emigrants Statue commemorates the many people who fled Scotland and sailed to far-off lands in search of a better life during the Highland clearances.

Timespan Heritage Centre
Dunrobin St
Mid-Mar-Oct: 10am-5pm daily; Nov-mid-Mar: noon-4pm Tue, 10am-3pm Sat & Sun **timespan.org.uk**

Red-roofed croft on the Applecross Peninsula

③⑨
Gairloch

🅰B3 🅸Gale Centre, Achtercairn 🅦galeaction forum.co.uk

Most visitors come to Gairloch, whose name comes from *Ghearr Loch*, meaning Short Loch, for its beaches, in particular the appropriately named Big Sand, which fronts an enormous campsite, but there's also much of cultural interest. A few paces along from the excellent visitor centre at Achtercairn, and housed within an old nuclear bunker, the new **Gairloch Heritage Museum** is a cut above your average museum, with beautifully presented collections pertaining to traditional Highland Life, though its most noteworthy section is the Poolewe Hoard, a dazzling assortment of bronze age artifacts which were discovered by a local farmer in 1877. Gairloch is also one of the best spots along the west coast for wildlife watching, with a couple of excellent outfits running dolphin and whale-watching excursions from the harbour at Charlestown.

Gairloch Heritage Museum

🚶🅿🏳 🅳Apr-Oct: 10am-6pm Mon-Sat (to 8pm Thu) 🅦gairlochmuseum.org

④⓪
Knoydart Peninsula

🅰B4 🅦visitknoydart.co.uk

Inaccessible by car, this remote Peninsula is tailor-made for those seeking a few days well and truly off the beaten track. The main walking route into Knoydart starts at Kinloch Hourn, at the far eastern end of Loch Hourn; most walkers break at Barisdale, where there's a bothy and a campsite. A second, much harder, route

Panoramic views over Loch Hourn and *(inset)* red deer on the slopes of ↓ Ladhar Beinn

begins at the western end of Lock Arkaig through Glen Dessary. For those who don't fancy the walk, there are regular ferries from Mallaig *(p245)* to Inverie, the area's one village of note and location for mainland Britain's most remote pub – as good a reason as any to make the effort to get here.

In 1997, the Knoydart Foundation was set up to buy and then manage the peninsula, and it took just two years before a community buyout was secured. Today, Knoydart is popular with more

---

DRINK

The Old Forge
Rural charm, hearty food, local ales, stunning views and no phone signal. Not only does the Old Forge have the distinction of being the most remote pub in Scotland and mainland Britain, it also happens to be one of the best.

🅰B4 🅰Inverie 🅦Weds 🅦theoldforge.co.uk

£ £ £

↑ Pub garden at Applecross village, a popular stop on the North Coast 500

experienced hillwalkers, drawn to the area by the prospect of chalking off one – or all – of the peninsula's four munros.

41
Applecross Peninsula

🅰B4 ⓦapplecross.uk.com

The Applecross Peninsula is not the easiest place to get to, but once you do get there, the views across the Sound of Raasay towards Skye (p222) are as glorious as any in Scotland. The peninsula can only be reached via two roads, the one from the south, across the *Bealach na Bà* (Pass of the Cattle), rated as one of the most exhilarating anywhere in Britain – and certainly a drive not to be missed. The coast road from the north is not nearly as dramatic, but it is no less enjoyable.

At the heart of the Applecross peninsula is the village of the same name, though beyond a small heritage centre and the local church there's not a whole lot to do, which is actually part of its appeal. You'd do well to settle in at the fabulous local pub, the Applecross Inn, and soak up the glorious views.

> Applecross is not the easiest place to get to, but the views across the Sound of Raasay towards Skye are as glorious as any in Scotland.

Eilean Donan Castle amid the stunning natural scenery of Glen Shiel ↑

42

Glen Shiel

🅰C4 🅰Skye & Lochalsh
🚆Kyle of Lochalsh 🚌Glen
Shiel 🛈Bayfield House,
Bayfield Rd, Portree;
(01478) 612992

Dominating one of Scotland's
most haunting regions, the
awesome summits of the Five
Sisters of Kintail rear into view
as the A87 enters Glen Shiel.
The Visitor Centre at Morvich
offers ranger-led excursions in
summer. Further west, and
sitting serenely at the confluence of three lochs – Alsh,
Long and Duich – romantic
Eilean Donan Castle is one of
the most memorable sights in
Scotland. After becoming a
Jacobite stronghold, it was
destroyed in 1719 by English
warships. Restored in the 19th
century, the re-created rooms –
among them the banqueting
hall and billeting room – hold
numerous exhibits such as a
lock of Bonnie Prince Charlie's
hair. The castle has also been
used as a film set, featuring
in both *Highlander* and the
James Bond epic *The World
is Not Enough*.

Eilean Donan Castle

🎟🏠🧒 🅰Off A87, near
Dornie 🕐Feb-Dec: daily
🌐eileandonancastle.com

43

Wester Ross

🅰C3 🅰Ross & Cromarty
🚆Achnasheen, Strath-
carron 🚌Gairloch 🌐visit-
wester-ross.com

Leaving Loch Carron to the
south, the A890 suddenly
enters the northern Highlands
and the wilderness of Wester
Ross. The Torridon Estate has
some of the oldest mountains
on earth (Torridonian rock is
over 600 million years old),
and is home to red deer, wildcats and wild goats. Peregrine
falcons and golden eagles
nest in the sandstone mass of
Beinn Eighe, above Torridon
village, with views over
Applecross towards Skye. The
Torridon Countryside Centre
offers guided walks in season.

Further north, the A832
cuts through the Beinn Eighe
National Nature Reserve,
Britain's oldest wildlife sanctuary. Remnants of the
ancient Caledonian pine forest
still stand on the banks and
isles of Loch Maree, sheltering
wildcats and pine martens.
Buzzards and golden eagles
nest above. **Beinn Eighe
Visitor Centre** has information on the reserve.

Along the coast, a series of
exotic gardens thrive in the
warming influence of the Gulf
Stream *(p55)*. The most
impressive of these is
Inverewe Garden.

Torridon Countryside Centre

🎟🅰🅰Torridon 📞(01445)
791368 🕐Apr-Sep: Sun-Fri

Beinn Eighe Visitor Centre

🅰Near Kinlochewe, on
A832 🕐Mar-Oct: daily
🌐nature.scot

44 🎟🥾🍽🏛

Inverewe Garden

🅰C3 🅰On A832, near
Poolewe, Ross-shire
🕐Daily (house: Apr-Oct)
🌐nts.org.uk

Over 130,000 visitors a year
come to this national treasure.
The gardens contain an extraordinary variety of trees,
shrubs and flowers from
around the world, despite its
latitude of 57.8° north.

Inverewe was started in
1862 by 20-year-old Osgood
Mackenzie after he was given
a large estate of exposed,
barren land next to his
family's holding. He began
by planting shelter trees then
created a walled garden using
imported soil. He found that
the climate, warmed by the
North Atlantic Drift from the

Gulf Stream, encouraged the growth of a range of exotic species.

By 1922, it had achieved international recognition as one of the world's great plant collections, and in 1952 was donated to the National Trust for Scotland. Now one of Scotland's leading botanical gardens, Inverewe has Blue Nile lilies, the tallest Australian gum trees in Britain and rhododendrons from China. There's colour all year, but the gardens are at their best between spring and autumn.

45
Ullapool

⚑ C3 🏛 Ross and Cromarty 🚌 Inverness 🚗🚕 ℹ Argyle St 🌐 ullapool.com

Located on a peninsula jutting into Loch Broom, Ullapool is one of the west coast's most attractive towns. It's also the largest town in the northwest Highlands, built as a fishing station by the British Fisheries Commission in 1788. Fishing remains a significant industry, particularly in winter, when East European "klondyker" factory shops moor in the loch. An afternoon's stroll here takes visitors through wide streets and past white-washed houses and palm trees. The town is also home to the **Ullapool Museum**, housed in an old church built by Thomas Telford. Exhibitions on crofting and the sea form the mainstay of the museum collection, while the local history walks run by the museum staff each Thursday are well worth joining in.

Ullapool Museum
♿🐕 🏠 7-8 West Argyle St ⏰ Apr-Oct: Mon-Sat 🌐 ullapoolmuseum.co.uk

EAT

Seafood Shack
The seasonal, open-air shack has become one of the west coast's most popular eateries, serving the likes of hot crab claws, lobster burger and tempura haddock wrap. Cash only.

🏠 West Argyle St, Ullapool ⏰ Apr-Oct 🌐 seafoodshack.co.uk

£££

DRINK

Ceilidh Place
Known for its live music, this restaurant/bar also offers a variety of tasty dishes like Loch Broom langoustines with lemon mayo, and venison with redcurrant pie and mash.

🏠 14 West Argyle St, Ullapool 🌐 theceilidh place.com

£££

The quaint Ullapool Museum, housed in an old church ↑

GREAT VIEW
Sango Bay

A popular stop on the North Coast 500 route, and for good reason. The stunning viewpoint over Sango Bay is easily accessed from the A838 at Durness. There is also a good campsite next to the beach if you can't bring yourself to leave.

46

Falls of Shin

C3 **Achany Glen**
(01549) 402888

A picturesque waterfall on the River Shin, the Falls of Shin attracts visitors every year to see Atlantic salmon leap on their upstream migration from mid-May to late autumn – in fact it's one of the best places anywhere in the UK to witness this remarkable phenomenon. From the car park by the state-of-the-art wood-clad visitor centre, a path heads down to a viewing platform high above the falls, from where you can watch transfixed as these majestic fish attempt to jump the thundering cascade. The visitor centre itself has an exhibition on the falls, and its famous inhabitants, as well as a superb restaurant, while there's an excellent children's playground and mini-golf course next door.

_____

47

Cape Wrath and the North Coast

C2 **Sutherland & Caithness**

The northern edge of main-land Scotland encompasses the full variety of Highland geography – rugged and mountainous moorlands, pristine white-sand beaches, dramatic rocky coastlines

Smoo Cave near Durness in Sutherland and *(inset)* its interior waterfall

↓

carved by ferocious north Atlantic waves and gently undulating sheep pastures as far as the eye can see.

Cape Wrath is alluring not only for its name but for its cliffs and its many sea stacks, swarming with sea-birds. In summer, the 13-km (8-mile) road leading to Cape Wrath is served by mini-bus, reached only by taking a ferry from the pier by the Cape Wrath Hotel.

At Durness is Smoo Cave, an awesome cavern hollowed out of limestone. **Smoo Cave Tours** run trips there. Just outside the town, a small community of artists has established the Balnakeil Craft Village, which displays pottery, wood carving, enamelwork, printmaking and paintings by local artists. Astonishingly white beaches follow along the coast, and the road then loops round Loch Eriboll, the deepest of Scotland's many sea lochs.

The **Strathnaver Museum** in Bettyhill explains the notor-ious Sutherland Clearances, which saw the forced evictions of over 15,000 people. At Rossal, 16 km (10 miles) south, a walk around an excavated village offers information on life in pre-Clearance days.

The main town here is Thurso, site of Northlands, the Scottish Nordic Music

EAT

Côte du Nord
An innovative nine course set dinner menu showcasing the finest local produce is served at this intimate restaurant on the very north coast of Scotland.

🅐C2 🏠The School House, 2 Kirtomy, Bettyhill 🕐Mar-Oct 🔲cotedunord.co.uk

£ £ £

Mac & Wild
The menu here focuses on quality cuts of Highland beef and venison and salmon, as well as veggie and vegan options.

🅐C3 🏠Falls of Shin Visitor Centre, Achany Glen 🔲macandwild.com

£ £ £

↑ Puffins are just some of the many species of seabirds found on Handa Island

---

Festival each September. John O'Groats is probably the most famous name on the map here. Even more rewarding are the cliffs at Duncansby Head and the Pentland Firth.

Smoo Cave Tours
⊗ ⊗ 🏠Durness 🕐Apr-Oct: daily 🔲smoocavetours.com

Strathnaver Museum
⊗ 🏠Clachan, Bettyhill 🕐Apr-Oct: Mon-Sat 🔲strathnavermuseum.org.uk

---

48

Dunnet Head

🅐C2 🏠Caithness

Britain's most northerly point, wild, windswept Dunnet Head

is characterized by stunning sandstone sea cliffs, its headland crowned by a lighthouse built by Robert Stevenson, grandfather of the author Robert Louis Stevenson, in 1831. From here, you're likely to encounter puffins, guillemots and kittiwakes among other spectacular bird-life. The nearby 16th-century **Castle of Mey** was the summer holiday home of the Queen Mother, which explains the preponderance of royal memorabilia dotted around this surprisingly modest residence; look out, too, for several watercolours painted by Prince Charles, who still visits at least once a year. The gardens here are also worth a lengthy stroll.

Castle of Mey
⊗ 🏠Clachan, Bettyhill 🕐May-late-Jul & mid-Aug-Sep: daily 🔲castleofmey.org.uk

---

49

Handa Island

🅐C2 🏠Sutherland 🚢From Tarbet (Apr-Aug: Mon-Sat) 🛈Scottish Wildlife Trust; (07920) 468572

This small yet dramatic Torridonean island just off Scourie on the north-west

coast, is an important breeding sanctuary for many species of seabirds. In past centuries its hardy people had their own queen and parliament, but the last few Handa residents were evacuated in 1847 when their potato crop failed. The island was also a burial ground as it was safe from the wolves which inhabited the mainland.

The island is now managed by the Scottish Wildlife Trust. Visitors can take the pedestrian ferry from Tarbet, and walk to the 328-ft- (100-m-) high northern cliffs to experience the intimidating antics of great and Arctic skuas (large migratory birds) swooping low overhead. Early in the year 11,000 pairs of razorbills and 66,000 pairs of guillemots also take up residence here. Handa's dramatic sandstone cliffs, pounded by the powerful Atlantic waves provide stunning ocean panoramas.

Did You Know?

The most northerly point of mainland Great Britain is Dunnet Head, not John O'Groats.

A DRIVING TOUR
ROAD TO THE ISLES

Distance 72 km (45 miles) **Stopping-off points**
Glenfinnan NTS Visitors' Centre (01397 722250) explains the Jacobite risings and serves refreshments; the Old Library Lodge in Arisaig offers excellent Scottish cuisine.

This scenic route goes past vast mountain corridors, breathtaking beaches of white sand and tiny villages to the idyllic town of Mallaig, one of the ferry ports for the isles of Skye, Rum, Eigg, Muck and Canna. In addition to stunning scenery, the area is steeped in Jacobite history.

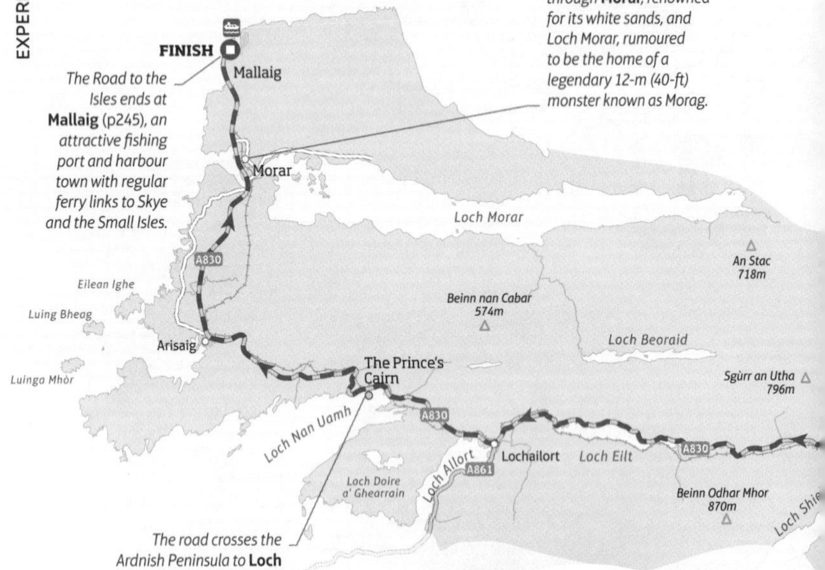

THE HIGHLANDS
AND ISLANDS

Locator Map
For more detail see p202

*The road continues through **Morar**, renowned for its white sands, and Loch Morar, rumoured to be the home of a legendary 12-m (40-ft) monster known as Morag.*

FINISH
Mallaig

*The Road to the Isles ends at **Mallaig** (p245), an attractive fishing port and harbour town with regular ferry links to Skye and the Small Isles.*

Morar

Loch Morar

An Stac
718m

Eilean Ighe

Luing Bheag

Beinn nan Cabar
574m

Loch Beoraid

Arisaig

Luinga Mhòr

Sgùrr an Utha
796m

The Prince's Cairn

A830

Loch Nan Uamh

Lochailort   Loch Eilt

A830

A830

Loch Doire
a' Ghearrain

Loch Allort

A861

Beinn Odhar Mhor
870m

Loch Shiel

*The road crosses the Ardnish Peninsula to **Loch Nan Uamh**, where a cairn marks the spot from which Bonnie Prince Charlie left for France in 1746 (p64).*

→

Glenfinnan Monument
to Jacobite warriors on
the banks of Loch Shiel

↑ A woman and her dog on the beautiful white sands of Morar

0 kilometres 5
0 miles 5

N ↑

*Looking east from the town of **Corpach**, across Loch Linnhe, there are fine views of Ben Nevis (p208).*

*A flight of eight locks, designed by Thomas Telford, forms the most spectacular part of the **Caledonian Canal** (p217).*

Finnan
Dubh Lighe
Fionnlighe
△ Aodann Chleireig 663m
Suileag
Glenfinnan
● Glenfinnan Monument
A830 Kinlocheil
Drumsallie
Loch Eil
Blaich
A861
A830
Corpach
Caol
Lochy
A82
Neptune's Staircase
Inverlochy
START ● Fort William
Loch Linnhe
A861
○ Upper Achintore
A82
C1164
Nevis
Ben Nevis 1345m △
C1162

*This 18-m- (60-ft-) high monument commemorates those who rose in support of Bonnie Prince Charlie in the 1745 Jacobite rebellion (p63). He first raised his standard in **Glenfinnan**.*

*Begin the tour at **Fort William**, which stands at the foot of Ben Nevis (p208), Britain's highest peak at 1,345 m (4,411 ft).*

Stob Bàn 999m △

NEED TO KNOW

Jacobite Express, Glenfinnan Viaduct

BEFORE
YOU GO

Things change, so plan ahead to make the most of your trip. Be prepared for all eventualities by considering the following points before you travel.

AT A GLANCE

CURRENCY
Pound Sterling (GBP)

AVERAGE DAILY SPEND

SAVE	SPEND	SPLURGE
£50	£125	£200+

BOTTLED WATER	CUP OF COFFEE	PINT OF BEER	DINNER FOR TWO
£1.00	£2.50	£4.50	£50

CLIMATE

The longest days occur May–Aug, while Oct–Feb sees the shortest daylight hours.

Temperatures average 15°C (59°F) in summer, and drop below 0 °C (32 °F) in winter.

October and November see the most rainfall, but heavy showers occur all year round.

ELECTRICITY SUPPLY
Power sockets are type G, fitting three-pronged plugs. Standard voltage is 230 volts.

Passports and Visas

For entry requirements to the UK, including visas, consult your nearest British embassy or check the **Visas and Immigration** page on the UK government website. For a stay of up to three months EU nationals and citizens of the US, Canada, Australia and New Zealand do not need a visa to enter the country.
Visas and Immigration
W gov.uk/browse/visas-immigration

Government Advice

Now more than ever, it is important to consult both your and the UK government's advice before travelling. The **UK Foreign and Common-wealth Office**, the **US State Department** and the **Australian Department of Foreign Affairs and Trade** offer the latest information on security, health and local regulations.
Australian Department of Foreign Affairs and Trade
W smartraveller.gov.au
UK Foreign and Commonwealth Office
W gov.uk/foreign-travel-advice
US State Department
W travel.state.gov

Customs Information

You can find information on the laws relating to goods and currency taken in or out of Scotland on the **UK Government** website.
UK Government
W gov.uk

Insurance

We recommend that you take out a fully comprehensive insurance policy covering theft, loss, medical care, cancellations and delays, and read the small print carefully.

Emergency treatment is usually free in the UK from the National Health Service (p277), and there are reciprocal arrangements in place with EEA member states, Australia, New Zealand and some other countries.

Vaccinations

No inoculations are needed for the UK.

Booking Accommodation

Scotland offers a variety of accommodation, from luxury five-star hotels to family-run B&Bs and budget hostels. Lodgings can fill up quickly and prices are higher in summer, especially in the Highlands and Islands and in Edinburgh during the festival season and over Hogmanay.

Camping is allowed almost anywhere in Scotland, so long as you are respectful of the community and leave the site as you found it. Be sure to familiarize yourself with the **Scottish Outdoor Access Code** before you set off.

Scottish Outdoor Access Code
W outdooraccess-scotland.scot

Money

Britain's currency is pound sterling (£). Scottish notes are different to those used in the rest of the UK, but they should be accepted outside Scotland too. Major credit, debit and prepaid currency cards are accepted, as are contactless payments, though they are not accepted on buses and other forms of public transport.

Tipping is not obligatory, but it is customary to leave a tip of 5–10 per cent if service is good.

Travellers with Specific Requirements

Modern sights tend to be accessible, but historic buildings may not be. **Capability Scotland** is Scotland's largest support organization for disabled people and **Tourism for All** is the UK's central source of travel information. **Disability Rights UK** lists accommodation. The AA has an **AA Disability Helpline** for members. **Can Be Done**, **Action on Hearing Loss** and the **Royal National Institute for the Blind** are resources for those with non-visible disabilities.

AA Disability Helpline
C (0800) 262050
Action on Hearing Loss
W actionhearingloss.org.uk
Can Be Done
W canbedone.co.uk
Capability Scotland
W capability-scotland.org.uk

Disability Rights UK
W disabilityrightsuk.org
Royal National Institute for the Blind
W rnib.org.uk
Tourism for All
W tourismforall.org.uk

Language

The official language is English, however Scotland is a multicultural country in which you will hear many languages spoken. Gaelic is now spoken by fewer than 1 per cent of Scots. Regional accents can be challenging, even for visitors from other Anglophone countries.

Opening Hours

COVID-19 The pandemic continues to affect Scotland and the rest of the UK. Some sights and hospitality venues are operating on reduced or temporary opening hours and require visitors to make advance bookings. Always check ahead before visiting.

Mondays Some museums and tourist attractions are closed for the day.
Sundays and Public Holidays Many shops close early, or for the entire day.
Winter Some accommodation establishments and other services in rural areas that cater mainly to tourists close from around October until the Easter school holidays.

PUBLIC HOLIDAYS	
New Year's Day	1 Jan
Bank Holiday	2 Jan
Good Friday	mid-Apr
May Day	Early May
May Bank Holiday	End May
Aug Bank Holiday	Early Aug
Christmas Day	25 Dec
Boxing Day	26 Dec

GETTING
AROUND

Public transport connects Scotland's cities, while trains and buses serve the regions and flights and ferries connect the mainland and islands.

AT A GLANCE

PUBLIC TRANSPORT COSTS

EDINBURGH

£1.80

Single Bus Journey

GLASGOW

£4.20

All-day Subway Ticket

CITY LINK EXPLORER PASS

£49

3 days unlimited travel on Scottish Citylink

SPEED LIMIT

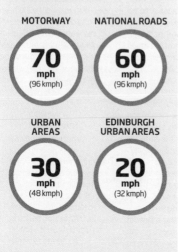

MOTORWAY

70 mph (96 kmph)

NATIONAL ROADS

60 mph (96 kmph)

URBAN AREAS

30 mph (48 kmph)

EDINBURGH URBAN AREAS

20 mph (32 kmph)

Arriving by Air

Three main international airports serve Scotland: Edinburgh, Glasgow, and Aberdeen. All are near their respective cities, with adequate transport links, including a tram service between Edinburgh Airport and the city. Glasgow Prestwick Airport handles mainly holiday flights to and from European destinations. Inverness Airport has a small number of flights from Amsterdam in addition to flights from London and other UK airports. Dundee has flights from London City. Scotland's other mainland airports include Wick, Campbeltown and Oban. The Northern and Western Isles are served by Kirkwall Airport in Orkney, Sumburgh Airport in Shetland, Stornoway Airport on Lewis, and smaller airports on Islay, Tiree, Benbecula and Barra.

Train Travel

International Train Travel

Edinburgh and Glasgow are the main hubs for rail travel to Scotland from the rest of the UK. There are connections at London St Pancras International for Eurostar services from mainland Europe. **London North Eastern Railway** then runs from London to Edinburgh, Dundee and Aberdeen. **Avanti West Coast** operates from London Euston to Glasgow and onward to Edinburgh, with some trains continuing to Inverness. **The Caledonian Sleeper** operates overnight services from London Euston to Glasgow, Edinburgh, Aberdeen, Inverness and Fort William. The **Interrail Great Britain Pass** offers a good deal on travel throughout Scotland and the rest of the UK for 3, 4, 6 or 8 days within a one month period.

Avanti West Coast
w avantiwestcoast.co.uk
Caledonian Sleeper
w sleeper.scot
Eurostar
w eurostar.com
Interrail Great Britain Pass
w interrail.eu
London North Eastern Railway
w lner.co.uk

Airport	Distance to city	Public Transport	Journey time	Price
Edinburgh	8 miles (13 km)	Airlink 100 Bus	45 mins	£4.50
		Tram	30 mins	£6.50
Glasgow	8 miles (13 km)	Airport Express 500 Bus	15 mins	£9.00
Aberdeen	7 miles (11 km)	Jet Service 727 Coach	30 mins	£3.70

JOURNEY PLANNER

Plotting the main driving routes by journey time, this map is a rough guide to driving between Scotland's main towns and cities. The times given reflect the fastest and most direct routes. Allow extra time for driving in bad weather and beware of rapidly changing weather conditions.

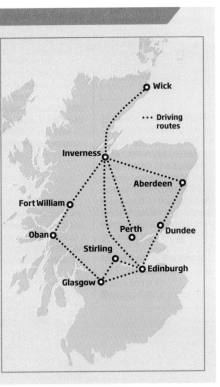

Aberdeen to Inverness	2.5 hrs
Edinburgh to Glasgow	1.25 hrs
Edinburgh to Dundee	1.25 hrs
Edinburgh to Aberdeen	3 hrs
Edinburgh to Inverness	3.5 hrs
Edinburgh to Stirling	1 hr
Glasgow to Stirling	3.5 hrs
Glasgow to Oban	2.5 hrs
Inverness to Fort William	1.5 hrs
Inverness to Wick	2.75 hrs
Perth to Inverness	2.5 hrs

Regional Trains

Lines within Scotland are coordinated by **National Rail**, with main stations in Glasgow, Edinburgh, Stirling, Perth, Dundee, Aberdeen, Inverness, Fort William and Oban. Thurso is Scotland's northernmost railway station. The West Highland Line terminates at Mallaig.

National Rail

W nationalrail.co.uk

Long-Distance Bus Travel

Long distance coaches connect major towns and cities with each other and with rural areas. Main operators are **Megabus** and **Scottish Citylink**.

Megabus

W uk.megabus.com

Scottish Citylink

W citylink.co.uk

Public Transport

Public transport in Scotland is a combination of private sector and city-operated services.

Most cities operate only bus systems. In Edinburgh buses are complemented by a single tram line and in Glasgow by a single subway circuit and a suburban rail network, all controlled by Strathclyde Partnership for Transport (SPT).

Public transport operators and **Traveline Scotland** provide ticket information, timetables and safety and hygiene measures for all public transport services across the country, as well as live updates on local services.

Traveline Scotland
🔳 travelinescotland.com

Public Transport Operators
Aberdeen: First Aberdeen
🔳 firstgroup.com/aberdeen
Dundee: Xplore Dundee
🔳 nxbus.co.uk
Edinburgh: Transport for Edinburgh
🔳 transportforedinburgh.com
Glasgow: SPT
🔳 spt.co.uk

Bus
Urban bus networks are generally fast, frequent and reliable. In most cities, a single fare applies for all bus travel within city limits. Multiple trip tickets and one-day travel passes are available in major cities. These can be bought online and stored on your phone. Single-trip tickets can be bought from the driver when boarding your bus but change is not given so you must pay the exact fare in cash. Public transport in rural areas is less extensive. Timetables are often designed around the needs of local workers and school students, so schedules are less convenient for visitors, with departures early in the morning and in late afternoon or early evening.

Tram
Edinburgh Trams connect Edinburgh International Airport with the city centre. There are plans to extend it as far as Leith by 2023.
Edinburgh Trams
🔳 edinburghtrams.com

Subway
Glasgow's **SPT Subway**, the only underground rail service in Scotland, comprises a 7 mile (10 km) loop connecting 15 stations in the city centre. Trains run every 4 minutes at peak times.

Tickets can be bought at any subway station. Single tickets are a fixed price and are valid on any journey. Savings can be made by purchasing a return (£3.30) or an all-day pass (£4.20).
SPT Subway
🔳 spt.co.uk/subway

Taxi

Cabs can be picked up at taxi ranks or hailed on the street. London-style black cabs display a yellow "taxi" sign which is lit up when the taxi is free. Fares are metered. "Private hire" cars must be booked by phone.

Driving

Travelling by car is by far the easiest way to explore beyond major cities.

Driving to Scotland
The journey to Edinburgh or Glasgow from London or main English ferry ports via the M1 and M6 motorways takes around 8–9 hours. If arriving by car ferry to Newcastle the A1 brings you to Edinburgh in around 2.5 hours.

Driving in Scotland
Scotland's roads are generally good, with motorways or dual carriageway highways connecting all major towns and cities. In remote areas some roads are single carriageway with designated passing places. Convoys of slow-moving caravans can slow up traffic in peak summer holiday season. Be aware that weather can change rapidly and driving conditions can deteriorate suddenly at any time of year. Driving in cities is not recommended; traffic is heavy and parking can be scarce.

Car Rental
To rent a car in Scotland you must be at least 21 years old (some renters insist on a minimum age of 25) and have held a valid licence for one year. Car rental agencies have outlets at main airports and in major towns and cities.

Rules of the Road
Drive on the left. Seat belts must be worn at all times and children must travel with the correct child restraint for their weight and size.

Mobile telephones may not be used while driving, except with a handsfree system, and third party insurance is required by law.

Overtake on the outside or right-hand lane and give priority to traffic approaching from the right. Give way to emergency service vehicles. It is illegal to drive and park in bus lanes.

On single-track roads which are wide enough for only one vehicle, pull into the nearest designated passing place on your left, or wait opposite a passing place on your right to allow an oncoming vehicle to pass. You should also use passing places to allow drivers to overtake.

Scotland's legal alcohol limit for drivers is lower than the rest of the UK's, at 50 mg of alcohol per 100ml (0.05 per cent BAC). Avoid drinking alcohol completely if you plan to drive.

Cycling

The trails of the Scottish Highlands are perfect for off-road riding, and there are great networks for mountain bikers across the country, not just in the Highlands. For a slightly less energetic ride, gentle, traffic-free trails follow old canal towpaths and former railway lines; perfect for families. **7Stanes** trails span the entirety of southern Scotland. Find traffic-free city and countryside bike routes on the website of the UK's National Cycle Network, **Sustrans**.

7Stanes
W forestryandland.gov.scot
Sustrans
W sustrans.org.uk

Bicycle Hire

Off road, touring and city bikes, bikes for younger children, and electrically assisted e-bikes can be rented from companies like **Biketrax** in Edinburgh and **EBS Cycle Centre** in Dundee. **Nextbike** is a cycle sharing scheme with 500 bikes available from more than 60 locations around Glasgow.

BikeTrax
W biketrax.co.uk
EBS Cycle Centre
W electricbikesscotland.com
Nextbike
W nextbike.co.uk

Bike Touring

Several companies operate guided and self-guided bike tours around Scotland. **Wilderness Scotland** offers guided cycling tours in scenic areas such as the Cairngorms, the Hebrides and the Great Glen, with a convenient support van to carry your luggage.

Wilderness Scotland
W wildernessscotland.com

Walking and Hiking

With a vast network of clearly way-marked footpaths, Scotland is a fantastic destination for walkers and hikers. Check the **Scottish Mountaineering Club**, **Scotways** and **Ramblers** for information specific to your route.

Scotland's mountains are easy to reach but bad weather can strike at any time, so planning and good preparation are essential. Ensure you have good hiking boots, warm waterproof clothing, a map and a compass. Tell someone where you're going and when you plan to return.

Walking is also an easy and enjoyable way to explore Scotland's compact city centres such as Edinburgh, Glasgow and Stirling, where most of the key sites are within walking distance of one another, and smaller cities such as Aberdeen, Dundee, Inverness, Perth and Stirling.

Boats and Ferries

There are no international car ferries direct to Scotland. However **DFDS Seaways** sails from Amsterdam to Newcastle in the north of England, only 100 km (64 miles) from the Scottish border. **P&O Ferries** sails between Larne in Northern Ireland and Cairnryan, around 130 km (80 miles) south of Glasgow and **Stena Line** sails from Belfast to Cairnryan.

For island hoppers, **Caledonian MacBrayne** (Calmac) offers passes valid for 8 days, 15 days or one month on its routes to western isles including Arran, Barra, Coll, Eigg, Harris, Islay, Mull, Raasay, Skye and Tiree. **NorthLink Ferries** sails to Stromness in Orkney from Scrabster and from Aberdeen to Kirkwall in Orkney and Lerwick in Shetland. **Pentland Ferries** offers car ferries to South Ronaldsay in Orkney from Gill's Bay, west of John O'Groats. **John O'Groats Ferries** operates a passenger-only service to South Ronaldsay. Smaller, independent ferry services operate between smaller islands and the mainland.

Caledonian MacBrayne
W calmac.co.uk
DFDS Seaways
W dfds.com
John O'Groats Ferries
W jogferry.co.uk
NorthLink Ferries
W northlinkferries.co.uk
P&O Ferries
W poferries.com
Pentland Ferries
W pentlandferries.co.uk
Stena Line
W stenaline.co.uk

SCOTLAND BY BOAT

Cruising on the Caledonian Canal and around the island and mainland ports of Scotland's scenic northwest coast is a fabulous way to see some of the country's finest scenery.

Caledonian Discovery
Operating two 12-passenger hotel barges, Caledonian Discovery offers one-week cruises on the Caledonian canal and the Great Glen Lochs.
W caledonian-discovery.co.uk

Hebridean Island Cruises
If you are looking to explore Scotland's Isles in style, these luxury all inclusive cruises tour the Western Isles aboard the Hebridean Princess, an elegant small cruise ship with just 30 cabins.
W hebridean.co.uk

PRACTICAL
INFORMATION

A little local know-how goes a long way in Scotland. Here you can find all the essential advice and information you will need during your stay.

AT A GLANCE

USEFUL NUMBERS

GENERAL EMERGENCY

999

POLICE (NON-EMERGENCY)

101

NHS 24 (NON-EMERGENCY)

111

TIME ZONE
GMT/BST
British Summer Time (BST) runs late March to late October.

TAP WATER
Unless otherwise stated, tap water in the UK is safe to drink.

WEBSITES AND APPS

Traffic Scotland
Use this app for real-time traffic conditions and road journey times anywhere in Scotland.

visitscotland.com
Scotland's official tourist board website

walkhighlands.co.uk
A useful tool for planning walks and hikes anywhere in Scotland

mwis.org.uk/scottish-forecast
Weather forecasts provided by the Mountain Weather Information Service

Personal Security

Scotland is generally safe, but petty crime does take place. Pickpockets work known tourist areas and busy streets. Use your common sense and be alert to your surroundings. If you have anything stolen, report the crime as soon as possible at the nearest police station. Get a copy of the crime report in order to make a claim on your insurance. Contact your embassy or consulate immediately if your passport is stolen or in the event of a serious crime or accident.

For emergency police, fire, ambulance services, or emergency mountain rescue, dial 999 (or 112). For medical help or non-emergency situations, dial 111.

Scots are generally accepting of all people, regardless of their race, gender or sexuality. In fact, Scotland has long been considered more socially progressive than its British neighbours.

LGBT+ rights are generally in line with the rest of the UK, which are considered among the most progressive in Europe. Same-sex marriage was legalized in Scotland in 2014 and Scotland is the first country in the world to include LGBT+ history and education in the school curriculum. Major Scottish cities have vibrant LGBT+ scenes, and since 2018 smaller towns and villages have launched their own Pride parades.

Despite all the freedoms that the LGBT+ community enjoy, acceptance is not a given. **LGBT Helpline Scotland** is a fantastic service that provides support and practical information for victims of homophobic abuse or hate crimes. If you do feel unsafe, the **Safe Space Alliance** pinpoints your nearest place of refuge.

LGBT Helpline Scotland
📞 0300 123 2523
🌐 lgbthealth.org.uk

Safe Space Alliance
🌐 safespacealliance.com

Health

The UK has a world-class healthcare system. For minor ailments go to a pharmacy or chemist. If you have an accident or medical problem requiring non-urgent medical attention you can

find details of non-emergency medical services on the **NHS** website. Alternatively, call NHS 24 at any hour on 111, or go to the nearest Accident and Emergency (A&E) department.

You may need a doctor's prescription to obtain certain pharmaceuticals. EU citizens can receive medical treatment in the UK free of charge, though this may change when the UK leaves the EU.

NHS
🆆 nhs.uk

Smoking, Alcohol and Drugs

Smoking and "vaping" are banned in all public spaces. However, many bars and restaurants have outdoor areas where smoking is permitted.

Alcohol may not be sold to or bought for anyone under 18 and it can only be purchased between the hours of 10am and 10pm, and 12:30pm and 10pm on a Sunday. The drink-drive limit (p274) is strictly enforced.

Possession of all recreational drugs, including psychoactive substances formerly known as "legal highs" and now classified as illegal, is a criminal offence.

ID

Visitors to the UK are not required to carry ID on their person. Passports are required for internal flights within the UK. You may be asked for photo ID when buying alcohol.

Visiting Places of Worship

Show respect by dressing modestly, especially when entering churches and religious buildings. Some remote areas of the Highlands and Islands are deeply religious.

Responsible Tourism

It is the law that every person, regardless of whether they are a local or visiting, should have access to the countryside in Scotland. As long as you act responsibly, you can walk, cycle, canoe and horse ride in all open land or waters. Be sure to familiarize yourself with the **Scottish Outdoor Access Code** before you set off.

Scottish Outdoor Access Code
🆆 outdooraccess-scotland.scot

Mobile Phones and Wi-Fi

Do not rely on mobile phones or other devices for navigation or emergency communications in remote areas where mobile reception can be intermittent. Free Wi-Fi hotspots are widely available in city centres. Cafés and restaurants will usually give you their Wi-Fi password on the condition that you make a purchase.

Visitors travelling to the UK with EU tariffs are able to use their devices abroad without being affected by data roaming charges. This situation may change once the UK has left the EU. Pay-as-you-go SIM cards are available at newsagents and supermarkets.

Post

Standard post is handled by the Royal Mail. There are post offices throughout Scotland, some in supermarkets or other stores. Larger post offices will open from 9am to 5:30pm on weekdays and until 12:30pm on Saturdays. You can also buy stamps in shops.

Taxes and Refunds

Stores offering tax free shopping will provide non-EU residents with a VAT 407 form which allows you to reclaim value added tax (VAT) on certain products. VAT is charged on most goods and services and is included in the price shown.

Discount Cards

If you plan to visit as many of Scotland's castles and stately homes as possible, the **Historic Environment Scotland Explorer Pass** provides access to over 70 attractions over a 3-, 7- or 14-day period. For those planning to travel extensively within Scotland, Scotrail's **Spirit of Scotland** pass offers unlimited train, bus and ferry transport over an 8-or 15-day period. The **Scottish Citylink Explorer Pass** offers 3-, 5- and 8-days unlimited travel on its coach network, as well as special offers on accommodation.

Historic Environment Scotland Explorer Pass
🆆 historicenvironment.scot
Scottish Citylink Explorer Pass
🆆 citylink.co.uk/explorerpass.php
Spirit of Scotland
🆆 scotrail.co.uk

INDEX

Index

SCOTTISH VOCABULARY

Gaelic is a Celtic language that is still spoken as a second language in the Highlands and Western Isles of Scotland. Estimates put the figure of Gaelic speakers throughout the country at around 60,000. The last decade has seen something of a revival of the language thanks to the encouragement of both education and broadcasting authorities. However the majority of people are most likely to come across Gaelic today in the form of place names. Words such as glen, loch, eilean and kyle are all still very much in use. English remains the principal language of Scotland. However the country's very distinct education, religious, political and judicial systems have given rise to a rich vocabulary that reflects Scottish culture. Many additional terms in current usage are colloquial. English as spoken by the Scots is commonly divided into four dialects. Central Scots can be heard across the Central Belt and the southwest of the country. As around a quarter of the population lives within 32 km (20 miles) of Glasgow, West Central Scots is one of the most frequently heard subdivisions of this dialect. Southern Scots is spoken in the east of Dumfries and Galloway and the Borders; Northern Scots in the northeast; and Island Scots in the Orkney and Shetland Islands.

PRONUNCIATION OF GAELIC WORDS

Letters	Example	Pronunciation
ao	craobh	this is pronounced similar to oo, as in cool
bh	dubh	"h" is silent unless at the beginning of a word in which case it is pronounced v, as in vet
ch	deich	this is pronounced as in the German composer Bach
cn	cnoc	this is pronounced cr, as in creek
ea	leabhar	this is pronounced e, as in get or a, as in cat
eu	sgeul	this is pronounced ay, as in say or ea, as in ear
gh	taigh-òsda	this is silent unless at the beginning of a word, in which case it is pronounced as in get
ia	fiadh	this is pronounced ea, as in ear
io	tiocaid	this is pronounced ee, as in deep or oo, as in took
rt	ceart	this is pronounced sht
th	theab	this is silent unless at the beginning of a word in which case it is pronounced h, as in house
ua	uaine	this is pronounced oo, as in poor

WORDS IN PLACE NAMES

ben	mountain
bothy	farm cottage
brae	hill
brig	bridge
burn	brook
cairn	mound of stones marking a place
close	block of flats (apartments) sharing a common entry and stairway
craig	steep peak
croft	small plot of farmland with dwellings in the Highlands
dubh	black
eilean	island
firth	estuary
gate/gait	street (in proper names)
glen	valley
howff	a regular meeting place, usually a pub
kirk	a Presbyterian church
kyle	a narrow strait of river
links	golf course by the sea
loaning	field
loch	lake
moss	moor

munro	mountain over 914 m (3,000 ft) high
strath	valley/plain beside river
wynd	lane
yett	gate

FOOD AND DRINK

Arbroath Smokie	small haddock that has been salted and then smoked
breid	bread
clapshot	mashed turnips and potatoes
clootie dumpling	rich fruit pudding
Cullen Skink	fish soup made from smoked haddock
dram	a drink of whisky
haggis	sheep's offal, suet, oatmeal and seasonings, usually boiled in the animal's intestine
Irn-Bru	popular soft drink
neeps	turnips
oatcake	a savoury oatmeal biscuit
porridge	a hot breakfast dish made with oats, milk and water
shortie	shortbread
tattie	potato
tattie scone	type of savoury pancake made with potato

CULTURAL TERMS

Burns Night	25 January is the anniversary of the birth of the poet Robert Burns, celebrated with a meal of haggis
Caledonia	Scotland
ceilidh	an informal evening of traditional Scottish song and dance
clan	an extended family bearing the same surname (last name)
first foot	the first person to enter a house after midnight on New Year's Eve
Highland dress	Highland men's formal wear including the kilt
Hogmanay	New Year's Eve
kilt	knee-length pleated tartan skirt worn as traditional Highland dress
Ne'erday	New Year's Day
pibroch	type of bagpipe music
sgian-dubh	a small blade tucked into the outside of the sock on the right foot worn as part of the traditional Highland dress
sporran	pouch made of fur worn to the front of the kilt
tartan	chequered wool cloth, different colours being worn by each clan

COLLOQUIAL EXPRESSIONS

auld	old
auld lang syne	days of long ago
Auld Reekie	Edinburgh
aye	yes
bairn	child
barrie	excellent
blether	chat
bonnie	pretty
braw	excellent
dreich	wet (weather)
fae	from
fitba	football
hen	informal name used to address a woman or girl
ken	to know; to have knowledge
lassie/laddie	a young woman/man
lumber	boyfriend/girlfriend
Nessie	legendary monster of Loch Ness
Old Firm	Celtic and Glasgow Rangers, Glasgow's main football teams
wean	child
wee	small

ACKNOWLEDGEMENTS

DK would like to thank the following for their contribution to the previous edition: Robin Gauldie, Juliet Clough, Keith Davidson, Alan Freeman, Sandie Randall, Alastair Scott and Roger Smith

The publisher would like to thank the following for their kind permission to reproduce their photographs:

(Key: a-above; b-below/bottom; c-centre; f-far; l-left; r-right; t-top)

123RF.com: Anton Ivanov 142bl; mirco1 36-7t; Oliver Taylor 127t.

21212: 72crb.

4Corners: Richard Burdon 19; Justin Foulkes 240-41; Fortunato Gatto 2-3; Susanne Kremer 146-47t; Maurizio Rellini 8clb; Riccardo Spila 92-93; Richard Taylor 4, 80-81t; Sebastian Wasek 200-01.

The Abbotsford Trust: 114-15, Angus Bremner 114bl, Angus Bremner 114cra.

Alamy Stock Photo: Action Plus Sports Images 58bl; AF archive 219bl; AJB 184t; Sally Anderson 156-57; Antiqua Print Gallery 60t; Archwhite 257br; Arterra Picture Library 20-21c, 252bc,/ Arndt Sven-Erik 210-11t; Sergio Azenha 43tr; Silvan Bachmann 35crb; Bailey-Cooper Photography 10ca; Fraser Band 215tr; John Bracegirdle 50-51t, 64-65t, 88-89b; Matthew Brown 128-29b; Richard Burdon 18c, 160-61; CCPhotography 147br; Angus Alexander Chisholm 265tr; Chronicle 63c, 63br; Classic Image 79bc, 117br; Clearview 118-19t, 252-53t; Gary Cook 133t, 250b; Creative Nature Media 128tl; Derek Croucher 248-49b; Ian Dagnall 24tl, 94-95b, 164t, 183tr, 254tl, 183tr; John Devlin 256bl; DGB 134bl, 267t; Jonathan Dorey - Scotland 260-261b; doughoughton 41tr; Eye Ubiquitous 52br, 147clb; eye35.pix 97tl; Keith Fergus 29br; Mark Ferguson 228t; Findlay 140cl, 172-73b; Alister Firth 46-47t; Slawomir Gawryluk 54-55t; geogphotos 239br; Ian Georgeson 74-75b, 82tl; GL Archive 61tr, 63bl, 158tr 63bl; David Gowans 213b; Tim Graham 246bl; The Granger Collection 172cra; Jeppe Gustafsson 224cra; Rik Hamilton 148-49b, 264b; Clare Hargreaves 47br; Hemis.fr 100tc,/ Cegalerba Nicolas 88tr,/ Bertrand Rieger 243t; Grant Henderson 30tl; Historic Images 78crb; Doug Houghton SCO 212tl; Image Scotland 65bl; imageBROKER 121cra,/ Markus Keller 244-45b; Vit Javorik 232-33b; John Peter Photography 22-23ca, 116-17t, 130-31b, 132b; 152-3b, 181br, 190tl, 199br; Pauline Keightley 45cl; Robert Kerr 165tr; Shahid Khan 75cl; Albert Knapp 175cr; Stefan Kusinski 79crb; LatitudeStock 11t; Thomas Lee 158b; Peter Lopeman 11br, 24-5t; De Luan 80crb; David Lyons 38-39t; Kevin Ma 41crb; Mark Sunderland Photography 107br, 179bc; Iain Masterton 46b, 98b, 106cl, 168br, 167t, 168-69t, 181cl, 194-95b, 261t; mauritius images GmbH 266br; Angus McComiskey 53crb, 186tl, 246-47t; MediaWorldImages 199tc; Henk Meijer 219cr; Bill Miller 119br; Rosaline Napier 104bl; Gerry Neely 221cb (Gabbro); Richard Newton 41cl; PA Images / Andrew Milligan 149tl; Chris Pancewicz 245tr; Ian Paterson 221clb; Charlie Phillips 255b; The Print Collector / Heritage Images / CM Dixon 197tr; Purepix 249tr; robertharding / Matthew Williams-Ellis 30-31bc; David Robertson 21ca, 176-77b; George Robertson 40-41b; RooM the Agency / marcoisler 28bl; Kay Roxby 179tl; Iain Sarjeant 166tl, 198br, 221crb; Scottish Viewpoint 43crb, 51cr, 117tr; Phil Seale 23tr, 135tr, 154-55b, 263b; Neil Setchfield 152tl; Duncan Shaw 64bc; Shine-a-light 151tl; shoults 214cra; Rod Sibbald 124-25; Antonio Siwiak 260clb; SJH Photography 87tl, 105tr; South West Images Scotland 59c; Stephen Saks Photography 122-23t; Eckhard Supp 48-9t; Timewatch Images 60br; travellinglight 22tr, 150b; UPI / John Angelillo 47cla; wanderluster 43cl; Sebastian Wasek 214-15b; Colin Waters 61bl; Monica Wells 155tr; Richard Wheeler 103tr; Arch White 103tr; Kenny Williamson 58br; Andrew Wilson 10clb, 13t;

Wim Wiskerke 22-3t; Allan Wright 42b, 122bl, 126bl; Alan Wylie 143cl; Ian Macrae Young 135br.

AWL Images: Robert Birkby 34-35tc, 54bl; Alan Copson 49crb, 144; Tom Mackie 22tl; Mark Sykes 113cra.

Bridgeman Images: A Lady in Black (oil on canvas), Cadell, Francis Campbell Boileau (1883-1937) / Art Gallery and Museum, Kelvingrove, Glasgow, Scotland 149c; Cromwell at Dunbar, 1650 (oil on canvas), Gow, Andrew Carrick (1848-1920) / Imperial Defence College, Camberley, Surrey, UK 63tr; Hadrian's Wall (gouache on paper), Green, Harry (b.1920) / Private Collection / Look and Learn 60bc; National Galleries of Scotland, Edinburgh 90cra.

Camera Obscura & World of Illusions, Edinburgh: 80cr.

Chivas Brothers: 48bl.

Dreamstime.com: Andreaobzerova 12-3b; Bobbrooky 226-27t; Anna Derewacz Czuprynska 37cl; Henner Damke 225b; Dnaveh 25tr; Sandro Fileni 76cl; Grahambraid 25tl; Henrywei 26cr; Holgers 35br; Helen Hotson 10-1b, 26t, 26crb; Jakphoto 12bl; Attila Jandi 95tl; Karol Kozlowski 79t; Licancabur 253br; Christoph Lischetzki 175tl; Martin Molcan 243cr; Mrmessy2 136-37, 18tl; Sueburtonphotography 242bl; Tinn Tienchutima 96-97b; Vaeenma 207cr; Stefano Valeri 189t, 257tl; Andrew Ward 234br; Jeff Whyte 87tr; Anastasia Yakovleva 216-17t.

Edinburgh Art Festival: John McKenzie/ Untitled, (2016) by Jonathan Owen, on display at the Burns Monument. Courtesy of the artist, Ingleby Gallery, Edinburgh 74bl.

Edinburgh International Book Festival: Robin Mair 40tr.

Getty Images: AFP / Andy Buchanan 91, 204b,/ Glyn Kirk 173tr; Bloomberg / Simon Dawson 207t; Kristian Buus 204-05t; Cultura / Leon Harris 31cl; Culture Club 62t, 63tl; Daniele Carotenuto Photography 102-03bc; De Agostini / DEA / S. Vannini 195crb; Matthew Williams-Ellis 59br; Ross Gilmore 65tr; Heritage Images 62clb, 63cra, 80clb; Hulton Archive 61tl,/ Heritage Images / Historica Graphica Collection 206cr; Samir Hussein 205br; Image by Peter Ribbeck 113t; Thomas Janisch 222t; Jeff J Mitchell 12t, 65br, 44-45bc, 74cr, 175tr, 205ca; Moment / Sam Spicer 28-9t; National Galleries of Scotland 80bc; Sarun Rojanakatanyoo 90bl; Steve Talas 17, 108-09; James Warwick 233cra; Westend61 13cr; Jon Wild 100-01b.

iStock / Getty Images: 1111IESPDJ 29cl, 22kay22 180cra; ALBAimagery 222br, 234-35t; AlbertPego 84t, 98-99t; ANNEYP 33tl; Ansaharju 16c, 68-69; argalis 77cra, 174-75b; benedek 120-21t; BrianPIrwin 94tl; Stephen Buwert 62bc; DavidGraham86 84br; DouglasMcGilvray 78bl; duncan1890 61bc, 79cb; E+ / JohnFScott 32cra,/ northlightimages 221clb; ewg3D 82-83bc; extravagantni 56-57t; font83 37br; fotoVoyager 26bl; FrankCornfield 159tr; Gannet77 65cra; Orietta Gaspari 170-71b; georgeclerk 31br, 45cb, 72t, 140t; Richard Heath 236-37b; iweta0077 32-33b; jikgoe 78tr; lucentius 6-7, 21tr, 24-25ca, 218, 230-31t, 232tr; malcphotolanc 61cla; mariofederrovici 229bl; miroslav_1 64tl; Moment / Jack Hoyer 264clb; Susanne Neumann 182-83b; pawel.gaul 77t; rechitansorin 59bl; Roxiller 49tr; Swen_Stroop 267-68; sunlow 196-97b; tane-mahuta 36br; theasis 8cla, 55crb, 140cr, 177tr; treasuregalore 143br; undefined 184-85b; Flavio Vallenari 262-63t; Chunyip Wong 220-21t.

Glasgow City Council: 42t, 140bl.

Glasgow Science Centre: 145cra; Martin Shields 145bl.

Glasgow Summer Sessions / TRNSMT FESTIVAL 2020: 44-45tc.

Go Ape: 53tr.

Historic Environment Scotland: 130tl.

National Museums Scotland: 86-87b, 87cra; 89tr, 89br; Peter Dibdin 72cr; Paul Dodds 120bl.

Penguin
Random
House

This edition updated by
Main Contributer Darren Longley
Senior Editor Alison McGill
Senior Designers Laura O'Brien, Vinita Venugopal
Project Editors Dipika Dasgupta, Danielle Watt
Project Art Editor Ankita Sharma
Assistant Editor Mark Silas
Indexer Hilary Bird
Senior Picture Researcher Sumita Khatwani
Assistant Picture Research Administrator Vagisha Pushp
Jacket Coordinator Bella Talbot
Jacket Designer Laura O'Brien
Senior Cartographic Editor Casper Morris
Cartography Manager Suresh Kumar
DTP Designer Rohit Rojal
Senior Production Editor Jason Little
Production Controller Rebecca Parton
Managing Editors Shikha Kulkarni, Hollie Teague
Deputy Managing Editor Beverly Smart
Managing Art Editors Bess Daly, Priyanka Thakur
Art Director Maxine Pedliham
Publishing Director Georgina Dee

First edition 1999

Published in Great Britain by Dorling Kindersley Limited, One Embassy Gardens, 8 Viaduct Gardens, London SW11 7BW

Published in the United States by DK Publishing, 1450 Broadway, Suite 801, New York, NY 10018

Copyright © 1999, 2021 Dorling Kindersley Limited
A Penguin Random House Company
21 22 23 24 10 9 8 7 6 5 4 3 2

A CIP catalogue record for this book is available from the British Library.

A catalogue record for this book is available from the Library of Congress.

ISSN: 1542 1554
ISBN: 978 0 2414 6262 1

Printed and bound in China.

www.dk.com

A NOTE FROM DK EYEWITNESS

The rapid rate at which the world is changing is constantly keeping the DK Eyewitness team on our toes. While we've worked hard to ensure that this edition of Scotland is accurate and up-to-date, we know that opening hours alter, standards shift, prices fluctuate, places close and new ones pop up in their stead. So, if you notice we've got something wrong or left something out, we want to hear about it. Please get in touch at travelguides@dk.com